Teacher Resource

Big Book of Writing Models

Program Authors
Lindamichelle Baron • Sharon Sicinski-Skeans

Modern Curriculum Press
Parsippany, New Jersey

Special thanks to the following schools for providing student writing samples:

Centre Ridge Elementary School, Centreville, VA

DeVargas Elementary School, San Jose, CA

Enterprise Elementary School, Cocoa, FL

Farmington Elementary School
Germantown, TN

Garfield Elementary School, Springfield, VA

Mandarin Oaks Elementary School
Jacksonville, FL

Martin Luther King Elementary School
Lancaster, PA

Mitchell K–6 Elementary School, Atwater, CA

Oak Street School, Basking Ridge, NJ

Red Bug Elementary School, Casselberry, FL

Red Rock Elementary School, Moab, UT

Riverdale Elementary School, Germantown, TN

Russell Primary School, Russell, KY

Shreve Island Elementary School
Shreveport, LA

West University Elementary School
Houston, TX

Special thanks to the following schools for research assistance:

Mount Prospect School, Basking Ridge, NJ

Oak Street School, Basking Ridge, NJ

Sawmill School, Tewksbury Twp., NJ

Special thanks to our Teacher Advisory Board:

Linda Prichard, Murfreesboro, TN

Theresa Langley, Cocoa, FL

Peggy Kearney, Baltimore, MD

Ted Jenes, Fort Collins, CO

Karen Carlson, Ledgewood, NJ

Susie Quintanilla, Houston, TX

Joyce Berube, Norcross, GA

Pat Sears, Virginia Beach, VA

Tracey Gomez, Tracy, CA

Executive Editor: *Betsy Niles*
Editors: *Donna Garinsky, Barbara Noe*
Designers: *Evelyn O'Shea, Bernadette Hruby*
Cover Design: *Evelyn O'Shea, Bernadette Hruby*
Cover Illustration: *Bernard Adnet*

Credits and Acknowledgments appear on page 224.

Modern Curriculum Press

An imprint of Pearson Learning
299 Jefferson Road, P.O. Box 480 • Parsippany, NJ 07054-0480
www.pearsonlearning.com • 1-800-321-3106

ISBN: 0-7652-2230-2

1 2 3 4 5 6 7 8 9 10   WC   10 09 08 07 06 05 04 03 02 01

Contents

The Forms of Writing

Take Note: Writing to Learn

Once Upon a Time: Writing to Tell a Story

Imagine That: Writing to Describe

Just the Facts: Writing to Inform

Welcome to The Write Direction
For Grades 1-5

Get ready to make the writing process one of the most enjoyable parts of your integrated Language Arts curriculum. *The Write Direction* is a student-centered writing program designed by writing experts. Program authors Sharon Elizabeth Sicinski-Skeans and Lindamichelle Baron are both authorities in the field. Their expertise and child-centered point of view helped to create a program that is not only teacher-friendly, but more important, student-friendly.

Dr. Sharon Elizabeth Sicinski-Skeans received a B.A. degree in English from Sam Houston State University, an M.Ed. in Curriculum and Instruction from the University of Houston-Park, and a Ph.D. at Texas A&M University in Curriculum and Instruction.

Dr. Lindamichelle Baron received a B.A. degree in Education from New York University, an M.A. in Reading, and an Ed.D. in Cross-Categorical Studies from Columbia University Teachers College.

In every lesson, students will see color photos of children their own age or famous authors who demonstrate that it is easy to be successful every step of the way. You will love the many options that appear before every unit in the Teacher Resource Guide for using *The Write Direction* in your classroom.

Look for these teacher-friendly features for support before each unit.

- Overview of Resources and Pacing Suggestions
- Making the Reading-Writing Connection
- The Classroom Writing Center

- Activities for Multiple Intelligences
- Assessment Options including Self-Assessment, Peer, and Teacher Evaluation Checklists, and Benchmark Papers with Rubrics for each Writing Process Lesson

---

Four key benefits of *The Write Direction* ensure writing success for you and your students:

Meets state writing standards

The Write Direction prepares your students for state and standardized writing assessments with more instruction and practice in the stages and forms of writing than any other program.

Guides teachers in teaching writing

The Write Direction's Teacher Resource Guides support teachers by taking the mystery out of teaching writing. Each guide provides simple 3-step core lesson plans for guaranteed success and addresses every writer's needs with proven teaching solutions through Meeting Individual Needs.

Provides easy time management

Whether you have five minutes, one hour, or six weeks, each *Write Direction* Unit Planner provides the teaching options, pacing suggestions, and assessment opportunities to suit diverse teaching styles and schedules.

Integrates the skills of grammar, usage, mechanics, and spelling

Skills for Super Writers practice books and Teacher Guides give third-, fourth-, and fifth-grade writers all the instruction, practice, and application of the skills they need to excel at state tests and become "super writers." In grades 1–5, minilessons at point of use provide meaningful instruction.

Program Components

United at last—a student-centered comprehensive instructional writing program and a fully correlated grammar, usage, mechanics and spelling practice program.

The Write Direction
⭐ Big Book of Writing Models
⭐ Teacher Resource Guide
⭐ Student Book (hardcover)
⭐ Transparencies

Skills for Super Writers
Grammar, Usage, Mechanics, and Spelling

⭐ Student Book
⭐ Teacher Guide

The Write Direction
links to CCC's

Developmentally Appropriate Program Components

	Grade 1	Grade 2	Grade 3	Grade 4	Grade 5
Big Book of Writing Models (17" x 22", spiral bound) Available for Grades 1 and 2; Grade 1 shown	⭐	⭐			
Teacher Resource Guide (9" x 12", spiral bound) Available for Grades 1–5; Grade 2 shown	⭐	⭐	⭐	⭐	⭐
Student Book (8 1/2" x 11") Available for Grades 3–5; Grade 3 shown			⭐	⭐	⭐
Skills for Super Writers Grammar • Usage • Mechanics • Spelling (8 1/2" x 11") Available for Grades 3–5; Grade 5 shown; Also available: Annotated Teacher Guide			⭐	⭐	⭐
Transparencies (8 1/2" x 11") Available for Grades 3–5; Grade 4 shown			⭐	⭐	⭐

The Write Direction
Scope and Sequence
Grades 1-5

WRITING PROCESS	Grade 1	Grade 2	Grade 3	Grade 4	Grade 5
Prewriting					
Brainstorm	•	•	•	•	•
• Draw	•	•	•	•	•
• Visualize	•	•		•	•
Quick Write			•	•	•
Make Lists	•	•	•	•	•
Use Journal or Log for Ideas	•	•	•	•	•
Identify Purpose	•	•	•		•
Identify Audience	•	•	•	•	•
Identify Form	•	•	•	•	•
Select Topic	•	•	•	•	•
Narrow Topic/Identify Main Idea			•	•	•
• Identify Character	•	•	•	•	•
• Identify Setting	•	•	•	•	•
• Identify Problem	•	•	•	•	•
• Identify Plot	•	•	•	•	•
Gather Information	•	•	•	•	•
• Make Lists	•	•	•	•	•
• Read Books, Journals, Logs	•	•	•	•	•
• Interview	•	•	•	•	•
• Research Library, Internet, CD-ROMs	•	•	•	•	•
• Take Notes			•	•	•
• Summarize			•	•	•
• Paraphrase				•	•
• Cite Sources		•		•	•
• Make Observations	•		•	•	•
• Use Charts (KWL Chart)		•	•	•	•
Organize Information			•	•	•
• Graphs		•	•	•	•
• Cluster Diagrams	•	•	•	•	
• Information Charts	•	•	•	•	•
• Diagrams	•	•	•	•	•
• Story Maps/Charts	•	•	•	•	•
• Time Lines			•	•	•
• Venn Diagrams			•	•	•
• Outlines			•	•	•
Design a Plan	•	•	•	•	•
Conference	•	•	•	•	•
• Share With a Partner or Group	•	•	•	•	•
• Listen	•	•	•	•	•
• Ask Questions	•	•	•	•	•
• Take Notes			•	•	•
• Consider/Incorporate Suggestions	•	•	•	•	•
Drafting					
Think About Your Subject	•	•		•	•
• Main Idea	•	•	•	•	•
• Character	•	•	•	•	•
• Setting	•	•	•	•	•

	Grade 1	Grade 2	Grade 3	Grade 4	Grade 5
Drafting (continued)					
• Problem	●	●	●	●	●
• Plot	●	●	●	●	●
Think About Your Audience	●	●	●	●	●
Think About Your Purpose	●	●	●	●	●
Think About Your Form	●	●	●	●	●
Think About Voice, Tone				●	●
Think About Language				●	●
Review Information				●	●
Use Drafting Checklist				●	●
Use Charts, Story Maps/Charts, Diagrams	●	●	●	●	●
Follow Plan or Outline	●	●	●	●	●
Include Beginning, Middle, End	●	●	●	●	
Organize Information Into Paragraphs					
• Write Topic Sentence That Tells the Main Idea	●	●	●	●	●
• Add Sentences That Support Main Idea: Descriptions (Sensory Details)	●	●	●	●	●
• Add Sentences That Support Main Idea: Facts/Reasons	●	●	●	●	●
• Add Sentences That Support Main Idea: Examples			●	●	●
• Add Sentences That Support Main Idea: Quotations				●	●
Support Opinions With Facts/Reasons			●	●	●
Sequence Ideas	●	●	●	●	●
Sequence Events	●	●	●	●	●
• Use Time-Order Words	●	●	●	●	●
• Use Transition Words		●	●	●	●
Write a Beginning That Grabs Reader's Attention	●	●	●	●	●
Write a Conclusion	●	●	●	●	●
• Resolve Problem			●	●	●
• Summarize			●	●	●
• Draw Conclusions			●	●	●
Cite Sources		●	●	●	●
Write a Title, Headline	●	●	●	●	●
Conference	●	●	●	●	●
• Share With a Partner or Group	●	●	●	●	●
• Listen	●	●	●	●	●
• Ask Questions	●	●	●	●	●
• Take Notes			●	●	●
• Consider/Incorporate Suggestions	●	●	●	●	●
Use Handwriting or Word Processing	●	●	●	●	●
Revising					
Review Purpose	●	●	●	●	●
Review Audience	●	●	●	●	●
Review Form	●	●	●	●	●
Review Tone, Voice, Language			●	●	●
Use Revising Marks	●	●	●	●	●
Use Revising Checklist			●	●	●
Revise to Elaborate	●	●	●	●	●
• Add Descriptive Details	●	●	●	●	●
• Add Facts/Reasons to Support Main Idea/Opinion	●	●	●	●	●
• Add Examples			●	●	●
• Add Dialogue, Quotation			●		●
• Add Sensory Details	●		●	●	●
• Add Humor				●	
• Add Flashback			●	●	●

	Grade 1	Grade 2	Grade 3	Grade 4	Grade 5
Revising (continued)					
• Expand Sentences With Adjectives, Adverbs	•	•	•	•	•
Revise to Clarify	•	•	•	•	•
• Rewrite a Confused Sentence or Section to Make Meaning Clear or to Maintain Focus	•	•	•	•	•
• Add Precise Adjectives, Adverbs, Verbs	•	•	•	•	•
• Add Vivid Adjectives, Adverbs, Verbs	•	•	•	•	•
• Add Facts/Reasons and Details to Clarify Opinion/Point of View		•	•	•	•
• Add Details to Describe Someone or Explain Something	•	•	•	•	•
• Delete Unimportant Information			•	•	•
• Rewrite to Suit Audience, Purpose, Form			•	•	•
Revise for Variety	•	•	•	•	•
• Vary Length of Sentence	•	•	•	•	•
• Vary Kind of Sentence			•	•	•
• Vary Beginning of Sentence	•	•	•	•	•
• Replace Overused Adjectives, Adverbs, Verbs	•	•	•	•	•
• Combine Short, Repetitive Sentences or Sentences With Similar Ideas		•	•	•	•
Revise to Create/Maintain Reader Interest	•	•	•	•	•
• Add Title That Makes Reader Want to Continue Reading	•	•	•	•	•
• Add Attention-Grabbing Beginning	•	•	•	•	•
• Include Strong Conclusion That Summarizes, Draws Conclusions, or Resolves Plot/Problem		•	•	•	•
Revise to Improve Organization	•	•	•	•	•
• Reorder Paragraph With Main Idea in the Beginning Followed by Details and Supporting Facts/Reasons			•	•	•
• Rewrite Beginning to Introduce Characters, Plot, Setting, Main Idea			•	•	•
• Rework Middle to Tell What Happens			•	•	•
• Rearrange Sentences/Paragraphs so Similar Ideas, Facts/Reasons, and Details Are Together	•	•	•	•	•
Revise to Improve Sequence	•	•	•	•	•
• Reconsider Sequence of Events and Ideas	•	•	•		•
• Add Time-Order Words	•	•	•	•	•
• Add Transitional Words				•	•
Conference	•	•	•	•	•
• Share With a Partner or Group	•	•	•	•	•
• Listen	•	•	•	•	•
• Ask Questions	•	•	•	•	•
• Take Notes			•	•	•
• Consider/Incorporate Suggestions	•	•	•	•	•
Editing and Proofreading					
Use Dictionary	•	•	•	•	•
Use Thesaurus			•	•	•
Use Proofreading Marks	•	•	•	•	•
Use Proofreading Checklist				•	•
Check Grammar and Usage	•	•	•		•
• Check Sentence Parts, Types, Structure	•	•	•	•	•
• Check for Sentence Fragments and Run-Ons		•	•	•	•
• Combine Sentences		•	•	•	•
• Check Parts of Speech and Their Usage	•	•	•	•	•
• Nouns	•	•	•	•	•
• Verbs	•	•	•	•	•
• Pronouns	•	•	•	•	•
• Adjectives	•	•	•	•	•
• Adverbs	•	•	•	•	•

	Grade 1	Grade 2	Grade 3	Grade 4	Grade 5
Editing and Proofreading (continued)					
• Prepositions			•	•	•
• Conjunctions			•	•	•
• Interjections				•	•
Check Mechanics	•	•	•	•	•
• Check Indention	•	•	•	•	•
• Check Capitalization	•	•	•	•	•
• Check Abbreviation			•	•	•
• Check Punctuation	•	•	•	•	•
• Period	•	•	•	•	•
• Question Mark	•	•	•	•	•
• Exclamation Point	•	•	•	•	•
• Comma	•	•	•	•	•
• Quotation Marks	•	•	•	•	•
• Apostrophe	•	•	•	•	•
• Italics and Underlining	•	•	•	•	•
• Colon			•	•	•
• Parentheses				•	•
• Check Handwriting/Neatness	•	•	•	•	•
Check Spelling	•	•	•	•	•
Conference	•	•	•	•	•
• Share With a Partner or Group	•	•	•	•	•
• Listen	•	•	•	•	•
• Ask Questions	•	•	•	•	•
• Take Notes			•	•	•
• Consider/Incorporate Suggestions	•	•	•	•	•
Publishing					
Make a List	•	•			
Create Captions	•	•			
Make a Story Silhouette			•	•	
Make Cutouts					
Create a Display	•	•	•		•
Create a Diorama			•		•
Make a Flip Book					•
Create a Bulletin Board	•		•		
Create a Poster	•		•	•	•
Make a Classroom Collection/Anthology/Encyclopedia	•	•	•	•	•
Make a Picture Dictionary	•				
Make a Picture Book					
Make a Book/Book Cover	•			•	•
Make a Notebook/Handbook	•	•			
Create a Storyboard				•	
Make a Mobile					
Illustrate Your Writing	•	•	•	•	•
Laminate Your Writing		•			
Frame Your Writing	•				
Create a Multimedia Document			•	•	•
Make a Picture Album	•		•		
Make a Poetry Gallery		•			
Make an Audio Recording	•	•	•		•
Make a Video Recording					•
Create a TV Commercial					•
Produce a News Broadcast	•	•			•
Create a Slide Show or Overhead Transparencies Presentation					•

	Grade 1	Grade 2	Grade 3	Grade 4	Grade 5
Publishing (continued)					
Create a Booklet, Pamphlet, or Brochure			●	●	
Print News Stories		●			
Create a Newsletter or Contribute to a Newsletter		●	●		●
Create a Newspaper	●				●
Create a Magazine/Revue			●		●
Create a Resource Rack or Binder	●	●			
Perform a Dramatization or Pantomime	●		●	●	●
Give an Oral Reading or Presentation	●		●	●	●
Have an Authors' Tea	●				
Put On a Puppet Show	●	●	●		
Perform a Radio Play or TV Talk Show					●
Perform a Skit or Stage Play			●	●	●
Perform a Song or Rap		●		●	
Conduct a Panel Discussion			●		●
Give a Speech			●	●	●
Make a Map			●		
Send a Letter	●	●	●	●	●
Send Electronic Mail		●	●		●
Submit Writing for Publication					●
Publish Writing Online		●	●	●	●
Make Your Own Letterhead or Stationery	●	●	●		●
Make Postcards	●				
Confer With a Published Author					●
Write a Monologue			●		
Present a Video Conference					●
Enter a Contest					●
Present a Science-Fiction Festival					●
Present a Poetry Festival	●				
Present a "Try It" Day	●				

FORMS OF WRITING

Writing to Learn

	Grade 1	Grade 2	Grade 3	Grade 4	Grade 5
Labels	●	●			
Lists	●	●	●	●	●
Captions	●	●			
Posters	●	●			
Picture Dictionary	●				
Notes			●	●	●
Log Entries	●		●	●	●
Journal Entries			●	●	●
Paragraphs			●	●	●
Summaries			●	●	●
Paraphrases			●	●	●
Graphs, Charts, Organizers			●	●	●
Diagrams and Outlines					●

Narrative Writing

	Grade 1	Grade 2	Grade 3	Grade 4	Grade 5
Narrative Paragraph			●	●	●
Story About Me	●				
Story About a Personal Event	●				
Story About a Best Friend	●				
Story About a Pet	●				
Personal Narrative		●	●	●	
News Story	●	●			

	Grade 1	Grade 2	Grade 3	Grade 4	Grade 5
Narrative Writing (continued)					
Folk Tale		•			
Picture Essay			•		
Riddles			•		
Jokes, Puns, and Terse Verse					•
Realistic Story		•	•	•	
Fantasy Story		•	•		
Fable			•		
Comic Strip				•	
Tall Tale				•	
Play Scene				•	
Story From History				•	
Biography					•
Science-Fiction Story					•
Mystery					•
Myth					•
Play					•
Descriptive Writing					
Descriptive Paragraph			•	•	•
Description of a Person	•	•			
Description of a Place	•				
Description of a Story Character	•				
Description of an Event		•			
Character Sketch			•	•	•
Setting			•		
Comparison		•	•		
Quatrain			•		
Free-Verse Poetry	•	•	•		
Shape Poem		•			
Haiku				•	
Limerick				•	
Diamante					•
Cinquain			•		•
Concrete Poem					•
Observation Report				•	
Compare-and-Contrast Description				•	
Compare-and-Contrast Essay					•
Eyewitness Account					•
Expository Writing					
Informative Paragraph			•	•	•
Book Report	•	•	•		
Friendly Letter and Envelope	•	•	•		
Thank-You Note	•				
Invitation		•			
Interview			•	•	
News Story					
How-to Paragraph			•	•	
Report	•	•			
Research Report			•	•	
Research Report With Citations					•
Problem-Solution Essay				•	•
Business or Formal Letter					•
Directions	•				•
Instructions		•			•

	Grade 1	Grade 2	Grade 3	Grade 4	Grade 5
Persuasive Writing					
Persuasive Paragraph			●	●	●
Book Review			●	●	
Advertisement/Poster				●	
Business Letter			●	●	
Poster				●	
Brochure			●	●	
Speech				●	●
Movie Review					●
Editorial Article					●
Point-of-View Essay					●
Commercial					●

INTEGRATED SKILLS

Writer's Craft	Grade 1	Grade 2	Grade 3	Grade 4	Grade 5
Alliteration		●	●	●	●
Analogy			●	●	●
Character		●	●	●	●
Characterization					●
Details—Sensory Words		●	●	●	●
Details—Examples			●	●	●
Dialogue		●	●	●	●
Exaggeration				●	●
Flashback					●
Foreshadowing and Suspense					●
Humor			●	●	●
Idioms				●	●
Language—Purpose/Audience	●	●	●	●	●
Language—Formal/Informal			●	●	●
Language—Literal/Figurative				●	●
Language—Slang/Dialect					●
Metaphor				●	●
Mood/Tone			●	●	●
Onomatopoeia			●	●	●
Order of Events and Ideas	●	●	●	●	●
Organization—Beginning, Middle, End	●	●	●	●	
Organization—Introduction, Body, Conclusion					●
Pacing					●
Personification			●	●	●
Plot	●	●	●	●	●
Point of View—First Person	●	●	●	●	●
Point of View—Third Person		●	●	●	●
Problem	●	●	●	●	●
Quotations					●
Reader Interest—Titles, Beginnings, Endings	●	●	●	●	●
Repetition				●	●
Rhyme	●	●	●	●	●
Rhyme—Assonance and Consonance					●
Rhythm			●	●	●
Sentence Variety—Beginnings	●	●	●	●	●
Sentence Variety—Kind, Length			●	●	●
Sentences: Combining and Expanding	●	●	●	●	●
Sentences: Transitions			●	●	●
Setting	●	●	●	●	●

	Grade 1	Grade 2	Grade 3	Grade 4	Grade 5
Writer's Craft (continued)					
Simile	•	•	•	•	•
Voice—Lyric and Narrative			•	•	•
Voice—Dramatic				•	•
Words—Precise Words, Descriptive/Vivid Words			•	•	•
Grammar and Usage					
Sentences					
Sentence Parts	•	•	•	•	•
• Simple Subjects	•	•	•	•	•
• Complete Subjects				•	•
• Compound Subjects				•	•
• (you) Understood			•	•	•
• Simple Predicates	•	•		•	•
• Complete Predicates				•	•
• Compound Predicates			•	•	•
• Direct and Indirect Objects					•
• Phrases					•
• Clauses					•
Sentence Structure	•	•	•	•	•
• Complete Sentences	•	•			
• Simple Sentences			•	•	•
• Compound Sentences			•	•	•
• Complex Sentences				•	•
• Fragments and Run-Ons				•	•
• Comma Splices					•
• Combining Sentences			•	•	•
• Expanding Sentences			•	•	•
• Word Order in Sentences				•	•
Sentence Types	•	•	•	•	•
• Declarative Sentences	•	•	•	•	•
• Interrogative Sentences	•	•	•	•	•
• Exclamatory Sentences	•	•	•	•	•
• Imperative Sentences			•	•	•
Nouns					
Common Nouns	•	•	•	•	•
Proper Nouns	•	•	•	•	•
Singular Nouns	•	•	•	•	•
Plural Nouns	•	•	•	•	•
Irregular Plural Nouns	•	•	•	•	•
Possessive Nouns	•	•	•	•	•
Verbs					
Action Verbs	•	•	•	•	•
Helping Verbs (be, have, do)			•	•	•
Linking Verbs			•	•	•
Main Verbs					•
Verb Tenses	•	•			
Present Tense	•	•			
Past Tense	•	•			
Future Tense			•	•	•
Irregular Verbs (bring, say, make)	•	•		•	•
Principal Parts: Regular Verbs					•
Participle					•
Subject-Verb Agreement (Singular and Plural Subjects)	•	•	•	•	•

	Grade 1	Grade 2	Grade 3	Grade 4	Grade 5
Verbs (continued)					
Subject-Verb Agreement (Simple and Compound Subjects)					•
Change of Tense			•	•	•
Problem Words (can, may, doesn't, don't)			•	•	•
Adjectives					
Common Adjectives	•	•	•	•	•
Proper Adjectives					•
Demonstrative Adjectives				•	•
Predicate Adjectives					•
Comparisons With Adjectives			•	•	•
Articles (a, an, the)			•	•	•
Adverbs					
Adverbs That Tell Where, When, and How	•	•	•	•	•
Comparisons With Adverbs			•	•	•
Problem Words (very/real, good/well)			•	•	•
Negatives				•	•
Double Negatives					•
Pronouns					
Personal Pronouns	•	•	•	•	•
Subject Pronouns			•	•	•
Object Pronouns			•	•	•
Problem Words: I and me	•		•	•	•
Possessive Pronouns	•	•	•	•	•
Demonstrative Pronouns			•	•	•
Reflexive Pronouns					•
Interrogative Pronouns				•	•
Agreement With Antecedents			•	•	•
Prepositions					
Prepositions			•	•	•
Prepositional Phrases			•	•	•
Object of Preposition					•
Conjunctions					
Coordinating Conjunctions			•	•	•
Interjections					•
Mechanics					
Capitalization					
First Word of Sentence	•	•	•	•	•
Pronoun I	•	•	•	•	•
First Word of Dialogue		•	•	•	•
First Word of Direct Quotations				•	•
Proper Noun	•	•	•	•	•
• Calendar items, days and months, holidays	•	•	•	•	•
• People's first and last names	•	•	•	•	•
• Family relationships				•	•
• Initials			•	•	•
Proper Adjectives					•
Titles of People	•		•	•	•
Titles of Books, Stories	•	•	•	•	•
Titles of TV Shows, Movies, Songs, Poems, Headlines			•	•	•
Abbreviations			•	•	•
Place Names	•	•			
Place Names and Geographical Features--streets, cities, states, countries			•	•	•

	Grade 1	Grade 2	Grade 3	Grade 4	Grade 5
Capitalization (continued)					
Organizations, Languages and Nationalities, Names of Historic Events					•
Letter and Envelope Parts	•	•	•	•	•
Outline Form			•	•	•
Citations					•
Abbreviation					
Streets and Cities, Months and Days			•	•	•
Titles			•	•	
Kinds of Businesses					•
Indention		•			
Punctuation					
Period	•	•	•	•	•
• At end of declarative/imperative sentences	•	•	•	•	•
• With abbreviations			•	•	•
• With initials			•	•	•
• In outline form			•	•	•
Question Mark	•	•	•	•	•
Exclamation Point	•	•	•	•	•
• Used with interjections					•
Comma	•	•	•	•	•
• In dates, addresses, letter parts	•	•	•	•	•
• In compound sentences			•	•	•
• In a series			•	•	•
• With numbers			•	•	•
• After introductory words, phrases			•	•	•
• After clauses				•	•
• With dialogue, direct quotations			•	•	•
Apostrophe	•	•	•	•	•
• In contractions	•	•	•	•	•
• In possessive nouns	•	•	•	•	•
Quotation Marks					
• In conversation	•	•	•	•	•
• In quotations		•	•	•	•
• In titles of stories, poems					•
Underlining/Italics					
• In titles of books, stories	•	•	•		
• In titles of movies, magazines, newspapers				•	•
• In stage directions				•	
Colon					
• In scripts				•	•
• In business letters after salutation			•	•	•
Parentheses					•
Spelling					
Closed and Open Syllable Constructions			•	•	•
Syllables in CVC and CVCe Words	•	•	•	•	•
Long Vowel Sounds and Letter Combinations	•	•	•		
Short Vowel Sounds and Letter Combinations	•	•	•		
Consonant Blends and Digraphs	•	•			
Endings s, es, ed, ing	•	•			
Endings s, es, ed, ing (Drop Final e)				•	•
Endings s, es, ed, ing (Double Final Consonant)	•	•	•	•	•
Endings s, es, ed, ing (Words Ending With y)			•	•	•
Endings s, es, ed, ing (Words Ending With Vowel + y)					•

Spelling (continued)	Grade 1	Grade 2	Grade 3	Grade 4	Grade 5
Prefixes (un, dis, re)	•	•			
Prefixes (pre, re, im, in, non, co)			•	•	•
Prefixes (de, dis, un, ex)			•	•	•
Rhyming Words	•	•			
Roots (drink, speak, read, happy)			•	•	•
Suffixes		•			
Suffixes (ness, full, ly, ion, able)			•	•	•
Schwa l			•	•	•
Schwa n			•	•	•
Compound Words	•	•	•	•	•
Homonyms and Problem Words (its/it's; their/they're/there)		•	•	•	•
Synonyms		•	•	•	•
Antonyms		•	•	•	•
High Frequency Words	•	•			
Phonograms and Word Families	•	•			

Reference Resources	Grade 1	Grade 2	Grade 3	Grade 4	Grade 5
Table of Contents	•	•			
Index		•			
Graphic Organizers		•			
Almanac				•	•
Map	•	•			
Atlas				•	•
Card Catalog		•	•	•	•
Computer Software, CD-ROMs, Electronic Media			•	•	•
Internet			•	•	•
Dictionary	•	•	•	•	•
Encyclopedia	•	•		•	•
Magazines			•	•	•
Outline		•	•	•	•
Thesaurus			•	•	•

The Write Direction: Grades 1 and 2 at a Glance

Teaching writing to young children is both a joy and a challenge. Children have vivid imaginations and a unique perspective on the world. They have thoughts, opinions, and feelings waiting to be given form. Your job as a teacher is to help children learn how to use words and language to express themselves through writing. The job of *The Write Direction* is to give you the tools and support you need to lead children to become independent, successful writers.

The Write Direction is a complete program that teaches writing using the writer's workshop model and the 5-stage writing process. Grades 1 and 2 cover the appropriate forms of writing: Writing to Learn, Writing to Tell a Story, Writing to Describe, and Writing to Inform. Under each category you will find the forms of writing most commonly covered in state standards and assessment tests.

The Write Direction contains writing-process lessons that invite children to write in various forms and for various purposes. The real student models, literature models, and graphic organizers in the *Big Book of Writing Models*, as well as blackline masters in the *Teacher Resource Guide* provide plenty of opportunity for instruction and practice. First- and second-grade children need interactive, hands-on materials. The Big Book allows children to experience a finished piece of writing done by someone their own age. Throughout the lessons, children have the opportunity to read and analyze these models and to use them as inspiration for their own writing.

The Write Direction for grades 1 and 2 includes:

Big Book of Writing Models features
- ◆ real student writing models
- ◆ literature models
- ◆ write-on/wipe-off charts

Teacher Resource Guide features
- ◆ a how-to section on using the writing process, including
  - • assessment
  - • journal writing
  - • conferencing
  - • minilessons
- ◆ lesson plans for every form of writing in the Big Book
- ◆ related literature titles
- ◆ suggestions for meeting the individual needs of children, including:
  - • Minilessons
  - • Writer's Block
  - • ESL Strategy
  - • Home-School Connection
  - • Writing Across the Curriculum
- ◆ expanded section of minilessons

How Does a Writer Grow?

Every Writer Is Different

It's the end of September—another new school year has begun. Joan Bennett, a first-grade teacher, is reading her class's first attempts at writing. As usual she is surprised by the wide range of abilities among children who are within a year of the same age.

◆ Take Sam, for instance. It's hard to believe that those random symbols, some of which look like letters, really mean anything. Yet Joan remembers that when she asked Sam to tell her about his writing he recounted a whole story about his cat. Sam has quite an imagination, and once his writing skills catch up, everyone will be able to enjoy his stories.

◆ Next, she looks at Maya's paper. In the middle of the page is a carefully drawn house with two small figures outside. Under the picture are several neatly written words that are phonetically spelled but accurate enough that Joan is able to read them. Maya has written about playing soccer with her sister. Maya is definitely ready for first grade.

◆ Then there's Todd. Todd is one of the older children in the class. Joan is impressed as she reads his account of a summer camping trip. Many of the words are spelled correctly, and Todd has included some interesting details and attempts at dialogue. He is clearly one of the more advanced writers in the class, and Joan hopes he will be an inspiration to the other children.

Writers Grow One Step at a Time

As an experienced teacher Joan knows that even though children of the same age can have widely different skills, research has demonstrated that they all learn to write by moving through specific developmental stages. On the following pages are real student writing models that show the natural development of writing skills.

The stages are based on the research of Joetta Beaver, Kathleen Taps, Mark Carter, and E. Jane Williams, authors of the *Developing Writer's Assessment (DWA)*. *DWA*, which is available from Celebration Press, is a complete assessment program that enables teachers to evaluate the strengths and needs of each writer and then use the information to plan instruction that moves children to the next level. By comparing your students' writing to the writing models that represent each level, you can see where your students are on target and where they may need extra help.

Student Writing Samples

On the following pages are levels 1 through 9 of the *DWA Continuum*, followed by student writing samples that represent each of those levels. These are the levels that correspond to kindergarten, first, and second grade.

Emerging Writers

Emerging writers create brief written messages of one simple sentence or less, which are based on their pictures. These writers are learning about the relationship of letters to sounds and the correspondence of written words to spoken words, as well as how to spell a few high-frequency words conventionally. They generally form a mixture of uppercase and lowercase letters that are, for the most part, the same size. Some of their words are unreadable without dictation. Emerging writers covers levels 1, 2, and 3.

Level 1

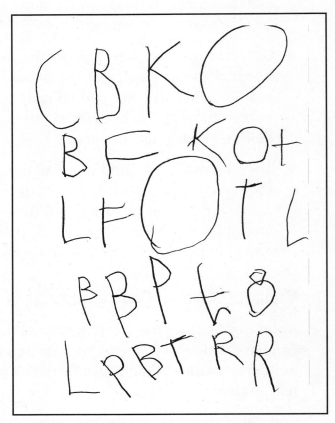

Spider was blue.
My other spider is black.
They are swinging.

Conventions

Sentence Structure Includes no evidence of intended message.

Directionality, Spacing, and Punctuation Places squiggles, other shapes, letterlike shapes, and/or letters randomly.

Letter Formation and Capitalization Forms squiggles, other shapes, and/or letterlike shapes.

Spelling Represents words using letterlike shapes and/or letters with no letter-sound correspondence to the intended word. Dictation needed to read all words.

Content

Supporting Details Includes no evidence of intended articles or modifiers.

Word Choice Includes no evidence of intended words.

Emerging Writers
Level 2

My baby chicken

Title _____ S a k X _____

(superscript: snakes)

S a k X   R n   l i v   i n   the

(superscript: snakes)

z o o.

Snakes can live in the zoo.

Conventions

Sentence Structure Includes 1 intended simple sentence.

Directionality, Spacing, and Punctuation Places letters and/or words in a left to right direction and leaves spaces between 3 or more words. May attempt punctuation.

Letter Formation and Capitalization Forms 2 or more words using lowercase letters.

Spelling Represents most words by recording 1 or more dominant sounds. May spell 2–3 different words conventionally. Dictation is needed to read some words.

Content

Supporting Details Includes 2 intended modifiers.

Word Choice Uses 4 or more intended routine words.

Early Writers

Early writers create short stories or informational pieces. They use a few compound and complex sentences and spell many one-syllable and some two-syllable words conventionally. These writers develop their ideas using primarily one strategy. They are learning to create stories that have simple beginnings, middles, and ends, and to use basic punctuation and capitalization. Early writers covers levels 4, 5, and 6.

Level 4

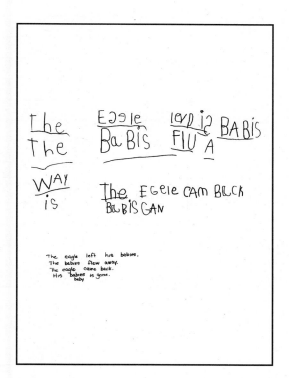

The eagle left his babies.
The babies flew away.
The eagle came back.
His babies (baby) is gone.

Conventions
Sentence Structure Includes 2–3 simple sentences or 1 complex / compound sentence.
Sentence Variation Begins all sentences with the same word.
Punctuation Ends 1 sentence or the story with a period.
Capitalization Capitalizes first word in 1 sentence; other letters may be inappropriately capitalized.
Spelling Spells 4–8 different words conventionally; dictation needed to read a few words.

Content
Opening Begins with an action or a fact in the first of 2–3 related thoughts or sentences.
Transitions Uses 1 transitional word or phrase to connect thoughts.
Development of Ideas Uses a glimmer of at least 1 strategy to develop an idea.
Supporting Details Includes 3–4 modifiers.
Word Choice Uses 1 precise word that is more exact in meaning.
Closing Stops abruptly with no ending after 2 or more related thoughts or sentences.

Early Writers
Level 5

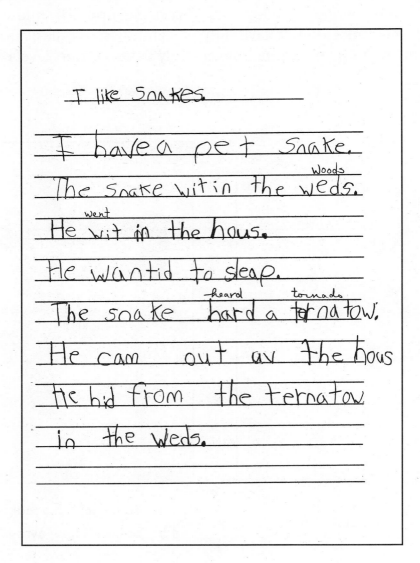

I like Snakes.

I have a pet snake.
The snake wit in the weds. [Woods]
He wit in the hous. [went]
He wantid to sleap.
The snake hard a ternatow. [heard] [tornado]
He cam out av the hous
He hid from the ternatow
in the weds.

Conventions
Sentence Structure Includes 4 or more simple sentences and/or 2 compound or complex sentences.
Sentence Variation Varies the way 2–3 sentences begin.
Punctuation Ends 2 to 6 sentences with periods.
Capitalization Capitalizes first word in 2 or more sentences. Other letters may be capitalized.
Spelling Spells 9 or more different one-syllable words conventionally.

Content
Opening Begins with an action or a fact in the first of 4 or more sentences.
Transitions Uses 2 different transitional words and/or phrases to connect thoughts or ideas.
Development of Ideas Uses 1 strategy somewhat effectively to develop an idea.
Supporting Details Includes 5 or more different modifiers.
Word Choice Uses 2 precise words that are more exact in meaning.
Closing Signals ending with "The End."

Early Writers
Level 6

> The Butterfly Who
> Had Beautyful Wings
> One day I was going for
> a walk. And then I saw
> a Butterfly So I decited
> to catch it And when I
> did I took it home and
> I got it in a jar
> for my pet and then
> I made hole in it so
> it could breath air.
> And when I was eating
> dinner it flaped it's
> wings to try to fly
> but it couldn't get
> away and when I went
> into my room I saw it's
> cool wings.
>
> And that is the end.

Conventions

Sentence Structure Includes 3 compound and/or complex sentences.

Sentence Variation Varies the way 4–5 sentences begin.

Punctuation Ends at least 7 sentences with periods or uses 2 or more forms of punctuation appropriately at times.

Capitalization Uses 2 or more forms of capitalization appropriately at times.

Spelling Spells 4 to 5 different two-syllable words conventionally.

Content

Opening Creates a brief context or introduction with 1 opening sentence.

Transitions Uses 3 different transitional words and/or phrases to connect thoughts or ideas.

Development of Ideas Uses 1 strategy somewhat effectively and at least a glimmer of 1 other strategy to develop ideas.

Supporting Details Supports 1 idea with details in at least 3 sentences.

Word Choice Uses 3–4 precise words that are more exact in meaning.

Closing Creates a logical ending or resolves the problem in at least 1 sentence; may include "The End."

Transitional Writers

Transitional writers begin their compositions by creating an introduction or a context. They use a variety of sentence structures. They spell many two-syllable and some multisyllable words conventionally, and they use basic punctuation and capitalization. These writers generally create brief endings. They are learning to use more than one strategy to develop ideas, to support and clarify ideas with details, and to organize their ideas into paragraphs. Transitional writers covers levels 7, 8, and 9.

Level 7

> A   Friend
> One day a Horse was grazing on some grass when an Elephant Shrew came along on the ground. The Horse said "Hello!" to the Elephant Shrew. The Elephant Shrew said "Hello!" back. Then they became friends. Then they went on a walk together. The Elephant Shrew went on the Horse's back! Then they went into

> a meadow where the Horse stoped to eat. Then the Horse said "Bye!" to the Elephant Shrew. The Elephant Shrew said "Bye!" to the Horse. Then the Horse went back to eating. And the Elephant Shrew went on a path to walk some more.

Conventions

Sentence Structure Includes 4–6 compound and/or complex sentences.

Sentence Variation Varies the way 6–7 sentences begin.

Punctuation Uses 3 forms of punctuation appropriately most of the time.

Capitalization Uses 3 forms of capitalization appropriately most of the time.

Spelling Spells 6 to 8 different two-syllable words conventionally.

Content

Opening Creates a context or introduction with 2 opening sentences.

Transitions Uses 4–5 different transitional words, phrases, and/or clauses to connect thoughts or ideas.

Development of Ideas Uses at least 2 strategies somewhat effectively to develop ideas.

Supporting Details Supports 2 ideas with details in at least 3 sentences; may be paragraphed.

Word Choice Uses 5–6 precise words or phrases that are more exact in meaning.

Closing Creates a brief closing (wrap-up, summary, conclusion) with at least 1 sentence. May include "The End."

Transitional Writers
Level 8

Title: Niagara Falls.

10/21/99

Dear Friend,

Have you been to Niagara Falls? I have. My whole family did. We stayed there for 3 days We went to the Falls in the summer of "99". We got there at 12:00 at night. We stayed in a motel called Horse Shoe Motel. Our motel was right next to a tower. The next day we went to the Maid of the Mist and the Cave of the Winds trip, it was cool. Then we went to a tourist store. My mom bought a picture of the Niagara Falls. After that we went out of the store and took a glaze at the Falls. My dad said the Canadian Falls real name is Horse Shoe Falls beca- use it is shaped like a horse shoe. When it was 8:00 we started to go back to the motel. When we entered to motel, my dad asked the person at the information desk what time the light show at the Falls would

begin. They said it started at 11:00 pm. Then we went to our room. We went back to the Falls at 11:09, and watched the light show. It was beautiful After the light show we went back to our room and went to bed. The next day was our last day to stay at Niagara Falls. We all woke up early and took a quick bath We got in our van and went to the Falls and took a last glaze and started home.

Conventions

Sentence Structure Includes 7–9 compound and/or complex sentences.

Sentence Variation Varies the way 8–9 sentences begin.

Punctuation Uses 4 forms of punctuation appropriately most of the time.

Capitalization Uses 4 forms of capitalization appropriately most of the time.

Spelling Spells 9 or more different two-syllable words conventionally.

Content

Opening Creates a context or introduction somewhat effectively with at least 3 opening sentences. May be paragraphed.

Transitions Uses 6–7 different transitional words, phrases, and/or clauses to connect thoughts or ideas.

Development of Ideas Uses 1 strategy generally effectively and at least 1 other strategy somewhat effectively to develop ideas.

Supporting Details Supports 3 ideas with details in at least 3 sentences. May be paragraphed.

Word Choice Uses 7–9 precise words or phrases that are more exact in meaning.

Closing Creates a somewhat effective closing (wrap-up, summary, conclusion) with at least 2 sentences.

The Pretty Butterfly

One summer day in the woods, Nadeine the catapillar said, "I wish I could fly like the rest of you." Billy the fly, Jesse the wasp, Daniel the bumble bee and Nathan the moth all said, "Keep dreaming! Nadeine said, "I know but I just can't help it!"

One day Nathan said, "come on Nadeine lets play throw the rock." But Nadeine said, "I can't I feel funny!" Then all of a sudden Nadeine was rolling up in something [what? (something)] happend to Nadeine! She was wraped up into a big brown ball!

A couple days later Jesse said, "It's not fun around here

any more because Nadeine's gone. "Yeah" said Billy "nothing is fun any more." I remember when she always... Then all of a sudden Nadeine popped out of the big brown ball! Everyone said, "It's Nadeine." Nadeine looked at herself "I have wings." said Nadeine "I can fly." "Great!" said Nathan "now we can play throw the rock! Then Daniel said, "now she is Nadeine the Butterfly!"

Conventions

Sentence Structure Uses a variety of sentences, including 10 or more compound and /or complex sentences.

Sentence Variation Varies the way 10–12 sentences begin.

Punctuation Uses 5–6 forms of punctuation appropriately most of the time.

Capitalization Uses 5 forms of capitalization appropriately most of the time.

Spelling Spells 4–5 different multisyllabic words conventionally.

Content

Opening Creates a context or introduction generally effectively with at least 3 opening sentences. May be paragraphed.

Transitions Uses 8–9 different transitional words, phrases, and/or clauses to connect thoughts or ideas.

Development of Ideas Uses 1 strategy generally effectively and at least 2 other strategies somewhat effectively to develop ideas.

Supporting Details Supports 4 ideas with details in at least 3 sentences; may be paragraphed.

Word Choice Uses 10–12 precise words and a few vivid or figurative phrases to clarify ideas and/or create a clearer image.

Closing Creates a generally effective closing (wrap-up, summary, conclusion) with at least 2 sentences.

Introducing the Writing Process in Grade 2

The writing process is made up of five stages that writers work through as they create a written piece. The stages are prewriting, drafting, revising, editing/proofreading, and publishing. Children do not move straight through these stages. They move back and forth as they rethink and revise their writing. You may wish to make a chart like the one below to hang in the classroom so that children become familiar with the stages of the writing process.

1. Prewriting

Prewriting is planning and getting ready to write.

- Brainstorm.
- Select a topic.
- Gather information.
- Think about what to say.
- Make a list, a web, or a picture.

2. Drafting

Drafting is putting ideas on paper.

- Use your writing plan as a guide.
- Write as much as you can think of.
- Don't stop to fix mistakes in spelling or grammar.

3. Revising

Revising is changing and improving your writing.

- Read over your writing.
- Make it clear.
- Add, move, or change information and ideas.

4. Editing and Proofreading

Editing and proofreading is giving the work a final check.

- Make sentences complete.
- Check spelling.
- Check capitals and ending punctuation.

5. Publishing

Publishing is sharing your work with others. There are many ways to publish your writing.

- Make a book.
- Draw a picture.
- Tell a story.
- Put on a play.
- Send a letter.

Using The Write Direction

The Extra Help First Graders Need

Because first graders are just beginning to read and write, they need extra support and repeated exposure to the process of writing. Students begin with modeled writing, where they analyze and discuss a student writing model or a literature model, and then move to shared and interactive writing, where they contribute either verbally or by writing themselves to create a group story. Finally they are ready for independent writing where they write on their own.

In each stage of the writing process:

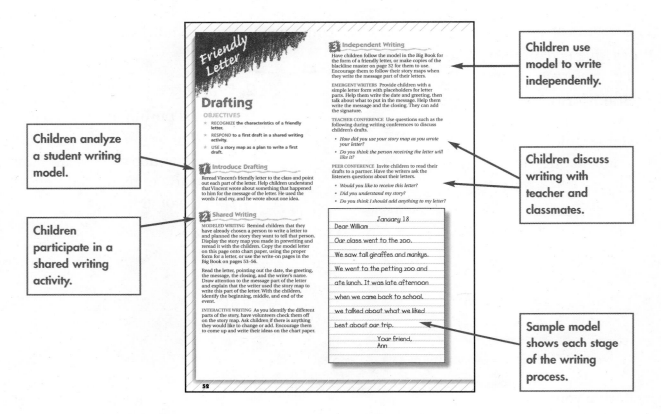

Children analyze a student writing model.

Children participate in a shared writing activity.

Children use model to write independently.

Children discuss writing with teacher and classmates.

Sample model shows each stage of the writing process.

The Role of Literature in Writing

Children learn about writing through example. They can watch other people write, read books, or have books read to them. In grade 1, lessons begin with writing models written and illustrated by real first graders. The model is shown in the child's own handwriting with the child's drawings to show the range of ability among children at this age and to make the writing more authentic.

Literature plays an important role in writing both as a model and as an inspiration. In the *Big Book of Writing Models*, student models are interspersed with literature models from noted children's authors.

Additional literature titles related to each form of writing are listed at the beginning of each unit. These books can serve as a springboard for the writing lesson, another example of a particular form of writing, or a source for a writing topic.

The Flexibility Second Graders Need

The Flexibility Second Graders Need

Like grade 1, grade 2 of *The Write Direction* features real student writing models as well as literature models. In grade 2, however, there are two kinds of lessons:

- ◆ lessons that model each stage of the writing process; and
- ◆ lessons that show only the finished model.

The lessons that model each stage of the writing process show the student writer's work at every stage of the writing process and can be used to guide children through the process with their own writing. These lessons generally take longer to complete.

The lessons that show only the finished model serve as examples of different forms of writing and can be used when time is a concern or when you don't want to take children through the whole process.

Lessons That Work for You

One of the strengths of *The Write Direction* is its flexibility. The forms of writing can be taught in the order they are presented or they can be adapted to fit your classroom curriculum. You may choose to work through the program in the order we suggest, or you may wish to teach some or all the forms of writing in a particular category. You may also pick and choose individual lessons as they relate to other subjects or classroom themes. Make a copy of the following chart to help you keep track of the forms of writing you've taught throughout the year.

Grade 1	
Form of Writing	**Date Taught**
Writing to Learn	Unit 1
Labels	
Lists	
Captions	
Posters	
Picture Dictionary	
Literature Log	
Writing to Tell a Story	Unit 2
Friendly Letter	
Story About Me	
Story About a Best Friend	
Story About a Pet	
News Story	
Writing to Describe	Unit 3
Description of a Person	
Description of a Place	
Free-Verse Poem	
Description of a Story Character	
Writing to Inform	Unit 4
Book Report	
Thank-You Note	
Report	
Directions	

Grade 2	
Form of Writing	**Date Taught**
Writing to Learn	Unit 1
Lists	
Captions	
Posters	
Literature Log	
Learning Log	
Observation Log	
Writing to Tell a Story	Unit 2
News Story	
Personal Narrative	
Folk Tale	
Realistic Story	
Fantasy	
Writing to Describe	Unit 3
Shape Poem	
Description of an Event	
Description of a Person	
Free-Verse Poem	
Comparison	
Writing to Inform	Unit 4
Instructions	
Invitation	
Friendly Letter	
Book Report	
Report	

The Writer's Workshop Model

The typical writer's workshop is a block of time scheduled each day for students to work on writing. The time block begins with a teacher-directed minilesson followed by children writing on their own. The teacher's role shifts from whole class instructor to a facilitator and promoter of writing. The instruction becomes individualized as children work at their own pace on different pieces of writing at different stages in the process.

Components of the Writer's Workshop

Whole Class Meeting/Minilesson – Many teachers begin the writer's workshop with a minilesson. *The Write Direction* provides a minilesson in each of the writing process lessons as well as many additional minilessons in the back of the *Teacher Resource Guide*. Minilesson topics can be an introduction to the lesson, an extension or a review of a topic, or a spontaneous discussion generated by the class.

Independent Writing/Teacher-Student Conferences – Suggested questions for teachers to ask during conferencing are provided for each stage of the writing process. Checklists to guide children as they work are offered for drafting, revising, and editing/proofreading.

Peer Conferences – Pairs or small groups of children share their writing with one another, exchanging ideas, asking questions, and making suggestions. Children listen and make comments in a way that other children understand and respect.

Group Share – This is one of the most important parts of the writer's workshop because it gives children the opportunity to validate their writing by sharing it with others. You may want to have an Author's Chair or a Share Chair in your room when several children are scheduled to share their writing on a given day. Sharing and publishing ideas are suggested for each lesson in *The Write Direction*.

Pacing the Writer's Workshop in Your Classroom

Whole Class Meeting	5 minutes
Shared & Independent Writing/ Teacher-Student Conferences	10–15 minutes
Peer Conferences	5 minutes
Group Share	5 minutes

Journal Writing

Why Write in a Journal?

A journal is a special place for children to write—words, lists, feelings, questions, ideas, drawings, even doodles. A journal can be a notebook, a composition book, or a few sheets of paper stapled together.

Why is journal writing important, even as early as first grade? Not only do writers get many of their ideas from their journals, but for young children, journal writing promotes fluency in thinking, writing, and reading. Putting words on paper makes thinking "visible." When a young child has a thought and writes it in words, he or she is thrilled when someone else can actually read those words and knows what the child is thinking. Writing that someone else can read validates the child's personal experiences and feelings.

Journal writing also encourages risk taking. When children write in their journals where spelling, grammar, and punctuation don't count, they try out new words and stretch their writing. As one teacher said, "When spelling doesn't count, I get a lot more stories about alligators and elephants than I do about cats."

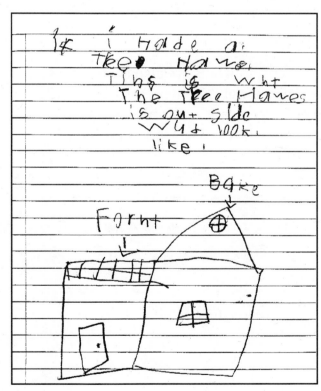

Early first-grade journal entry

If I had a
treehouse
this is what
the tree house
is outside
would look like.
Front. Back.

Late first-grade
journal entry

Journal Writing

How to Get Started

Children should have the opportunity to write in their journals every day, even if it's just for a few minutes. Start with five minutes and gradually expand it to fifteen. Sometimes children will write a lot, other times they may write one sentence or just draw a picture.

How do you encourage children who are reluctant to write? Model writing for them. Share a few sentences from your own journal with the class. Let them see you write. Write in your journal when they are writing in theirs. For children whose writing skills are not developed, allow them to draw pictures in their journals and dictate the words while you write them down.

Some teachers use a prompt to start journal writing, but an even more effective approach is a short group prewriting session. Talk about journals and why you write in them—to remember important experiences and to express your thoughts and feelings. Then ask, "What can we write about today?" Share an idea with the class and encourage them to come up with others. Before long, everyone will have something to write about.

Journals as a Record of Progress

In addition to being a good source for writing ideas, journals are also a valuable assessment tool. Over the year a journal provides a longitudinal record of a child's writing development. It can help you identify children's strengths and needs. For example, if children can read back what they have written, it is a good indication of their ability to match letters and sounds.

On Thursday me and my dad wednt to the Bronx Zoo. We sar a poler bare. It was siting on a rock and then a duck flow in the water. The poler bare sir ckiled

the water. Then he jumped in the water. When he jumped in the water the duck flue out. It was so funny. I hyd a graet time.

Second-grade journal entry

Conferencing

Making the Most of the Teacher Conference

Listening, really listening, is the key to a good conference. Listening means not only hearing the words but reading body language and voice tone, knowing the history of the current piece of writing, and the child's progress with this piece. Your ultimate goal is to help the writer. Respond to the writer, not to the writing.

Conferencing can happen quickly as you walk around the room stopping at a few children's desks, or it can be a more formal discussion at a neutral table or desk elsewhere in the room. Try to conference with each child at least once a week—more frequently if possible.

Here are some suggestions for successful conferencing.

- ◆ Keep conferences short.
- ◆ Listen and learn from the children. Allow them to do the talking.
- ◆ Tell the child what you've understood. Ask questions to find out what you don't understand.
- ◆ Give encouraging and genuine responses. Avoid overpraising.
- ◆ Keep the conference focused by talking about only one or two issues.
- ◆ Emphasize the child's accomplishments, rather than focusing on the deficiencies.
- ◆ Use the conference to gently nudge the child—to keep the writer writing.

Sample Teacher/Student Conference

EMILY: I'm stuck.

MISS F: Is this the same story you were stuck on yesterday?

EMILY: Yes. (*sigh*)

MISS F: Emily, I have an idea. You seem to be stuck on this piece, so why don't you put it away for a while? See if you can write about something else. Look in your journal for ideas.

EMILY: There is one thing I could write about.

MISS F: What's that?

EMILY: I went to a restaurant last night. It had flowers by the front door. (*Emily's thoughts ramble, and one topic leads to another and another.*)

MISS F: Is there something about the restaurant you'd like to write about?

EMILY: Yes, I just remembered. I got a dollhouse for my birthday, and my dad made some furniture to go in it.

MISS F: Could you write about that? Your dollhouse? And the new furniture?

EMILY: Yes, I think I will.

Making the Most of Peer Conferencing

Peer conferencing, even for first and second graders, is a beneficial experience and an important part of the writing process. It gives children an opportunity to share their writing with their peers, exchange ideas, ask questions, and offer suggestions. By helping other writers, they are learning about writing and honing their own skills.

Establish guidelines for peer conferencing from the beginning so that children know what is expected of them. As a group, discuss how to act in a conference. Make a chart and post it in the classroom.

How to Conference

★ Listen quietly.
★ Tell what you like about the writing.
★ Ask questions about things you don't understand.
★ Make suggestions if the writer wants them.

Start by modeling a conference during group sharing. Give each child in the group an index card with a question mark drawn on one side and a smiling face drawn on the other. When the writer has finished sharing his or her story, hold up your card—the smiling face if you liked the story, the question mark if there's something more you want to know or something that isn't clear. Children will model your behavior and hold up the same card. When they do, ask them why they liked the story or what they have a question about.

When children are ready to conference in small groups or in pairs they can use the cards. Children need to learn to listen to each other when they read. This may take some time with young children but as one teacher explained, even if a child is not listening the writer still benefits by hearing his or her own writing read aloud.

As children take turns reading their writing, they will learn to listen to and appreciate each other's writing. Eventually the index cards can be replaced with written questions or checklists children can use to evaluate their own and others' writing.

Sample Peer Conference

A classmate listens as six-year-old Adam reads the beginning of his story out loud.

ADAM: We go on a big bus. It took us to the game. The Cougars and the Knights played. The score was 35 to 21. We saw men with painted faces at the game. There was a bathroom on the bus. There were lots of people on the bus. I ate a hot dog with ketchup at the game.

SARAH: It isn't about one thing. It goes hippie-hop from one thing to the next. It's all mixed up.

Sarah assured Adam that with Jaws's (the classroom stapler) help, he could take his book apart and put the pages in a more logical order.

Minilessons

What Is a Minilesson?

Minilessons are exactly what the name implies—brief instructional lessons that last sometimes only a minute and rarely over five minutes. The benefit of minilessons is that children are learning skills in context and when they need them. Good minilessons respond to the situation and the needs of the writer at a particular point in time.

Let the children lead you. Observe and listen to discover opportunities for learning. When children want to add information but give up because their page is full, recognize the opportunity to teach several minilessons on adding information. When the glue is disappearing and everyone wants to use the stapler at once, a minilesson on managing materials would be appropriate. When children don't know what to write next, present a minilesson on ways to get back on track.

Remember, minilessons are not just lessons that are presented once and then forgotten. The same topic can be covered again and again—in other lessons, in different contexts, from a new perspective. These lessons help children develop and become more skillful writers. *The Write Direction* provides minilessons in each lesson at point of use. These are generally related to a skill in the lesson. There is also a collection of minilessons on related writing skills at the end of the *Teacher Resource Guide*. These can be used at any time and are ideal for reviewing skills or expanding a lesson.

Minilessons can be broken down into four areas.

◆ **Basic Skills** These are fundamental skills that all young children need to learn in order to read and write, such as
- left-to-right progression
- spacing between sentences
- size of words

◆ **Writing Process** These are strategies and skills that facilitate the writing process, such as
- conferencing
- managing time
- making revisions

◆ **Writer's Craft** These are techniques that improve writing, such as
- using dialogue
- adding colorful vivid words
- varying the beginning of sentences

◆ **Language Skills** These are the conventions of grammar, usage, mechanics, and spelling that clarify the writer's words for the reader. They include
- capitalizing the first word in a sentence
- using punctuation marks at the end of sentences
- making subjects and verbs agree

Minilessons

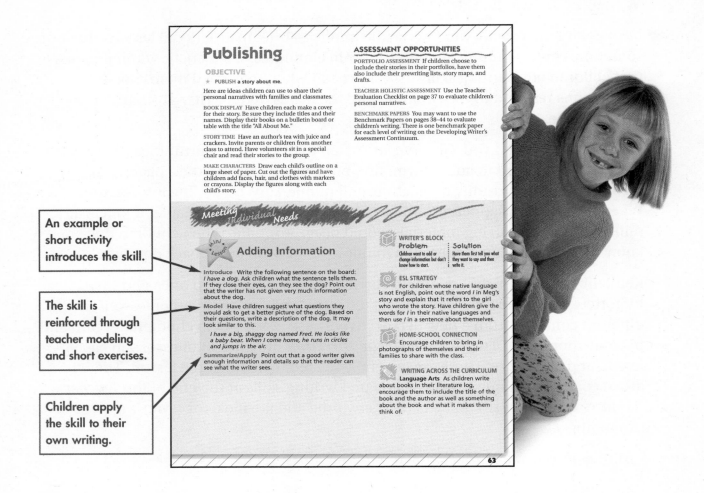

An example or short activity introduces the skill.

The skill is reinforced through teacher modeling and short exercises.

Children apply the skill to their own writing.

Ways to Present Minilessons

Minilessons should be short and fun and grab children's attention. There are many ways to present minilessons.

- ◆ Direct presentation

- ◆ Role play

- ◆ Demonstration by a child

- ◆ Compiling lists from the group

- ◆ Teacher writing in front of the class

- ◆ Telling past classroom experiences

Some minilessons should be presented to the entire class; others might be better presented to a small group. In some cases, one particular child may be in need of an individual minilesson. If you see that several children are struggling with a concept such as dialogue, take them aside and present a quick minilesson on quotation marks. If one child is misusing the writing center, he or she should have a minilesson about caring for and using the supplies at the center. Minilessons are flexible and can be taught as the need arises.

Take Note: Writing to Learn

Contents

RESOURCES

TEACHING PLANS

Writing to Learn

Unit Planner

WRITING FORM	MINILESSONS				
	Basic Skills/ Writing Process/ Writer's Craft	**Grammar, Usage, Mechanics, Spelling**	**Writing Across the Curriculum**	**Meeting Individual Needs**	**Assessment**
Lesson 1 LISTS pp. 18–19 (2 days)	• Numbering a List, 19		• Science, 19	• Writer's Block, 19 • ESL Strategy, 19 • Home-School Connection, 19	• Self-Assessment Checklist, 12 • Teacher Evaluation Checklist, 13 • Peer Evaluation Checklist, 14 • Teacher Conferencing, 18
Lesson 2 CAPTIONS pp. 20–21 (2 days)	• Size of Words and Letters, 21		• Social Studies, 21	• Writer's Block, 21 • ESL Strategy, 21 • Home-School Connection, 21	• Self-Assessment Checklist, 12 • Teacher Evaluation Checklist, 13 • Peer Evaluation Checklist, 14 • Teacher Conferencing, 20
Lesson 3 POSTERS pp. 22–23 (3 days)	• Using Illustrations, 23		• Health, 23	• Writer's Block, 23 • ESL Strategy, 23 • Home-School Connection, 23	• Self-Assessment Checklist, 12 • Teacher Evaluation Checklist, 13 • Peer Evaluation Checklist, 14 • Teacher Conferencing, 22
Lesson 4 LITERATURE LOG pp. 24–25 (2 days)	• Using Books and Stories to Get Ideas for Writing, 25		• Social Studies, 25	• Writer's Block, 25 • ESL Strategy, 25 • Home-School Connection, 25	• Self-Assessment Checklist, 12 • Teacher Evaluation Checklist, 13 • Peer Evaluation Checklist, 14 • Teacher Conferencing, 24
Lesson 5 LEARNING LOG pp. 26–27 (2 days)	• Graphic Organizers, 27		• Math, 27	• Writer's Block, 27 • ESL Strategy, 27 • Home-School Connection, 27	• Self-Assessment Checklist, 12 • Teacher Evaluation Checklist, 13 • Peer Evaluation Checklist, 14 • Teacher Conferencing, 26
Lesson 6 OBSERVATION LOG pp. 28–29 (2 days)	• Making and Recording Observations, 29		• Social Studies, 29	• Writer's Block, 29 • ESL Strategy, 29 • Home-School Connection, 29	• Self-Assessment Checklist, 12 • Teacher Evaluation Checklist, 13 • Peer Evaluation Checklist, 14 • Teacher Conferencing, 28

Making the Reading-Writing Connection
Writing to Learn

You may want to add the following books to your classroom library. Each category of books represents one form of writing children will be introduced to in *Writing to Learn*. The books serve as models for good writing and are valuable resources to use throughout each lesson. The suggested titles offer reading opportunities for children of varying reading abilities and are labeled as follows.

 Easy—books with a readability that is below second-grade level, but with content of interest to second graders

 Average—books with an average readability level that can be read independently by most second-grade students

Challenging **Challenging**—books with above-average readability for more proficient students or books that can be read aloud to students

Use literature to introduce a writing form, as a model of successful writing, to enhance minilessons, to focus on grammar and usage, and to expand each lesson.

LISTS

Moonbear's Pet
by Frank Asch. Simon & Schuster Books for Young People, 1997. Bear and his friend Little Bird find a pet in the pond. Bear thinks of a list of names for his new pet fish. Little Bird lists the presents he brings to the newly-named "Splash."

Nate the Great and Me: The Case of the Fleeing Fang
by Marjorie Weinman Sharmat. Yearling Books, 2000. Nate lists his ideas to help him solve the case of Fang, the missing dog.

What Do Authors Do?
by Eileen Christelow. Clarion Books, 1995. A humorous book that explains the different ways authors write and that shows the writing process, step by step. Part of the process is making lists of ideas.

CAPTIONS

From Seed to Plant
by Gail Gibbons. Holiday House, 1991. Labels and captions help to tell the story of how seeds transform into full plants.

The Berenstain Bears and Too Much Vacation
by Stan & Jan Berenstain. Random House, 1989. The Berenstain Bears have an interesting problem-filled vacation in a remote mountain cabin. Later, they laugh over their pictures, to which they have added funny captions.

Dr. Amelia's Boredom Survival Guide: First Aid for Rainy Days, Boring Errands, Waiting Rooms, Whatever!
by Marissa Moss. Pleasant Company Publications, 1999. Amelia keeps a journal on how to stop boredom. In it she draws and writes captions for her drawings.

POSTERS

Arthur's Pet Business
by Marc Brown. Econo-Clad Books, 1999. Arthur the aardvark starts a pet business to show he is responsible enough to own a dog. He makes posters to advertise his new venture.

Missing: One Stuffed Rabbit
by Maryann Cocca-Leffler. Albert Whitman & Co., 1998. Coco the stuffed rabbit and his diary go home with a second-grader. When he is missing after a shopping trip, all the children make posters to help find him.

Chicken Little
by Stephen Kellogg. William Morrow & Co., 1987. Foxy Loxy's plot to capture Chicken Little and the others is foiled when Chicken Little recognizes the fox from a "wanted" poster.

LOGS

Franklin Goes to Day Camp
by Paulette Bourgeois. Scholastic, 1998. Franklin records his observations in a diary as he attends camp.

Emily's First 100 Days of School
by Rosemary Wells. Hyperion Books for Children, 2000. From charts to numbers to kisses, there's something different each day to help Emily count the first 100 school days.

How We Crossed the West, The Adventures of Lewis and Clark
by Rosalyn Schanzer. National Geographic Society, 1997. Presents simplified versions of the daily logs that the famous explorers kept as they made their journey to the Pacific Northwest.

The Classroom Writing Center
Writing to Learn

As children learn about different ways they will be *Writing to Learn*, consider the following suggestions for your classroom writing center.

◆ Use all kinds of posters to decorate your writing center. To manage the number of children using the center, post a sign-up list. Include a list of center rules. Display photos of children learning to write with captions written by children. Make available picture dictionaries and create an ongoing word wall nearby.

◆ Have children help label containers for writing supplies, such as pencils, pens, markers, writing paper, drawing paper, construction paper, tag board and poster board, index cards, glue sticks, stick-on labels, rubber stamps, ink pads, stickers, and glitter pens.

◆ Make available drawing software for children to use. Software that includes stamps will allow children to stamp pictures to create picture/word lists and to write captions and rebus-style sentences.

◆ Provide blank books for children to decorate and use for a variety of purposes, including literature logs, learning logs, and observation logs. A colorful construction paper cover can be assigned for each kind of log.

The Stages of the Writing Process

Consider using the following activities as children explore the various writing forms in this unit.

A Prewriting Activity for Lists and Learning Log Entries To introduce a new unit of study in a content area such as science or social studies, have children list in their learning logs ideas they would like to learn. As the unit progresses, children can check off items in their lists and write ideas and draw pictures to tell about what they have learned.

A Drafting Activity for Literature Log Provide quiet time in the writing center or reading corner for children to write in their literature logs. Create and post a sign like the one to the right to remind children what to include in a log entry.

A Publishing Activity for Posters Display children's posters along a wall. Have children arrange the posters in groups, placing posters with similar themes together.

Writing in Your Literature Log
- What story or book did you hear or read?
- What did you like? What did you not like?
- What do you think of the characters?
- What does the story make you think about?

Graphic Organizers

The following blackline masters can be used to help children with various unit lessons. Make copies for use in the writing center and transparencies to use with an overhead projector. Complete and display an example of each organizer.

Blackline Master	Purpose	Writing Form
List, page 6	Prewriting or Drafting: collection sheet	Lists
Captions, page 7	Prewriting or Drafting: collection sheet	Captions
Literature Log, page 8	Prewriting or Drafting: collection sheet	Literature Log
Observation Log, page 9	Prewriting or Drafting: collection sheet	Observation Log

Create a Bulletin Board

◆ Use the bulletin board to introduce and display the forms of writing children will be doing: lists, captions, and posters, and literature, learning, and observation logs. Title the board: "*We Are Writing to Learn!*"

◆ Design the bulletin board to resemble a garden with six sections. Each section has a garden marker labeled with one form of writing. Other garden signs can include: *Plotting Good Writing* and *See how our writing grows!*

◆ Provide an example of each kind of writing when you introduce *Writing to Learn*. These samples can be published pieces or writing of your own. Over time, replace the samples with children's writing. Change the writing often so that each child's writing is eventually displayed.

List

A list can help you when you write.

_____

1. _____

2. _____

3. _____

4. _____

5. _____

Captions

Draw pictures. Then write captions for them.

Literature Log

Use this page to write about books you've read.

Title of book: _____

Author's name: _____

What the book is about: _____

_____

_____

_____

What the book makes me think about: _____

_____

_____

_____

_____

Observation Log

Write about what you see around you. You can draw pictures, too. Don't forget the date.

Date _____

_____

_____

_____

_____

Date _____

_____

_____

_____

_____

Connecting Multiple Intelligences

Writing to Learn

The following activities focus on specific prewriting and publishing ideas for children who demonstrate intelligence in different ways: talent and skill with words (linguistic), with numbers (logical-mathematical), with pictures (spatial), with movement (bodily-kinesthetic), with people (interpersonal), with self (intrapersonal), with music (musical), and/or with nature (environmental or naturalist).

Linguistic
Prewriting — Search through an observation log to find a topic to make a poster.
Publishing — Create a book of lists. Each page is devoted to a list of words that relate to a topic.

Logical-Mathematical
Prewriting — Arrange letter cards to form words before writing the words in a list.
Publishing — Include a chart or picture graph to illustrate a point on a poster.

Spatial
Prewriting — Draw sketches in an observation log and include captions at a later time.
Publishing — Include pictures or labeled diagrams in learning log entries.

Bodily-Kinesthetic
Prewriting — Act out the main idea of a drawing or picture before writing a caption about it.
Publishing — Cut out words from magazines to paste on tag board to create a list.

Environmental (Naturalist)
Prewriting — Select an outdoor setting to record observations in a log.
Publishing — Write about books with nature themes in your literature log.

Writing to Learn

Intrapersonal
Prewriting — Choose an event you have or will participate in to create a poster.
Publishing — Make a book of lists that name favorite things. Decorate each list in a special way.

Interpersonal
Prewriting — Interview others to get ideas for lists of words related to particular topics.
Publishing — Work with a partner to read a book and write about it in a literature log.

Musical
Prewriting — Listen to a tape recording of a story and write about it in a literature log.
Publishing — Listen to a musical recording. Write a list of all the things the music makes you think about.

Evaluating Student Writing
Writing to Learn

The Write Direction offers a variety of assessment options. The following are short descriptions of the assessment opportunities available in this unit. Just select the assessment option that works best for you.

Types of Assessment	Writing Lessons
Checklists Self-Assessment, Teacher, and Peer Evaluation Checklists help children refine their writing at each writing process stage.	• Self-Assessment Checklist, page 12 • Teacher Evaluation Checklist, page 13 • Peer Evaluation Checklist, page 14
Teacher and Peer Conferencing Throughout each lesson in this unit, there are opportunities to interact with children, informally questioning them about their progress and concerns. Children also have opportunities to interact with one another to ask questions, share ideas, and react to their partner's writing.	• Lists, page 18 • Captions, page 20 • Posters, page 22 • Literature Log, page 24 • Learning Log, page 26 • Observation Log, page 28

Self-Assessment Checklist

Writing to Learn

Name of Writer _____

Date _____

Type of Writing _____

Use this checklist when you are revising, or editing and proofreading
- **lists**
- **captions**
- **posters**
- **literature logs**
- **learning logs**
- **observation logs**

	YES	NO	Ways to Make My Writing Better
Did I have the right kind of information in my writing?	☐	☐	
Did I write the information correctly?	☐	☐	
Do I need to move things around to make my writing easier to understand?	☐	☐	
Will I be able to understand and use this information later?	☐	☐	

Teacher Evaluation Checklist
Writing to Learn

Name of Writer _____

Date _____

Writing Mode _____

Use this checklist when you are evaluating a child's
- **lists**
- **captions**
- **posters**
- **learning log**
- **literature log**
- **observation log**

	YES	NO	Recommendations to Child
Is the writing developed according to the guidelines of the writing form?	❑	❑	
Does the writing include enough information?	❑	❑	
Is there too much information?	❑	❑	
Is the information recorded correctly?	❑	❑	
Is the information recorded so that the child will be able to understand and use it later?	❑	❑	
Is the handwriting legible?	❑	❑	
Was the work done neatly?	❑	❑	

Peer Evaluation Checklist
Writing to Learn

Name of Writer _____

Name of Writing Partner _____

Conference Date _____

Type of Writing _____

Use this checklist during revising, or editing and proofreading conferences for
- **lists**
- **captions**
- **posters**
- **literature logs**
- **learning logs**
- **observation logs**

	What My Writing Partner Said	Ways to Make My Writing Better
Did I include the right kind of information?		
Is there anything I should take out?		
Is there anything I should add?		
Is there something I can do to make my writing easier to understand?		
Do you think I will be able to use this information later?		

Home Letter

Dear Family,

Your child is about to begin Unit 1 in our writing program called *The Write Direction*. In this unit, "Writing to Learn," your child will use writing as a tool for learning. Writing lists is something we all do every day. Making a poster and writing captions is a way to share information.

Your child will also begin to keep written logs to record what he or she thinks about books that are read, ideas about science and social studies topics or experiments, and observations.

Here are some ways to help your child use writing to learn.

1 Have your child make lists to help remember things, such as a things-to-do list or a homework checklist, and to help them plan things, such as a list of things to take on a family trip or to a birthday party.

2 Have your child help you write captions for family album photos.

3 Provide your child with a special journal or notebook to record thoughts, experiences, and feelings. Ask them to share their school logs with you.

4 Work together to create special posters or banners to celebrate family milestones such as birthdays and anniversaries.

5 Visit the library to find books to read together. Here are some to look for.
- ◆ *Weather Words and What They Mean* by Gail Gibbons. Holiday House, 1990. Basic weather words and concepts are introduced, such as wind, moisture, and temperature.
- ◆ *I Took My Frog to the Library* by Eric Kimmel. Viking Penguin, 1990. Each day a girl visits the library and takes a different pet. The results are always the same—disastrous!

Sincerely,

Carta para el hogar

Estimada familia,

Su hijo/a está a punto de comenzar la Unidad 1 de nuestro programa de escritura titulado *The Write Direction*. En esta unidad, "La escritura para aprender," su hijo/a usará la escritura como instrumento de aprendizaje. Hacer listas es algo que hacemos todos los días. Hacer un cartel y pies de grabados es una forma de comunicar información.

Su hijo/a también va a comenzar a mantener diarios de escritura para anotar lo que él o ella piensa y siente acerca de los libros que se leen, ideas sobre temas de ciencias o de estudios sociales o experimentos y observaciones.

He aquí algunas sugerencias que le pueden servir a su hijo/a para usar la escritura para aprender.

1 Pídanle a su hijo/a que haga listas para ayudarse a recordar cosas, tales como listas de cosas que hacer o una lista de las tareas, y ayúdenle a planear cosas, tales como lo que se debe llevar en un viaje de la familia, o una lista de cosas para un cumpleaños.

2 Pídanle a su hijo/a que los ayude a escribir pies para las fotos del álbum familiar.

3 Den a su hijo/a una libreta o cuaderno especial donde anotar experiencias, pensamientos y sentimientos. Pídanle que les muestre su diario hecho en la escuela.

4 Juntos, hagan carteles para fiestas especiales de la familia, tales como cumpleaños y aniversarios.

5 Visiten la biblioteca para buscar libros que puedan leer juntos. He aquí algunos libros que pueden buscar.

- ◆ *Weather Words and What They Mean* por Gail Gibbons. Holiday House, 1990. Se presentan palabras y conceptos básicos del clima, tales como viento, humedad y temperatura.
- ◆ *I Took My Frog to the Library* por Eric Kimmel, Viking Penguin, 1990. Cada día, una niña visita la biblioteca trayendo una mascota diferente. Los resultados son siempre iguales—¡un desastre!

Sinceramente,

TAKE NOTE:

Writing to Learn

Writing to Learn

Introduction

To help children think about the different ways they write to learn, do an activity like the following. Show children a soccer ball and a pencil. Ask if they know what one has to do with the other. Have children pretend they have all joined a soccer team. Then ask the following questions.

★ You will need to buy special equipment to play on a team. How will you remember what you need?

★ You will want to know the names of your team members and their phone numbers. How will you remember them?

★ How will you keep track of when and where each game will be played? What if you need directions to the field? How will you remember how to get there?

★ You don't want to forget how to do a certain play. What can you do to remember it?

★ You see a poster announcing a soccer camp. What do you do to find out about the camp?

Talk with children about the importance of writing down information to find out something new, to remember ideas, and to share what you know. Emphasize that writing is not only for school subjects, but is something people do everyday at home, on the job, and at play. Invite children to give examples of times when they have made a list or jotted down ideas they wanted to remember.

Explain to children that over the next few weeks they will learn more about the different ways they write to learn by writing lists and captions, making posters, and writing in logs to remember books they have read and ideas they have learned in science, social studies, and math. Point out classroom examples of each kind of writing. Remind children that writing is something we all do every day, because writing is a great way to share, learn, and remember important things.

Lists

Things to Write About

1. losing my tooth
2. playing soccer
3. going to the zoo
4. helping my grandfather
5. making a birdhouse

There are so many things to write about.

Colin Washington
Texas

OBJECTIVES

★ **RECOGNIZE** the characteristics and purposes of lists.

★ **RESPOND** to a model list written by a student writer.

★ **WRITE** a list.

Begin the Lesson

Invite children to suggest places they might like to visit on a class trip. List their responses on the board, numbering each item. Then review the list with the class. Point out that a list is a good way to brainstorm ideas and to remember information.

Discuss a Writer's Model

MEET THE WRITER Show children the list, "Things to Write About," on page 2 of the Big Book of Writing Models and introduce the writer, second-grader Colin Washington. Read aloud Colin's comment and discuss his purpose for writing the list. Help children understand that Colin made the list to help him think about and remember ideas he might want to write about.

TALK ABOUT THE MODEL Invite volunteers to read aloud the items on Colin's list. Talk about how looking at the list will help Colin decide what to write. Then discuss how the list is organized. Lead children to notice that each item is numbered sequentially and written on a different line. Also clarify that a list does not have to be written in complete sentences.

Write and Confer

Have children make their own lists of ideas for writing. (See page 6 for a blackline master.) Suggest that they look through their journals and think about favorite people, places, things, activities, and events. Then they can make a list of all the ideas they could write about. Remind children to number their items and write each one on a new line.

TEACHER CONFERENCE As children work on their lists, ask questions such as the following.

- *Why would it be a good idea to look at your list if I asked you to write a story?*

- *What other kinds of lists could you make?*

- *How do lists help you at school?*

ASSESSMENT OPPORTUNITIES

SELF-ASSESSMENT Have children complete the Self-Assessment Checklist on page 12.

PEER EVALUATION Have children use the Peer Evaluation Checklist on page 14.

TEACHER HOLISTIC ASSESSMENT Use the Teacher Evaluation Checklist on page 13 to evaluate children's lists.

Numbering a List

Introduce Have children look at Colin's list on page 2 of the Big Book. Direct children's attention to the numbers and the different idea written after each number. Then write Colin's ideas in a single line on the board. Invite children to tell which version is better. Point out that numbering a list keeps the list organized and tells how many items are in the list.

Model Demonstrate how to number a list. Write the words *Class List* on the board. Then write the numeral 1 and your name on the first line of the list. Invite children, one by one, to add their names to the list. Remind children to write the next consecutive number before they write their name.

Summarize/Apply Review with children that numbered lists can help them organize and remember their ideas. Encourage children to write numbered lists when they brainstorm ideas to write about or organize information for writing.

WRITER'S BLOCK

Problem	Solution
Children have difficulty thinking of ideas for their lists of things to write about.	Suggest that children look at pictures and favorite books or talk to friends and family about things they've done or like to do to generate ideas.

ESL STRATEGY

Allow children whose native language is not English to dictate their lists to partners or parent volunteers. Then have children copy their lists to practice writing in English.

HOME–SCHOOL CONNECTION

Suggest that children help family members to write and use lists for everyday tasks, such as grocery shopping, completing chores, and planning family outings.

WRITING ACROSS THE CURRICULUM

Science Reinforce the idea that some lists children use in school show what they know or have learned, such as spelling lists and word lists. Encourage children to write lists in their journals or learning logs, such as ideas they learned in science.

Leaves We Eat	Roots We Eat
lettuce	potatoes
cabbage	carrots
spinach	radishes
parsley	turnips

Captions

Our class went to the Statue of Liberty.

We had to take a boat to get there.

Did you know the statue is over 151 feet tall?

I drew these pictures about our trip. The captions tell what happened.

CAPTIONS

Ashley Thomas
New York

Captions 3

OBJECTIVES

★ RECOGNIZE the characteristics and purpose of captions.

★ RESPOND to model captions written by a student writer.

★ WRITE captions.

1 Begin the Lesson

Gather several photos or large pictures that lend themselves to having captions added, such as sports or family trip pictures. Display the pictures and ask children to tell what is going on in each. Write their responses on the board in the form of captions, such as *Jake hit a home run for the Rockets* or *This is one of the gorillas at the zoo.*

2 Discuss a Writer's Model

MEET THE WRITER Show children the pictures and captions on page 3 of the Big Book of Writing Models and introduce writer Ashley Thomas, who is a second-grade student. Invite a volunteer to read aloud what Ashley has to say about her pictures and why she wrote the captions.

TALK ABOUT THE MODEL Invite volunteers to read aloud Ashley's captions. Point out that each caption is written just below the picture. Have children compare what is written in the caption to what is shown in the picture. Ask children if they would know what each picture is about without the caption. Help children understand that a caption uses words, phrases, or sentences to tell about a picture and can make the picture more interesting.

3 Write and Confer

Have children write captions for pictures they cut out of magazines and newspapers. Children can glue the pictures onto construction paper and then write a caption below each one. Encourage children to find pictures that can be grouped together. You may wish to have children use copies of the blackline master on page 7 for their pictures and captions. Remind children that a caption is a phrase or a sentence that explains or adds information about a picture.

TEACHER CONFERENCE As children work on their captions, ask questions like the following.

* *How did you decide what to write for each caption?*
* *What information will the reader learn from your caption?*

PEER CONFERENCE Encourage partners to read each other's captions and tell what they like about them.

ASSESSMENT OPPORTUNITIES

SELF-ASSESSMENT Have children complete the Self-Assessment Checklist on page 12.

PEER EVALUATION Have children use the Peer Evaluation Checklist on page 14.

TEACHER HOLISTIC ASSESSMENT Use the Teacher Evaluation Checklist on page 13 to evaluate children's captions.

Size of Words and Letters

Introduce On posterboard write captions under four pictures using different-sized print: large, regular, tiny, and regular but with varying letter sizes. Invite children to suggest which caption is easiest to read and give reasons why. Explain that the second caption is easiest to read because the words are the right size and the letters are all the same size.

Model Have children review the pictures and captions on page 3 of the Big Book. Point out that the captions are large enough to read easily, but not so large that they don't fit on the page. The words' letters are also all about the same size.

Summarize/Apply Have children review the captions they have written for their pictures. Ask them to decide if their words and letters are easy to read. Encourage them to make changes if needed.

WRITER'S BLOCK

Problem	Solution
Children have difficulty choosing words that tell about the most important details of the pictures.	Help children understand that a caption is like a sign that gives a little information. Discuss the most important idea the picture shows. Use words children mention and model how to turn the words into a caption.

ESL STRATEGY

Using word lists and other writing resources in the classroom, have children write single-word labels for each picture. As children tell you more about each picture, model how to add words to write phrases or sentences for their captions.

HOME–SCHOOL CONNECTION

You may want to suggest that children help older family members write captions for photos in a family album or write captions for pictures drawn at home or colored in coloring books.

WRITING ACROSS THE CURRICULUM

Social Studies Have children write captions for a bulletin-board display or a mural that shows pictures of a topic you are currently studying.

Posters

My poster tells all about our book fair.

Do you like to read?

Come to the

School Book Fair!

Monday, November 16

10:00 a.m. - 2:00 p.m.

in the library

POSTERS

4   Writing to Learn   Luis Cardona
Mississippi

OBJECTIVES

★ **RECOGNIZE** the characteristics and purposes of posters.

★ **RESPOND** to a model poster written by a student writer.

★ **MAKE** a poster.

Begin the Lesson

Display a variety of posters in the classroom. Also invite children to describe posters they have seen in the community or while on a trip. Decide if each poster announces an event or shares an important idea. Help children understand that a poster is a good way to get peoples' attention in order to share information.

Discuss a Writer's Model

MEET THE WRITER Direct children's attention to the poster shown on page 4 of the Big Book of Writing Models and introduce the writer, Luis Cardona, who is in second grade. Invite a volunteer to read aloud what Luis says about his poster. Discuss with children whether Luis made the poster to announce an event or to share an important idea.

TALK ABOUT THE MODEL Have the class read and discuss Luis's poster. Ask what words Luis uses to tell important information. Discuss what the writer does to draw attention to his message, such as using large print and colorful drawings. Help children understand that a poster should be interesting to look at and easy to read, and it should share important information.

Write and Confer

Invite children to make posters about a school activity. Have them brainstorm ideas, such as a field trip, field day, family night, science fair, carnival, or bake sale. List the ideas, then let children choose one or use their own. As they plan their posters, remind them to include information such as *who, what, when, where,* and *why.*

After children draw their plans on large paper, have partners check for facts and spelling. Then children will be ready to use bright colors, pictures, and interesting titles to get readers' attention.

TEACHER CONFERENCE To check their understanding of posters, ask children questions such as the following.

- *How did you decide what to include on your poster?*
- *Why do you think people will read your poster? How will it catch their attention?*
- *What will people learn from your poster?*

ASSESSMENT OPPORTUNITIES

SELF-ASSESSMENT Have children complete the Self-Assessment Checklist on page 12.

PEER EVALUATION Have children use the Peer Evaluation Checklist on page 14.

TEACHER HOLISTIC ASSESSMENT Use the Teacher Evaluation Checklist on page 13 to evaluate children's posters.

Using Illustrations

Introduce Display several illustrated posters. Invite children to identify the main message or purpose of each poster. Then have them suggest reasons why the illustrations were used. Lead children to conclude that the illustrations make the poster more interesting and easier to understand.

Model Have children look at Luis's illustrations in his poster on page 4 of the Big Book. Invite them to suggest why Luis drew these pictures. Guide them to understand that the illustrations reinforce the purpose of the poster—to encourage readers to come to the book fair.

Summarize/Apply Suggest that children review their own posters and add more illustrations if needed. Remind them that their illustrations should attract readers who are looking at the poster from far away.

WRITER'S BLOCK

Problem	Solution
Children write words that are too small or are misspelled.	Use a pencil to lightly draw writing lines on the poster board. Also encourage children to write and draw in pencil before adding color. That way they can easily adjust letter size and correct mistakes as needed.

ESL STRATEGY

Have children with differing language proficiencies work together to create a poster. Have them share responsibilities and discuss each step of the writing process.

HOME–SCHOOL CONNECTION

Have children share their posters with family members. Encourage them to discuss the importance of each piece of information they included.

WRITING ACROSS THE CURRICULUM

Health To reinforce the idea of using posters to share information, have children select a healthy habit they have learned, such as brushing their teeth, eating healthy foods, or exercising. Invite them to create a poster encouraging others to develop this habit.

Literature Logs

OBJECTIVES

★ RECOGNIZE the characteristics and purposes of literature logs.

★ RESPOND to a model log entry written by a student writer.

★ WRITE in a literature log.

1 Begin the Lesson

Display popular books that children have read. Invite each child to choose a book and briefly tell what the book is about and what the story reminds him or her of. Encourage children to also tell what they liked and didn't like about the stories. Record responses for a few books on the board. Tell children they can write ideas like these in a special notebook called a literature log.

2 Discuss a Writer's Model

MEET THE WRITER Show children the literature log entry on page 5 of the Big Book of Writing Models and introduce the second-grade writer, Tanika Brown. Invite a volunteer to read aloud what Tanika says about her purpose for writing about books. Point out that Tanika can always reread what she has written in her literature log to help her remember the books she has read.

TALK ABOUT THE MODEL Read Tanika's log entry aloud. Discuss the kinds of information that Tanika included, starting with writing the date, the book title, and the author's name. Then Tanika tells about the main character and what she did. Invite volunteers to suggest reasons why Tanika wrote about this book. Point out that the main character reminded Tanika of a person she knew, her Aunt Rita.

Share with children that the stories, characters, and settings that writers write about in their literature logs can also be good sources for writing ideas.

LITERATURE LOG

January 16

Miss Rumphius
by Barbara Cooney

Today I finished reading Miss Rumphius. The main character reminds me of my Aunt Rita. This is why. Miss Rumphius traveled around the world. Then she went to live by the sea. My Aunt Rita travels too. She lives by a lake. My aunt loves to plant flowers, just like Miss Rumphius. When I grow up, I'm going to plant flowers, too.

I like to write about books I've read. It helps me remember them.

Tanika Brown
Indiana

Literature Log 5

3 Write and Confer

Have each child write a log entry about a book she or he has read or listened to in school or at home. (See page 8 for a blackline master.) Display the Big Book model as children write. Remind them to date their entries and begin with the book title and author's name. Encourage them to write about something they like in the book and how they feel about the book. They may wish to write about something or someone the book reminds them of.

TEACHER CONFERENCE To check their understanding of literature logs, ask children questions such as these.

• *What kinds of things did you write about the book you read? Why should you include the date and the book's title and author?*

• *Does the story remind you of anything?*

• *How might you use your literature log to help you write stories of your own?*

ASSESSMENT OPPORTUNITIES

SELF-ASSESSMENT Have children complete the Self-Assessment Checklist on page 12.

PEER EVALUATION Have children use the Peer Evaluation Checklist on page 14.

TEACHER HOLISTIC ASSESSMENT Use the Teacher Evaluation Checklist on page 13 to evaluate children's literature logs.

Mini Lesson

Using Books and Stories to Get Ideas for Writing

Introduce Display a list of writing ideas that relate to a favorite children's story, for example: *How to Plant Beans, My Giant Friend, Goldie the Goose,* and *How to Play a Harp.* Invite children to guess what story you used to get those ideas. (*Jack and the Beanstalk*) Then explain that stories are a good source of ideas for writing.

Model Review with children Tanika's literature log entry on page 5 of the Big Book. Remind them that a literature log is a good source of ideas for writing. Then invite children to suggest story ideas based on Tanika's entry, such as a story about flowers, traveling, or aunts. List children's ideas on the board.

Summarize/Apply Encourage children to review their literature logs and look for ideas for writing. Suggest they list two or three ideas. Invite volunteers to share their ideas and tell how they thought of them.

WRITER'S BLOCK

Problem	Solution
Children only summarize the story and do not include personal reactions.	Guide children by asking if the story or characters remind them of something that happened to them or someone they know and to include this information in their writing.

ESL STRATEGY

Have children draw pictures to show what they like about the book. As children talk about their drawings, help them with vocabulary and sentence structure to write captions in their logs.

HOME-SCHOOL CONNECTION

Encourage children to keep a literature log at home. Suggest they work with family members to write about books they read together.

WRITING ACROSS THE CURRICULUM

Social Studies Have children read and respond to folk tales and fairy tales from different cultures around the world. Encourage children to record the place of origin for each story. Point out the places on a world map.

November 12

The Magic Fan
by Keith Baker

Today I read The Magic Fan. It is a book about a boy from Japan. He has a magic fan that shows him how to make things. I like the fans in the book. They lift up and show cool pictures. I wish I had a magic fan. I would make lots of things, too.

Learning Logs

I write about things I'm learning in class in my learning log.

October 5

Different Shapes

Circles are round. They do not have any corners.

A triangle has three sides and three corners.

A rectangle has four sides and four corners. My desk is a rectangle.

A square also has four sides and four corners.

What is the difference between a rectangle and a square?

6   Writing to Learn

Felicia Espinoza
Arkansas

OBJECTIVES

★ **RECOGNIZE** the characteristics and purposes of learning logs.

★ **RESPOND** to a model log entry written by a student writer.

★ **WRITE** in a learning log.

1 Begin the Lesson

On the board, write a topic children are learning about in school. Have children brainstorm what they know about the topic and questions they wonder about the topic. Record their responses on the board. Then explain the purpose of a learning log: It is a notebook in which you write about subjects like math, science, social studies, and language arts.

2 Discuss a Writer's Model

MEET THE WRITER Have children look at the learning log entry on page 6 of the Big Book of Writing Models and introduce the writer, Felicia Espinoza, who is in the second grade. Let children read what Felicia says about her writing. Ask children to look at the title of Felicia's log entry and then her pictures, which suggest the subject she wrote about.

TALK ABOUT THE MODEL Read Felicia's entry aloud. Invite volunteers to retell the facts that Felicia wrote. Then direct children's attention to the question at the end of the entry. Introduce the idea that a learning log is a good place to record facts you want to remember and questions you would like answered.

3 Write and Confer

Have children make a learning log by dividing and labeling a notebook into sections, one for each subject. Then have them write about a topic they are learning in class. Remind children to include questions they have about the topic. If possible, have children write in their logs immediately after a lesson.

TEACHER CONFERENCE As children work on a log entry, ask questions like the following. Make sure children understand that a learning log can help them think about and recall what they have learned.

* *Why did you choose to record these facts and questions in your learning log?*

* *How will you get the answers to your questions?*

* *How might you use your learning log?*

ASSESSMENT OPPORTUNITIES

SELF-ASSESSMENT Have children complete the Self-Assessment Checklist on page 12.

PEER EVALUATION Have children use the Peer Evaluation Checklist on page 14.

TEACHER HOLISTIC ASSESSMENT Use the Teacher Evaluation Checklist on page 13 to evaluate children's learning logs.

Graphic Organizers

Introduce Using red, blue, and green chalk or markers, make a simple color chart. In the left column draw one color circle for each color. In the right column write each color's name. At the top of the chart, add the title "Colors." Invite children to look at the chart and suggest why it is a good way to record information.

Model Explain that pictures can often give information more easily than words or sentences. Have children recall the shapes Felicia drew in her log entry on page 6 of the Big Book. Begin a new chart and invite volunteers to draw Felicia's shapes on the left and write their labels on the right. Ask children how the chart helps to organize the information.

Summarize/Apply Point out that writers often use charts to organize their ideas because the pictures and words in them help to make the ideas easy to understand. Suggest that children use graphic organizers like charts when they record information in their learning logs.

WRITER'S BLOCK

Problem

Children do not record or review information in their learning logs.

Solution

Encourage partners to work together, motivating each other to think about and record what they've learned. Point out that the information in their logs may help them when completing a worksheet or a test.

ESL STRATEGY

Help children with subject-specific vocabulary. Give them content-area word lists to glue onto the inside covers of their learning logs. Include picture cues to help children identify and remember the meanings of the words.

HOME–SCHOOL CONNECTION

Have children take home their learning logs at the end of the week. Invite them to share their entries with family members and discuss what they have learned during the week. Encourage children to add new entries about school topics that they have learned more about after sharing them with their families.

WRITING ACROSS THE CURRICULUM

Math Have children record notes and questions about math concepts they are learning in class. Encourage them to draw or write examples in their log entries.

Addition

$\square + \square = 6$

$\bigcirc + \square = 5$

$\square$ is the same number.

$\bigcirc$ is a different number.

The number sentences are $3 + 3 = 6$ and $2 + 3 = 5$.

Observation Logs

OBJECTIVES

★ **RECOGNIZE** the characteristics and purposes of observation logs.

★ **RESPOND** to a model log entry written by a student writer.

★ **WRITE** in an observation log.

1 Begin the Lesson

Invite children to describe what they see, hear, smell, and feel in the classroom. Write today's date and record their observations on the board. Then explain the purpose of a special notebook called an observation log in which you use your senses to write about the things around you. Point out that writing in an observation log can help you pay attention to the world around you and help you to discover and write about new things.

2 Discuss a Writer's Model

MEET THE WRITER Show children the log entries on page 7 of the Big Book of Writing Models and introduce the writer, second-grader Nikki Liu. Have children look at the pictures on the page and predict what Nikki observed and wrote about in her observation log. Help children understand that Nikki wrote notes and drew pictures to help her remember what she observed on three different days.

TALK ABOUT THE MODEL Have volunteers read aloud Nikki's observations. Point out the date of each entry and talk about why it is important to include a date each time you write. Invite children to identify the descriptive words that Nikki used to tell about the color, sound, texture, and actions of the ducks. Encourage children to predict what Nikki might write next.

March 5
I saw a brown duck sitting on a nest by the creek.

Quack!

I like to write about interesting things I see.

March 6
Today I saw the father duck. He has a dark green head. He quacked loudly when I got too close.

March 10
The eggs hatched! I peeked into the nest and saw 6 fuzzy ducks. One egg has not hatched yet.

Nikki Liu
New Mexico

Observation Log 7

3 Write and Confer

Have children record their observations of the school. Children might choose to record what they observe in the classroom, in another part of the school building, or outdoors on the playground. Remind them to use all their senses—sight, hearing, smell, taste, and touch. Point out that it's not necessary to write complete sentences. You might want to encourage children to draw pictures. (See the blackline master on page 9.)

TEACHER CONFERENCE Invite children to read their entries aloud and show any pictures they have drawn. Ask questions such as the following.

- *Which senses did you use to observe the people, places, and things around you?*

- *What new things did you discover by writing in your log?*

- *How do you think you might use this information later?*

ASSESSMENT OPPORTUNITIES

SELF-ASSESSMENT Have children complete the Self-Assessment Checklist on page 12.

PEER EVALUATION Have children use the Peer Evaluation Checklist on page 14.

TEACHER HOLISTIC ASSESSMENT Use the Teacher Evaluation Checklist on page 13 to evaluate children's observation logs.

Mini Lesson

Making and Recording Observations

Introduce Have a volunteer perform a simple experiment in front of the class, such as putting food coloring in water or dropping two items from the same height. Have children use their senses to describe what is happening during the experiment. Record their observations on chart paper. Then explain to the class that they have just made and recorded observations.

Model Have children reread the model on page 7 of the Big Book. Ask them to identify the different senses Nikki used to observe the ducks. Help children understand that when they observe a moving object, they should write their observations quickly so they don't miss anything. Suggest that they write short phrases and sentences and draw simple pictures.

Summarize/Apply Remind children to write quickly but accurately when they record observations. Encourage them to make and record observations every day and to use all their senses to observe the things around them.

WRITER'S BLOCK

Problem	Solution
Children write only visual descriptions of their surroundings.	Suggest that children close their eyes and focus on what they hear, feel, and smell. Encourage children to write at least two or three details using these senses.

ESL STRATEGY

Suggest that children draw what they see, hear, smell, or feel. Then guide them as they write descriptive words to tell about their observations. Suggest words for each of the senses. For example, ask: *Did it feel soft or rough? Did the plant look green or yellow? Was it tall or short?*

HOME–SCHOOL CONNECTION

Encourage children to write in their observation logs during family outings and vacations. Have family members help children record observations of people, places, and things.

WRITING ACROSS THE CURRICULUM

Social Studies Have children record their observations during a class field trip. Encourage them to write about interesting sights, sounds, smells, and textures. Schedule moments during the trip when children can write in their logs.

> April 15
>
> I am at a museum right now. We are here on a class field trip. The museum is very noisy because lots of people are talking. There are so many things to see. The dinosaurs are huge! I got to touch a real dinosaur fossil. It felt like a hard rock.

Revising and Editing Marks

≡	capitalize
∧ or ∨	add
—	remove
⊙	add a period
/	make lowercase
◯	spelling mistake
↻	move

Once Upon a Time: Writing to Tell a Story

Contents

Writing to Tell a Story

MINILESSONS

WRITING FORM	Basic Skills/ Writing Process/ Writer's Craft	Grammar, Usage, Mechanics, Spelling	Writing Across the Curriculum	Meeting Individual Needs	Assessment
Lesson 1 NEWS STORY pp. 48–49 (3–4 days)	• Adding Facts to Support Main Idea, 49		• Science, 49	• Writer's Block, 49 • ESL Strategy, 49 • Home-School Connection, 49	• Self-Assessment Checklist, 42 • Teacher Evaluation Checklist, 43 • Peer Evaluation Checklist, 44 • Teacher and Peer Conferencing, 49
Lesson 2 PERSONAL NARRATIVE pp. 58–67 (6–10 days)	• Beginning, Middle, and End, 59 • Point of View, 61 • Order of Events, 63	• Capitalization— First Word of Sentence, 65	• Language Arts, 59 • Social Studies, 61 • Science, 63 • Reading, 65	• Writer's Block, 59, 61, 63, 65 • ESL Strategy, 59, 61, 63, 65 • Home-School Connection, 59, 61, 63, 65	• Rubric, 67 • Benchmark Papers, 54–57 • Self-Assessment Checklist, 52 • Teacher Evaluation Checklist, 53 • Peer Evaluation Checklist, 44 • Portfolio, 67 • Teacher and Peer Conferencing, 59, 60, 62, 64
Lesson 3 FOLK TALE pp. 68–71 (3–4 days)	• Characters and Setting, 69		• Science, 69	• Writer's Block, 69 • ESL Strategy, 69 • Home-School Connection, 69	• Self-Assessment Checklist, 42 • Teacher Evaluation Checklist, 43 • Peer Evaluation Checklist, 44 • Teacher and Peer Conferencing, 71
Lesson 4 REALISTIC STORY pp. 80–89 (6–10 days)	• Plot, 81 • Planning a Composition Using a Story Map, 83 • Sequencing Events by Cutting and Pasting Sentences, 85	• Capitalization— Names, 87	• Art, 81 • Science, 83 • Social Studies, 85 • Language Arts, 87	• Writer's Block, 81, 83, 85, 87 • ESL Strategy, 81, 83, 85, 87 • Home-School Connection, 81, 83, 85, 87	• Rubric, 89 • Benchmark Papers, 76–79 • Self-Assessment Checklist, 74 • Teacher Evaluation Checklist, 75 • Peer Evaluation Checklist, 44 • Portfolio, 89 • Teacher and Peer Conferencing, 81, 82, 84, 86
Lesson 5 FANTASY pp. 90–92 (3–4 days)	• Identifying Form— Real vs. Make-Believe, 91		• Science, 91	• Writer's Block, 91 • ESL Strategy, 91 • Home-School Connection, 91	• Self-Assessment Checklist, 42 • Teacher Evaluation Checklist, 43 • Peer Evaluation Checklist, 44 • Teacher and Peer Conferencing, 92

Making the Reading-Writing Connection
Writing to Tell a Story

You may want to add the following books and magazines to your classroom library. Each category of books or magazines represents one form of writing children will be introduced to in *Writing to Tell a Story*. The books and magazines serve as models for good writing and are valuable resources to use throughout each lesson. The suggested titles offer reading opportunities for children of varying reading abilities and are labeled as follows.

 Easy—books or magazines with a readability that is below second-grade level, but with content of interest to second graders

 Average—books or magazines with an average readability level that can be read independently by most second-grade students

 Challenging—books or magazines with above-average readability for more proficient students or those that can be read aloud to students

Use literature to introduce a writing form, as a model of successful writing, to enhance minilessons, to focus on grammar and usage, and to expand each lesson.

NEWS STORY

Time for Kids: News Scoop Edition
by Time, Inc. Time for Kids, a magazine for second and third graders from the creators of TIME magazine, contains a variety of news stories and articles with kid appeal.

The Furry News: How to Make a Newspaper
by Loreen Leedy. Holiday House, 1990. The animals write, edit, and print a newspaper about news that they are interested in.

Deadline! From News to Newspaper
by Gail Gibbons. Ty Crowell Co., 1987. Go behind the scenes of a small daily newspaper as the people at work rush to make their deadlines.

PERSONAL NARRATIVE

Ice-Cold Birthday
by Maryann Cocca-Leffler. Price Stern Sloan, 1992. The story of a great snowfall that nearly ruins a little girl's birthday party is told in first person. The day is saved when the snow turns into a big surprise.

How Many Stars in the Sky?
by Lenny Hort. Mulberry Books, 1997. A boy tells how he and his father set off into the night on an unexpected journey to count the stars.

Anthony Reynosos: Born to Rope
by Martha Cooper and Ginger Gordan. Clarion Books, 1996. Anthony tells of his life in Arizona and the passing down of rodeo traditions from father to son.

FOLK TALE

The Hatseller and the Monkeys
by Baba Wagué Diakité. Scholastic, 1999. This West African folk tale is about a hatseller whose hats are stolen by mischievous monkeys. The hatseller cleverly outwits the monkeys to get his hats back.

Goldilocks and the Three Bears
by James Marshall. Puffin Books, 1988. Goldilocks is a naughty little girl in this inventive retelling of the familiar tale.

And It Is Still That Way: Legends Told by Arizona Indian Children
Compiled by Byrd Baylor. Cinco Puntos Press, 1998. American Indian children retell tribal legends in their own words.

REALISTIC STORY

William's Doll
by Charlotte Zolotow. HarperCollins, 1972. A boy wants a doll but is forbidden it until his grandmother intervenes.

The Bat in the Boot
by Annie Cannon. Orchard Books, 1996. A baby bat that fell into a boot is rescued first by two children then by its mother.

Sleep Out
by Carol and Donald Carrick. Clarion Books, 1973. A young boy bravely plans to sleep outside alone for the first time.

FANTASY

Danny and the Dinosaur
by Syd Hoff. HarperTrophy, 1993. This is the classic tale of the young boy Danny and his new-found friend, a dinosaur.

Hey, Al
by Arthur Yorinks. Sunburst, 1989. A school janitor and his dog take off on an adventure of a lifetime to an island in the sky.

Cloudy With a Chance of Meatballs
by Judi Barrett. Aladdin Paperbacks, 1982. A grandfather tells a fantasy story about the fictional town of Chewandswallow and the strange weather encountered by its citizens.

The Classroom Writing Center
Writing to Tell a Story

As the school year progresses and children are learning about *Writing to Tell a Story*, you may want to enhance your writing center to promote story writing.

◆ Set up a puppet theater with materials to make stick, paper bag, finger, and sock puppets for dramatizing children's stories, stories they are planning, or stories they have shared with the class.

◆ In the listening station, make available tape recordings of stories. Enlist the help of family members to record stories. Also invite family members, especially grandparents, to send in recordings of personal stories they'd like to share.

◆ Make available drawing software that enables children to add text to drawings they have made or to stamps they have used.

◆ Display books that exemplify the kinds of writing in this unit: news stories, personal narratives, folk tales, realistic stories, and fantasies. See page 33 for a list of suggested books.

◆ Provide an Author's Chair. Make it special with a decorative label.

◆ Create a "Story Wall": Hang mural paper. Add the words *Story Wall*. Provide markers and crayons for children to draw and write freely.

The Stages of the Writing Process

Consider the following activities as children engage in writing stories.

A Prewriting Activity for a Realistic Story
Display interesting pictures from magazines or newspapers. Have small groups or partners create a plan for a story about one of the pictures.

A Drafting Activity for Writing Stories
Make a tips chart that suggests ways to begin a story. Your chart might look like the one to the right.

A Revising Activity for a News Story
Post the words *Who, What, When Where, Why or How* on colorful cards by a desk labeled *Editor's Desk*. Children can take turns using the desk to make sure they have answered each question in their stories.

> How to Start a Story
> 1. Have the main character introduce himself or herself.
> 2. Describe where the story takes place.
> 3. Begin a folk tale with *Once upon a time* . . . or *Long, long ago* . . .
> 4. Begin with a sentence that makes your readers want to read on:
> *Today was the worst day of my life!*

A Publishing Activity for a Story
Provide patterns for children to use to make shape books or set out completed story books.

Graphic Organizers

The following blackline masters can help children with parts of the lessons in this unit. Make copies for the writing center and transparencies for use with an overhead projector. Display a completed example of each organizer if desired.

Blackline Master	Purpose	Writing Form
Story Map, page 36	Designing a Plan: story map	All narrative forms
Real and Make-Believe, page 37	Prewriting: gathering ideas	Fantasy
Facts Chart, page 38	Prewriting: gathering and ordering ideas	News Story
Story Chart, page 39	Designing a Plan: story chart	All narrative forms

Create a Bulletin Board

◆ Create a bulletin-board display with the title *"We Are Writing to Tell a Story!"*

◆ Distribute kid-shaped cutouts for children to color to resemble themselves. If desired, they can affix a photo for a face. Display the cutouts at the bottom of the board, along with the sentence *We are storytellers!* inside a speech balloon.

◆ Create five sections on the bulletin board by using different background colors to resemble a quilt. Label each section with the name of one form of writing, including News Story, Personal Narrative, Folk Tale, Realistic Story, and Fantasy.

◆ Display examples of published pieces for each form of writing. Gradually replace the samples with children's writing.

Name _____   **Date** _____

Story Map

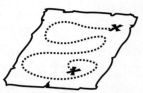

Use the map to plan your story.

Beginning

↓

Middle

↓

End

Name _____ Date _____

Real and Make-Believe

Write descriptions of real things on the left. Change them to make-believe things on the right.

Real	Make-Believe
1.	1.
2.	2.
3.	3.
4.	4.
5.	5.

Name _____ Date _____

Facts Chart

Write facts about something that happened or will happen.

Event: _____

What?	
Who?	
When?	
Where?	
Why/How?	

Story Chart

Write important details about your story.

Event: _____

Characters

Setting

Problem

Ending

Connecting Multiple Intelligences
Writing to Tell a Story

The following activities focus on specific prewriting and publishing ideas for children who demonstrate intelligence in different ways: talent and skill with words (linguistic), with numbers (logical-mathematical), with pictures (spatial), with movement (bodily-kinesthetic), with people (interpersonal), with self (intrapersonal), with music (musical), and/or with nature (environmental or naturalist).

Linguistic
Prewriting — Read aloud books or listen to tape recordings of different kinds of stories.
Publishing — Become a storyteller to share a story you have written.

Logical-Mathematical
Prewriting — Draw a series of numbered boxes to create a picture timeline for your story.
Publishing — Make an accordion-style book to publish your story.

Spatial
Prewriting — Draw simple sketches to plan a story map. Then go back and add key words.
Publishing — Write your story text on several pages and add illustrations to create a book.

Bodily-Kinesthetic
Prewriting — Act out your story plan to figure out how the characters will solve the problem.
Publishing — Dress like the character in your folk tale or fantasy as you tell or read it.

Writing to Tell a Story

Environmental (Naturalist)
Prewriting — Plan a news story that has something to do with a nature theme.
Publishing — Add drawings to show the importance of nature or animals in your folk tale or fantasy.

Intrapersonal
Prewriting — Look through classroom books to get ideas for a folk tale or fantasy.
Publishing — Make a tape recording of your story for others to use in a listening station.

Interpersonal
Prewriting — Talk with a small group to plan ideas for a story you will write.
Publishing — Display your writing in an "author of the week" showcase.

Musical
Prewriting — Plan to write a story about yourself or characters who have an experience with music.
Publishing — Include music or singing as you share a story you have written.

Evaluating Student Writing
Writing to Tell a Story

The Write Direction offers a variety of assessment options. The following are short descriptions of the assessment opportunities available in this unit. Just select the assessment option that works best for you.

Types of Assessment	Complete-Process Writing Lessons	Short-Process Writing Lessons
Rubric Specific characteristics of a writing form are used to develop a 4-point scale for evaluating children's writing (4–Well Developed, 3–Adequately Developed, 2–Partially Developed, 1–Undeveloped). Children's writing is compared with the characteristics to determine a rating point.	• Personal Narrative, page 67 • Realistic Story, page 89	
Benchmark Papers Annotated and scored student writing models are provided as benchmarks for evaluating children's writing. Children's published writing can be compared with these models for assessment.	• Personal Narrative, pages 54–57 • Realistic Story, pages 76–79	
Checklists Self-Assessment, Teacher, and Peer Evaluation Checklists help children refine their narrative writing at each writing process stage.	• Self-Assessment Checklist for Personal Narrative, page 52 • Teacher Evaluation Checklist for Personal Narrative, page 53 • Self-Assessment Checklist for Realistic Story, page 74 • Teacher Evaluation Checklist for Realistic Story, page 75 • Peer Evaluation Checklist, page 44	• Self-Assessment Checklist, page 42 • Teacher Evaluation Checklist, page 43 • Peer Evaluation Checklist, page 44
Portfolio Assessment Children's work generated throughout the writing process may be used in creating a portfolio illustrating their progress as writers. Strategies and tips for assessment using a portfolio appear in each lesson. Suggested pieces for a portfolio include completed writing and works-in-progress, logs, journals, and checklists.	• Personal Narrative, page 67 • Realistic Story, page 89	
Teacher and Peer Conferencing Throughout each lesson in this unit, there are opportunities to interact with children, informally questioning them about their progress and concerns. Children also have opportunities to interact with one another to ask questions, share ideas, and react to their partner's writing.	• Personal Narrative, pages 59, 60, 62, 64 • Realistic Story, pages 81, 82, 84, 86	• News Story, page 49 • Folk Tale, page 70 • Fantasy, page 92

Self-Assessment Checklist
Writing to Tell a Story

Name of Writer _____

Date _____

Type of Writing _____

Use this checklist when you are revising, or editing and proofreading a
- **news story**
- **folk tale**
- **fantasy**

	YES	NO	Ways to Make My Writing Better
Is there anything I should add or take out?	☐	☐	
Are the events in the middle of the story in the correct order?	☐	☐	
Did I write in complete sentences?	☐	☐	
Does my writing have a clear beginning, middle, and end?	☐	☐	
Have I spelled words correctly?	☐	☐	
Did I use punctuation marks and capital letters correctly?	☐	☐	

Teacher Evaluation Checklist
Writing to Tell a Story

Name of Writer _____

Date _____

Writing Mode _____

Use this checklist when you are evaluating a child's
- **news story**
- **folk tale**
- **fantasy**

	YES	NO	Recommendations to Child
Is the topic appropriate for this story line?	☐	☐	
Is the writing focused on the topic?	☐	☐	
Does the writing have a clear beginning, middle, and end?	☐	☐	
Is the sequence of events clear?	☐	☐	
Are the events presented in the correct order?	☐	☐	
Does the writer adhere to the conventions of			
grammar?	☐	☐	
usage?	☐	☐	
spelling?	☐	☐	
punctuation?	☐	☐	
capitalization?	☐	☐	
Is the handwriting legible?	☐	☐	
Was the work done neatly?	☐	☐	

Peer Evaluation Checklist
Writing to Tell a Story

Name of Writer _____

Name of Writing Partner _____

Conference Date _____

Type of Writing _____

Use this checklist during revising or editing and proofreading conferences for a
- **news story**
- **personal narrative**
- **folk tale**
- **realistic story**
- **fantasy**

	What My Writing Partner Said	**Ways to Make My Writing Better**
What did you like best about my story?		
Is there anything missing from my story?		
Is there anything I should take out of my story?		
What do you think I can do to make my story more interesting?		
Did you understand what happened in the story?		

Home Letter

Dear Family,

Are you a family of story readers? Maybe your favorite reading material is the newspaper or a story about a real person. Your children probably enjoy reading and hearing tales of fantasy and folklore.

Your child will be learning about writing different kinds of stories, such as a news story, a story about themselves, a folk tale, a realistic story, and a fantasy. You can look forward to reading these stories as your child works on planning, drafting, revising, editing, and publishing them.

Here are some ways you can support your child's story writing.

1 Ask your child to tell about his or her day at school. Your child's recollections of what was learned, friends played with, the lunch menu, and new experiences is a form of oral storytelling.

2 If your child has use of a computer at home, create a family newsletter to send out periodically. Involve every family member in deciding on a name and logo for your newsletter and in writing family stories. Scan in favorite photos, too.

3 Read books that are examples of different kinds of stories. Here are a few books to look for, but ask your local librarian to help you find folk tales, fantasy stories, and stories with realistic characters to read together.

◆ *The Art Lesson* by Tomie dePaola. G. P. Putnam's, 1989. In this touching story about the author's own childhood, Tommy knows he wants to be an artist when he grows up. He draws pictures everywhere. His friends think he's the best artist ever.

◆ *The Acorn Tree and Other Folktales* by Anne Rockwell. Greenwillow Books, 1995. This collection of traditional tales is told in an easy-going manner that is perfect for reading aloud to the whole family.

Sincerely,

Carta para el hogar

Estimada familia,

¿Son ustedes una familia de lectores de cuentos? Tal vez el material de lectura favorito de ustedes sea el periódico o un relato acerca de una persona real. A sus hijos probablemente les guste leer y oir cuentos de fantasía y de folclor.

Su hijo/a va a estudiar la escritura de diversos tipos de cuentos, tales como un artículo noticioso, un relato acerca de ellos mismos, un cuento tradicional, un cuento realista o una fantasía. Pueden participar en la lectura de estos cuentos cuando su hijo/a comience a planificar la escritura, a hacer el borrador, revisarlo, editarlo y publicarlo.

He aquí algunas sugerencias que les pueden servir para apoyar la escritura de cuentos por parte de su hijo/a.

1. Pídanle a su hijo/a que relaten su día en la escuela. Una forma oral de contar cuentos, es relatar lo que aprendió, los amigos con que jugó, el menú del almuerzo y nuevas experiencias.

2. Si su hijo/a tiene acceso a una computadora en casa, creen un boletín familiar para enviarlo periódicamente. Involucren a todos los familiares en decidir el nombre y el logotipo del boletín y en la redacción de los artículos. Añadan también sus fotos favoritas.

3. Lean libros que sean ejemplos de diferentes tipos de cuentos. He aquí varios que son buenos, pero pídanle ayuda al bibliotecario para hallar libros de cuentos tradicionales, cuentos de fantasía y cuentos con personajes reales que puedan leer juntos en casa.
   - *The Art Lesson* por Tomie dePaola, G.P. Putnam's, 1989. En este cuento emotivo acerca de la niñez del propio autor, Tommy sabe que quiere ser artista cuando crezca. Él hace dibujos por todos lados. Sus amigos creen que él es el mejor artista del mundo.
   - *The Acorn Tree and Other Folktales* por Anne Rockwell. Greenwillow Books, 1995. Esta colección de cuentos tradicionales se relata de manera fácil, lo que la hace idónea para la lectura en voz alta con toda la familia.

Sinceramente,

ONCE UPON A TIME:

Writing to Tell a Story

Writing to Tell a Story

Introduction

Introduce *Writing to Tell a Story* by having children close their eyes and think back as far as they can remember. Prompt them by asking if they can think back to first grade or kindergarten. Maybe they can remember their first day of school or their fourth birthday. Maybe they can think back farther to when they were first walking and learning to talk. Then invite children to share stories of their earliest memories.

Choose one child's story or use a story of your own and ask questions such as the following.

★ **Who is in the story?**

★ **When and where did it happen?**

★ **What happened first? Next?**

★ **How did the story end?**

★ **What do you think about this story?**

Point out to children that everyone has a great story to tell. Some stories, such as the ones they just shared, are about real people and things that happened. Other stories are made up by writers who tell about characters and things that happen that seem real or are make-believe. Explain that over the next weeks, they will be writing different kinds of stories. As you share the following information to preview each form of writing, show an example from your classroom library.

★ A **news story** tells about an important event that just happened.

★ In a **personal narrative** the writer tells a true story about something that happened to him or her.

★ A **folk tale** is a story that has been told by people over and over again for many years. Nobody knows for sure who the author is.

★ A **realistic story** tells about made-up characters and things that could really happen.

★ A **fantasy** is a make-believe story that could not really happen.

News Story

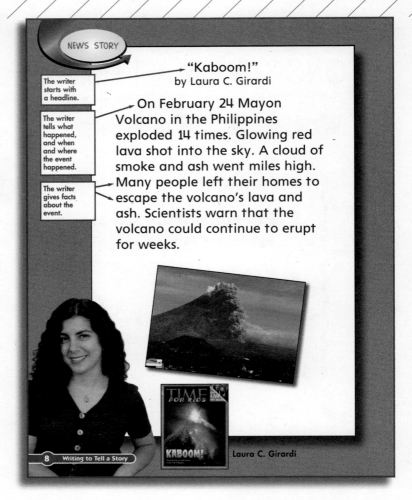

NEWS STORY

The writer starts with a headline.

The writer tells what happened, and when and where the event happened.

The writer gives facts about the event.

"Kaboom!"
by Laura C. Girardi

On February 24 Mayon Volcano in the Philippines exploded 14 times. Glowing red lava shot into the sky. A cloud of smoke and ash went miles high. Many people left their homes to escape the volcano's lava and ash. Scientists warn that the volcano could continue to erupt for weeks.

8   Writing to Tell a Story

Laura C. Girardi

OBJECTIVES

★ **RECOGNIZE** the characteristics of a news story.

★ **RESPOND** to a model of a news story written by a published author.

★ **PLAN, WRITE,** and **REVISE** a news story.

★ **USE** a fact chart to organize ideas.

1 Begin the Lesson

Share a news article that would interest children. Work with children to recognize the facts in the story by filling in a chart such as the following.

What?	Madison Elementary School Fair
Who?	children, teachers, parents
When?	October 12
Where?	school cafeteria and playground
Why or How?	raised money for school field trips

Help children understand that when writers tell a story with facts about an event that just happened, it is called a news story.

2 Discuss a Writer's Model

MEET THE WRITER Using page 8 of the Big Book of Writing Models, introduce the magazine writer, Laura C. Girardi. Explain that this writer gathered information and wrote a news story for a magazine called *Time for Kids*. Point out her byline in the article.

TALK ABOUT THE MODEL Read the news story to the class. Use the callouts to point out important facts about the event. Ask questions like the following to get children thinking about the characteristics of a news story.

• *What is the main idea of the news story?*

• *What facts are explained in this news story?*

• *How do you think the writer got her facts?*

• *Does the writer tell what she feels about the event, or does she tell only facts?*

Emphasize the importance of writing facts, rather than opinions. Invite children to suggest ways that news story writers gather their facts, such as by talking to people, watching the event, and reading about it.

Discuss the headline "Kaboom!" and tell children that writers often include a headline, or title for a news story, that will get the reader's attention and give clues about the story's main idea.

3 Write and Confer

INDEPENDENT WRITING Children can write their own news stories using Laura Girardi's model as a guide.

MAKE A PLAN Suggest that children brainstorm topics by thinking about recent important events. Once children choose the best idea for a news story, they can make a fact chart to plan their story (see page 38 for a blackline master).

WRITE IT DOWN As children write, remind them to answer the questions *Who?, What?, Where?, When?,* and *Why/How?* and include a headline and a byline.

LOOK IT OVER Have children check to make sure they have included all the facts about the event, beginning with the most important details. They can then check for spelling, punctuation, and capital letters.

TEACHER CONFERENCE To help children see ways to improve their news stories, ask questions such as these.

- *How did you begin your news story?*
- *Did you tell your readers all the facts?*
- *Is your headline interesting?*

PEER CONFERENCE Have partners read their news stories to each other. Ask them to listen for sentences that answer *who, what, where, when,* and *why/how.*

SHARE YOUR WORK Have children prepare final drafts using a word-processing program. Suggest they use a different font for the headline. Print out the stories and compile them into a class newsletter. Small groups could also present their news stories by role-playing newscasters.

ASSESSMENT OPPORTUNITIES

SELF-ASSESSMENT Have children complete the Self-Assessment Checklist on page 42.

PEER EVALUATION Have children use the Peer Evaluation Checklist on page 44.

TEACHER HOLISTIC ASSESSMENT Use the Teacher Evaluation Checklist on page 43 to evaluate children's news stories.

Meeting Individual Needs

Mini Lesson

Adding Facts to Support Main Idea

Introduce Tell two brief facts about a recent school event. Ask: *Did I tell everything important that happened? What other facts could I add to tell more about the event?* Invite children to suggest more details. Explain that writers revise their news stories by adding details to tell more about the main idea.

Model Read aloud Laura Girardi's news story on Big Book page 8. Have children raise their hands each time they hear a fact that tells more about the main idea—the Mayon Volcano. Jot the facts on the board as children restate them in their own words. Help children understand that a fact is a statement that can be proven true or false.

Summarize/Apply Explain that writers of news stories use facts to support the main idea so readers can know what happened. Encourage children to add important details to their news stories when they revise.

WRITER'S BLOCK

Problem	Solution
Children feel overwhelmed by the amount of information they need to include in their news stories.	Have children look at their fact charts and write a sentence to answer each question. Then they can add a few details they think may be important to readers.

ESL STRATEGY
Children acquiring English can work with fluent partners to plan and write a news story about an event familiar to both.

HOME–SCHOOL CONNECTION
Invite children to share their news stories with family members, and have them identify the facts that explain *who, what, where, when,* and *why/how.*

WRITING ACROSS THE CURRICULUM
Science As children research science topics, they might want to form *who, what, where, when,* and *why/how* questions as a way to guide their research.

What are dinosaurs?
Who studies dinosaurs?
When did dinosaurs live?
Where are dinosaur fossils found?
How and why did dinosaurs become extinct?

Writer's Workshop Planner

Personal Narrative

WRITING PROCESS STAGE	MINILESSONS			
	Writer's Craft; Grammar, Usage, Mechanics, Spelling	Writing Across the Curriculum	Meeting Individual Needs	Assessment
Prewriting pp. 58–59 (1–2 days)	Organization—Beginning, Middle, and End, page 59	Language Arts, page 59	Writer's Block ESL Strategy Home-School Connection	• Teacher and Peer Conferencing, page 59
Drafting pp. 60–61 (2–3 days)	Point of View—First-Person, page 61	Social Studies, page 61	Writer's Block ESL Strategy Home-School Connection	• Self-Assessment Checklist, page 52 • Peer Evaluation Checklist, page 44 • Teacher Evaluation Checklist, page 53 • Teacher and Peer Conferencing, page 60
Revising pp. 62–63 (1–2 days)	Order of Events, page 63	Science, page 63	Writer's Block ESL Strategy Home-School Connection	• Self-Assessment Checklist, page 52 • Peer Evaluation Checklist, page 44 • Teacher Evaluation Checklist, page 53 • Teacher and Peer Conferencing, page 62
Editing & Proofreading pp. 64–65 (1–2 days)	Capitalization—First Word of Sentence, page 65	Reading, page 65	Writer's Block ESL Strategy Home-School Connection	• Self-Assessment Checklist, page 52 • Peer Evaluation Checklist, page 44 • Teacher Evaluation Checklist, page 53 • Teacher and Peer Conferencing, page 64
Publishing pp. 66–67 (1 day)				• Benchmark Papers, pages 54–57 • Rubric, page 67 • Portfolio, page 67

Suggestions for Planning Each Day

- Whole Class Meeting/Minilesson (5–10 minutes)
- Independent Writing/Teacher-Student Conferences (30–40 minutes)
- Peer Conferences (5–10 minutes)
- Group Share (5–10 minutes)

Connecting Multiple Intelligences
With the Stages of the Writing Process

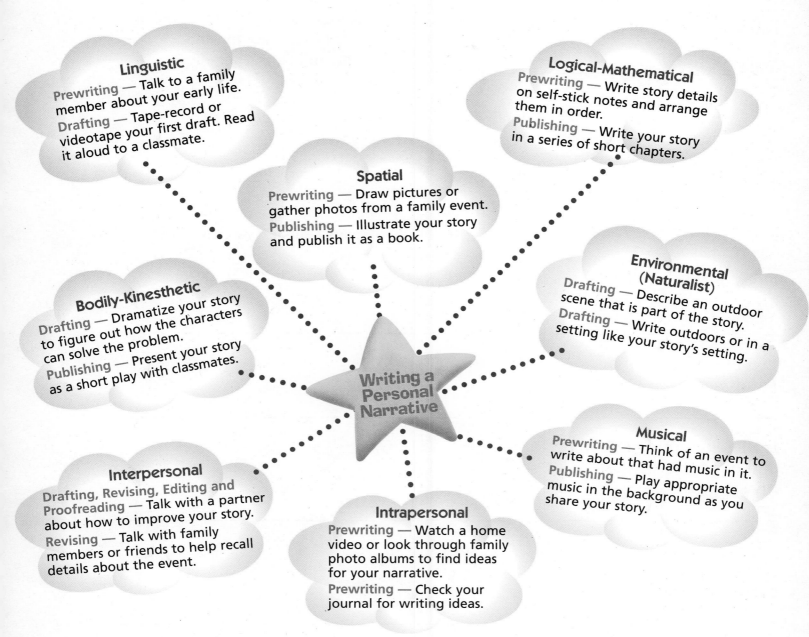

Linguistic
Prewriting — Talk to a family member about your early life.
Drafting — Tape-record or videotape your first draft. Read it aloud to a classmate.

Logical-Mathematical
Prewriting — Write story details on self-stick notes and arrange them in order.
Publishing — Write your story in a series of short chapters.

Spatial
Prewriting — Draw pictures or gather photos from a family event.
Publishing — Illustrate your story and publish it as a book.

Bodily-Kinesthetic
Drafting — Dramatize your story to figure out how the characters can solve the problem.
Publishing — Present your story as a short play with classmates.

Environmental (Naturalist)
Drafting — Describe an outdoor scene that is part of the story.
Drafting — Write outdoors or in a setting like your story's setting.

Writing a Personal Narrative

Interpersonal
Drafting, Revising, Editing and Proofreading — Talk with a partner about how to improve your story.
Revising — Talk with family members or friends to help recall details about the event.

Intrapersonal
Prewriting — Watch a home video or look through family photo albums to find ideas for your narrative.
Prewriting — Check your journal for writing ideas.

Musical
Prewriting — Think of an event to write about that had music in it.
Publishing — Play appropriate music in the background as you share your story.

Assessment Options

In this complete-process lesson, a variety of assessment tools are provided, specific to the personal narrative form. Annotated benchmark papers, corresponding to a 4-point evaluation rubric, are included to help you better rate children's papers. Self-Assessment, Peer, and Teacher Checklists will help make Teacher and Peer Conferences more productive and useful to children.

- Benchmark Papers, pages 54–57
- Evaluation Rubric, page 67
- Teacher and Peer Conferencing, pages 59, 60, 62, 64
- Self-Assessment Checklist, page 52
- Peer Evaluation Checklist, page 44
- Teacher Evaluation Checklist, page 53
- Portfolio Assessment, page 67

Self-Assessment Checklist
Writing a Personal Narrative

Name of Writer _____

Date _____

Type of Writing _____

Use this checklist when you are revising, or editing and proofreading a **personal narrative**.

	YES	NO	Ways to Make My Writing Better
Does my story tell about an experience I had?	☐	☐	
Did I use the words *I* and *me*?	☐	☐	
Is there anything I should add to or take out of my story?	☐	☐	
Are the things that happened told in the correct order?	☐	☐	
Is my story written in complete sentences?	☐	☐	
Have I spelled words correctly?	☐	☐	
Did I use punctuation marks and capital letters correctly?	☐	☐	

Teacher Evaluation Checklist
Writing a Personal Narrative

Name of Writer _____

Date _____

Writing Mode _____

> Use this checklist when you are evaluating a child's **personal narrative**.

	YES	NO	Recommendations to Child
Is the story clearly focused on the writer's own experiences?	☐	☐	
Is the story presented from the writer's point of view?	☐	☐	
Does the story include the writer's personal reactions?	☐	☐	
Is the sequence of events clear?	☐	☐	
Does the story have a clear, well-integrated beginning, middle, and end?	☐	☐	
Does the writer adhere to the conventions of			
grammar?	☐	☐	
usage?	☐	☐	
spelling?	☐	☐	
punctuation?	☐	☐	
capitalization?	☐	☐	
Is the story legible?	☐	☐	
Was the work done neatly?	☐	☐	

Benchmark Paper 1

Writing a Personal Narrative

A Hard dicesoin

Check your spelling.

Is there more you could tell about this experience?

Hello my name Tomer and I'm here to tell you about a Hard dicisen. Me and my brothr went to the video store. I wanted one game but my brothr wanted anothr. We wanted a video game. We kept on arguing until we picked anothr game.

How did you feel about this experience? Were you glad you and your brother were able to work things out?

Rating Point 1: Undeveloped Personal Narrative

This personal narrative is focused on something the writer experienced and is written from the author's point of view. There is a sequence of events but no details are provided and there is not enough content to make this a story. The author's reaction is not included.

Benchmark Paper 2
Writing a Personal Narrative

Sleepover

Once I had a sleepover party. I wated outside for evry one to come. Everyone came. we had hamburgers for dinner. we ate cake and opend prezents. We made t sherts and Anana and some other girls went outside for a tresher hunt! we went to sleep but people were talking. Kacie and Samanta and other girls cold not sleep. Finaly evryon stoped talking and went to sleep.

Capitalize the first word of a sentence.

Check your spelling.

Use time-order words to make the sequence of events clear.

Did you have fun at your party?

Rating Point 2: Partially Developed Personal Narrative
The story is focused on something that the writer experienced and is written from the author's point of view. The sequence of events is not completely clear. The beginning, middle, and end are evident but run together. Although there are numerous spelling errors, the reader can understand the story.

Benchmark Paper 3
Writing a Personal Narrative

The Sleepover

Use complete sentences.

One day my friend Winston was coming over for a sleepover. I didn't know how it was going to feel. Maybe scary, fun. I don't know. By the time Winston came over, we played, and after that Winston and I watched the TV show Gueniess World Records. Then, my mom put us to sleep. But the problem was, we couldn't get to sleep. We talked to each other and watched TV. But my mother kept cheking on us and said, "Turn off the TV. Winston's got a baseball game tomorrow" and then we finally fell asleep.

Use a comma at the end of a quotation.

How did you finally fall asleep?

Rating Point 3: Adequately Developed Personal Narrative
The story is clearly focused on the writer's personal experience and is written from the writer's point of view. The writer includes his feelings about the experience. The sequence of events is clear. A problem is stated and developed, but there is no real solution. There are minor errors in grammar, spelling, and mechanics.

Benchmark Paper 4
Writing a Personal Narrative

Good choice of topic for a story.

Capitalize words in a title.

Two funfilled Days

One day my mom came into my room and told me that we were going to the Frio Rio (witch means Cold water) with our wonderful cousins. The next weekend we went to our cousins. The first thing Kate and Clay said to me when we got there was "Get in your bathing suit and come with us!" I got into my bathing suit and went outside to the lake. My Uncle Rich, my cousin Clay, my brother Kyle, and Brooke were all ready to go swimming. Then Uncle Rich said, "Better watch out for the snapping fish. Just kidding." But that's when I got the picture of a fish biting me. I suddenly didn't want to go swimming "Come on Taylor," Brooke begged. But I said, "No, I'll just watch." The next morning I got into my bathing suit and put my clothes on over it. When I got to the kitchen everyone was heading out the door. I grabbed a piece of toast and joined them. When we got to the Frio Rio we all got water tubes and went down to the river. I froze when I saw the water. It was full of little fish! I thought about the snapping fish. Just then Clay went in and all the fish scattered away. I dove in with him climbed in the tube and floated down the river. THE END

Good details about how you felt.

Were you still scared?

Rating Point 4: Well-Developed Personal Narrative
The story is clearly focused on an important personal experience and is written from the writer's point of view with good details about the writer's reactions. The sequence of events is clear. A problem is stated, developed, and resolved. There are minor errors in grammar, spelling, and mechanics.

Personal Narrative

Prewriting

OBJECTIVES

★ RECOGNIZE the characteristics and purpose of a personal narrative.

★ RESPOND to a prewriting plan written by a student writer.

★ BRAINSTORM and SELECT a topic for a personal narrative.

★ USE a story map to organize the beginning, middle, and end of a personal narrative.

 Begin the Writer's Workshop

Invite children to think about something special that happened to them at home or at school and ask for volunteers to briefly share their experiences with the class. Make a list of their topics on the board. Your list might look something like this.

> going to a new school
> losing my front teeth
> visiting my cousin
> getting a new dog
> learning to ride a bike
> hitting a home run

Read the list and ask how the topics are alike. Explain that when writers write about something that happened to them, it's called a personal narrative.

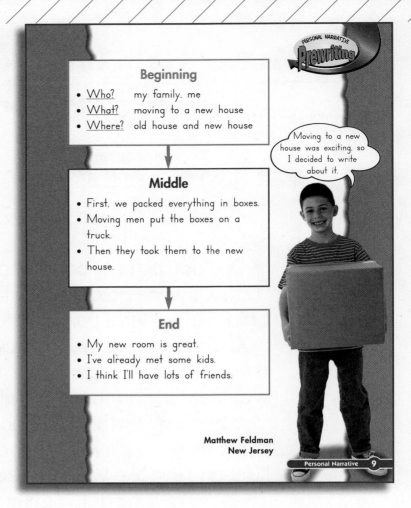

Beginning
- Who?   my family, me
- What?   moving to a new house
- Where?   old house and new house

Moving to a new house was exciting, so I decided to write about it.

Middle
- First, we packed everything in boxes.
- Moving men put the boxes on a truck.
- Then they took them to the new house.

End
- My new room is great.
- I've already met some kids.
- I think I'll have lots of friends.

Matthew Feldman
New Jersey

Personal Narrative 9

Discuss a Writer's Model

MEET THE WRITER Point out the photograph on page 9 of the Big Book of Writing Models. Introduce Matthew Feldman and explain that he is a second grader and that he wrote a personal narrative about an exciting experience—moving to a new house.

Explain that Matthew went through several steps to write his story. Point out that Matthew's model will help them as they learn to write personal narratives.

BRAINSTORM Discuss with children that the first step in writing is to select a topic. Talk about different ways to find a topic, including brainstorming, reading their journals or logs, talking to family members, or exchanging ideas with classmates.

SELECT A TOPIC Children can make a list of possible topics and then choose the one they like best. Encourage them to pick a favorite experience that they remember in detail and want to share.

DESIGN A PLAN Focus on Matthew's story map on page 9. Point out that Matthew uses the map to keep the events of his story in the order that they happened. Ask the following questions.

- *What does Matthew tell about in the beginning of his story?*

- *What words does he use to keep the events in the right order?*

- *What happens at the end? How does he tell how he felt?*

3 Prewrite and Confer

INDEPENDENT WRITING Give children blank story maps to fill out. (See page 36.) Remind them to tell who is in the story, where it takes place, and what it is about in the beginning.

TEACHER CONFERENCE Use questions like the following to help children improve their writing plans.

- *Why did you choose this topic to write about?*
- *Are the events in the order that they happened? How can you tell that?*
- *Do you have enough information?*

PEER CONFERENCE Have partners share their story maps. Remind them what to do in a conference.

- *Listen quietly to the other person's story.*
- *Tell what you like about the story.*
- *Ask questions if there is something you don't understand.*

Meeting Individual Needs

Mini Lesson

Organization— Beginning, Middle, and End

Introduce To review the idea of beginning, middle, and end with children, draw a simple picture of a train with an engine, boxcars, and a caboose. Point out that the engine is at the beginning of the train, the boxcars are in the middle, and the caboose is at the end. Have volunteers come to the board and point out the beginning, middle, and end of the train.

Model Have children look at Matthew's story map and show how it is divided into three stages. Point out that the beginning tells who the characters are, where the story takes place, and what it is about. The middle tells what happens next, and the end tells how everything works out. Have volunteers identify the information in each part of Matthew's story.

Summarize/Apply Explain that dividing a story into a beginning, middle, and end helps writers keep the events in order and reminds them not to leave anything out.

WRITER'S BLOCK

Problem	Solution
Children may list events but have trouble keeping them in order.	Suggest that they use the time-order words *first, next, then,* and *last* to link events and keep them in order.

ESL STRATEGY

Pair children with varying language proficiencies and have them help each other create story maps. Encourage them to act out the events of their stories and write them in order.

HOME–SCHOOL CONNECTION

Encourage children to share their story maps with their families and ask them to suggest more details.

WRITING ACROSS THE CURRICULUM

Language Arts Children may find story maps helpful when they write about books they have read.

Today Was a Terrible Day
by Patricia Reilly Giff

Who?   Ronald, Miss Tyler

What?   Ronald had a terrible day

Where? at school

1. Ronald ate the wrong sandwich.
2. Then he splashed water on a girl.
3. Last, he broke a flower pot.

Drafting

OBJECTIVES

★ **IDENTIFY** the characteristics of a personal narrative in a first draft of a student model.

★ **FOLLOW** a writing plan to write a first draft of a personal narrative.

 Continue the Writer's Workshop

Invite children to pretend they are going on a search to find buried treasure. Ask them what they would need to have ready to take with them. Elicit that they would need a compass to tell the direction, a shovel to dig with, and most important, a map to tell them where to find the treasure.

Explain that as writers they also need to get ready. They need to have pencils and paper, a topic to write about, and a story map to follow.

 Discuss a Writer's Model

Read Matthew's first draft on pages 10–12 of the Big Book of Writing Models to the class. Point out the colored lines with arrows and explain how they show the beginning, middle, and end of Matthew's story. Refer children back to Matthew's story map and show how he included all the information in his story and how he used the map to keep the details in order.

IDENTIFY CHARACTERISTICS OF A PERSONAL NARRATIVE Point out the following characteristics of a personal narrative.

- *Tells a story about something that happened to the writer*

- *Has a beginning, middle, and end*

- *Tells events in the order that they happened*

- *Is written in the first person*

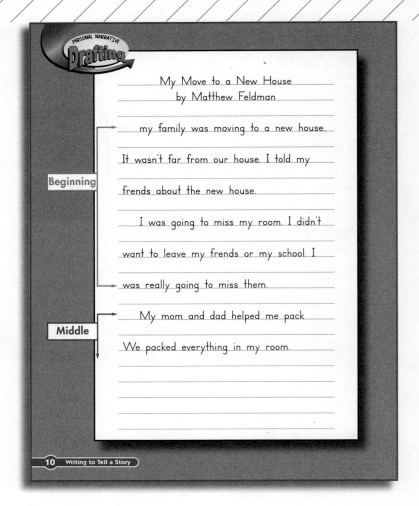

My Move to a New House
by Matthew Feldman

Beginning

my family was moving to a new house. It wasn't far from our house. I told my frends about the new house.

I was going to miss my room. I didn't want to leave my frends or my school. I was really going to miss them.

Middle

My mom and dad helped me pack

We packed everything in my room.

10 Writing to Tell a Story

3 Draft and Confer

THINK LIKE A WRITER As children prepare to write their first drafts, have them ask themselves the following questions.

- *What topic am I writing about?*

- *Who will read my story?*

- *Why am I writing about this experience?*

- *What do I have to remember about writing a personal narrative?*

INDEPENDENT WRITING Have children refer to their story maps as they write their first drafts. Remind them that this is the time to get their ideas on paper and not to worry about spelling or punctuation. Suggest that they store their first drafts and story maps together in their portfolios.

TEACHER CONFERENCE As children write, ask questions to help them.

- *Who is your personal narrative about?*

- *Where does it take place?*

- *Did you tell the story in the order it happened?*

PEER CONFERENCE Have children work in pairs and read their drafts to each other. Suggest that the writer ask the listener questions.

- *What do you think of the topic I chose for my story?*

- *Is there anything else I should add?*

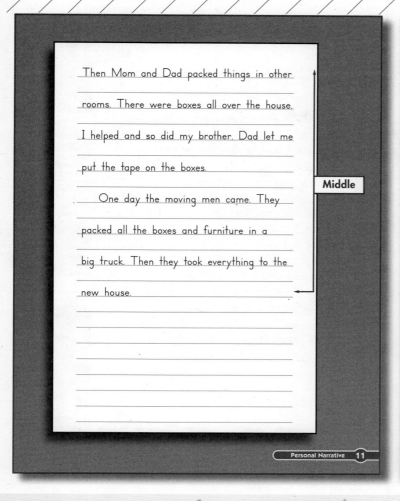

Then Mom and Dad packed things in other rooms. There were boxes all over the house. I helped and so did my brother. Dad let me put the tape on the boxes.

One day the moving men came. They packed all the boxes and furniture in a big truck. Then they took everything to the new house.

Middle

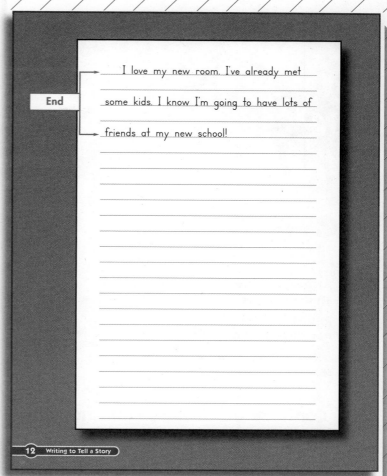

End

I love my new room. I've already met some kids. I know I'm going to have lots of friends at my new school!

Meeting Individual Needs

Point of View— First-Person

Introduce Write the following sentences on the board.

I like to read.

Andrew likes to draw.

Point out that the first sentence tells about something you, the writer, likes to do, and the other sentence tells about something another person likes to do.

Model Explain that when you write about yourself, you use the words *I, me,* and *my,* and when you write about someone else, you use their name or *he/she.* Point out that personal narratives are written from the writer's point of view.

Summarize/Apply As children write their first drafts, remind them that they are writing about something that happened to them and to use the words *I, me,* and *my.*

WRITER'S BLOCK

Problem	Solution
Children erase mistakes or start a new sheet of paper every time they make a change.	Remind them to draw a line through any words they want to change instead of erasing or starting over.

ESL STRATEGY

Children may find that it is easier to write words they don't know in English in their native languages first and then change them later.

HOME–SCHOOL CONNECTION

Communicate to family members that the purpose of a first draft is to get ideas down on paper and that corrections will be made later.

WRITING ACROSS THE CURRICULUM

Social Studies Have children pretend they are living in another country or time period and write about their lives.

My name is Jack. I am a shoemaker in Williamsburg, Virginia.

Revising

OBJECTIVES

★ **ANALYZE** a model to see how a student writer revised his writing.

★ **REVISE** a first draft of a personal narrative to clarify ideas.

★ **USE** time-order words to show the sequence of events.

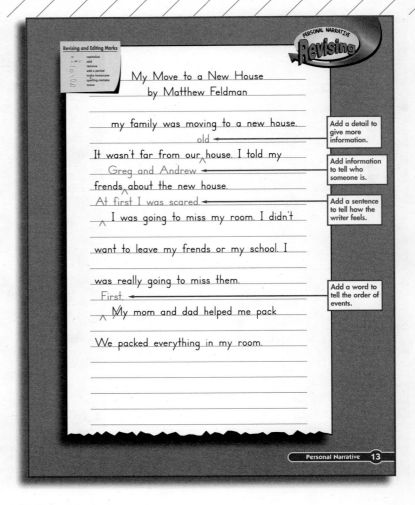

Revising and Editing Marks
= capitalize
∧ or ∨ add
remove
⊙ add a period
make lowercase
○ spelling mistake
move

My Move to a New House
by Matthew Feldman

my family was moving to a new house.
                                    old ←   *Add a detail to give more information.*
It wasn't far from our house. I told my
Greg and Andrew ←   *Add information to tell who someone is.*
frends about the new house.
At first I was scared ←   *Add a sentence to tell how the writer feels.*
    I was going to miss my room. I didn't

want to leave my frends or my school. I

was really going to miss them.
First,   *Add a word to tell the order of events.*
    My mom and dad helped me pack

We packed everything in my room.

Personal Narrative **13**

1 Continue the Writer's Workshop

Remind children that writers use special marks to show the changes they want to make in their writing. Point out the symbols for adding and removing information found in the chart on page 13 of the Big Book of Writing Models. (See also page 30 in the Teacher Resource Guide.) You may also want to review the symbol for making a capital letter lowercase.

2 Discuss A Writer's Model

Read the excerpt of Matthew's revised draft on Big Book page 13. When you get to the end of the page, point out the torn paper border and explain that this is only part of Matthew's story.

Ask children to look at the revising and editing marks Matthew used to show what he added or changed. Use the callouts to explain why Matthew made the changes he did. Ask children if they think his changes improved his personal narrative by making it clearer.

3 Revise and Confer

As children revise their drafts, have them keep in mind the following questions.

- *Do I have a beginning, middle, and end?*
- *Have I told about the characters, setting, and what the story is about?*
- *Did I tell the story in the order that it happened?*
- *Did I use time-order words to make the sequence of events clear?*

TEACHER CONFERENCE If children have difficulty seeing ways to improve their drafts, ask questions such as these.

- *How did you organize your story?*
- *Have you included enough information about the characters, setting, and what happens in your story?*
- *Have you told how the experience made you feel?*

PEER CONFERENCE Have partners read their first drafts to each other. Suggest that writers ask listeners the following questions.

- *Does my story make sense?*
- *Is there anything else I need to add?*

Order of Events

Introduce Write the following sentences on the board.

I went outside.

I put on my shoes.

I put on my socks.

Read the sentences, then ask children if the order of the sentences makes sense.

Model Have volunteers put the sentences in order, using words like *first, next, after,* and *last.* Their responses should look something like this.

First, I put on my socks.

Next, I put on my shoes.

Then, I went outside.

Summarize/Apply Point out that Matthew added the word *first* to tell the order in which they packed the boxes. Writers use time-order words to link events and to make the order in which they happened clear to the reader.

WRITER'S BLOCK

Problem	Solution
Children have recounted the events but not included their feelings about the experience.	Ask children what the best part of the experience was and how it made them feel. Suggest they include this information in the story.

ESL STRATEGY

To check the sequence of events, have children act out what happens in their narratives.

HOME–SCHOOL CONNECTION

Encourage children to share their revised narratives with their families and explain why they made certain changes.

WRITING ACROSS THE CURRICULUM

Science Encourage children to record the steps of an experiment or a set of instructions, using time-order words as in the following example.

How to Plant a Seed

First, fill a cup with some dirt.

Next, add the seeds.

Then, cover them with more dirt.

Last, give them some water.

Editing and Proofreading

OBJECTIVES

★ **ANALYZE** a model to understand how a student writer revised his writing.

★ **EDIT** and **PROOFREAD** a draft for grammar, usage, mechanics, and spelling.

★ **USE** a capital letter at the beginning of a sentence and a punctuation mark at the end.

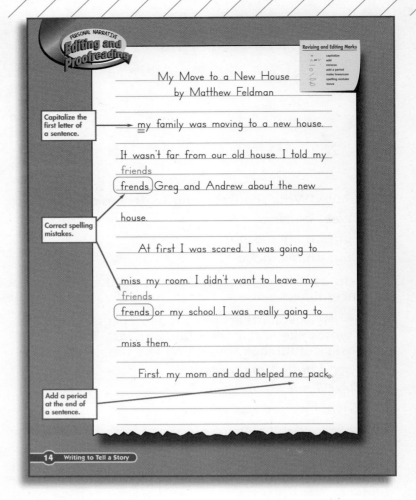

My Move to a New House
by Matthew Feldman

Capitalize the first letter of a sentence.
my family was moving to a new house.

It wasn't far from our old house. I told my friends

Correct spelling mistakes.
~~frends~~ Greg and Andrew about the new house.

At first I was scared. I was going to miss my room. I didn't want to leave my friends ~~frends~~ or my school. I was really going to miss them.

First, my mom and dad helped me pack.

Add a period at the end of a sentence.

14 Writing to Tell a Story

 Continue the Writer's Workshop

Explain to children that now is the time for them to go back and check their writing to correct spelling mistakes, add punctuation marks, or change words to improve their language.

Review the chart of revising and editing marks on page 14 of the *Big Book of Writing Models*, pointing out the symbols for capitalizing a letter, adding a period or other punctuation mark, and correcting a spelling mistake. (See also the blackline master on page 30 of this Teacher Resource Guide.)

 Discuss a Writer's Model

Review the excerpt of Matthew's revised draft on Big Book page 14. Ask children to look at the revising and editing marks he used to make corrections. Use the callouts to explain why Matthew made the changes he did. Ask children if Matthew missed any mistakes and if they think his changes improved his narrative.

3 Edit, Proofread, and Confer

As children revise their drafts, have them keep in mind the following questions.

- *Have I spelled words correctly?*
- *Did I begin sentences with a capital letter?*
- *Is there a punctuation mark at the end of each sentence?*
- *Did I put quotation marks at the beginning and end of every quotation?*

TEACHER CONFERENCE As children share their drafts with you, ask questions such as these.

- *What words did you have trouble spelling?*
- *How did you make sure that your punctuation marks are correct?*
- *Are there any other words you want to change?*

PEER CONFERENCE Have partners exchange drafts and read them slowly, looking for any problems the writer might have missed. Suggest that writers ask readers the following questions.

- *Did I miss anything?*
- *Is my handwriting clear?*
- *What would be a good picture to draw to go with my story?*

Capitalization—First Word of Sentence

Introduce Have children read the part of Matthew's narrative that is found on Big Book pages 11–12. Point out the capital letters at the beginning of every sentence. Explain that the capital letter tells where a new sentence begins.

Model Draw attention to Matthew's edited draft on page 14 of the Big Book. Point out the sentence that does not begin with a capital letter. Talk about the symbol Matthew uses to show that the letter needs to be changed.

Summarize/Apply Remind children that a capital letter tells readers that a new sentence is beginning. Have them check their writing to make sure each sentence begins with a capital letter.

WRITER'S BLOCK

Problem	Solution
Children still use invented spelling and have too many words to correct.	Suggest that they choose only three or four words to correct. They may wish to add the new words to their word lists or picture dictionaries.

ESL STRATEGY
Pair children with varying language proficiencies and have them work together to correct misspelled words in their drafts.

HOME–SCHOOL CONNECTION
Invite children to share their edited drafts with their families and explain some of the changes they made.

WRITING ACROSS THE CURRICULUM
Reading As children write in their literature logs, remind them to capitalize the first word in a sentence and put a punctuation mark at the end.

Oct. 9

Sparky's Bone
by Claire Daniel

Sparky is a dog. She digs a big hole to hide her bone. The next day she can't remember where she put her bone.

Personal Narrative

Publishing

OBJECTIVE

★ PUBLISH a personal narrative.

1 End the Writer's Workshop

Explain that publishing is the last step of the writing process. This is when writers share their work with other people and they want it to be the best it can be.

2 Discuss a Writer's Model

Have children look at Matthew's final draft on pages 15–17 of the Big Book of Writing Models. Point out that all mistakes were corrected, there are no crossed out words, and his writing is neat and legible. Discuss the illustrations, explaining that they make his story interesting and colorful as well as adding information.

3 Publish and Celebrate

Talk about different ways children might publish their writing. Use the publishing suggestions to the right as a guide. Discuss the steps for each option. Then give children some time to decide which one they will use or allow them to come up with their own ideas. Provide materials as needed.

Set aside a special time for a publishing celebration during which children can read, display, or perform their personal narratives. You may wish to add to the celebration by decorating the classroom, inviting family members or other classes to attend, and making a videotape.

> My Move to a New House
> by Matthew Feldman
>
> My family was moving to a new house. It wasn't far from our old house. I told my friends Greg and Andrew about the new house.
> At first I was scared. I was going to miss my room. I didn't want to leave my friends or my school. I was really going to miss them.

Personal Narrative 15

Publishing Ideas

STORY TIME

Have children take turns sitting in the Author's Chair and reading their stories to the class. Encourage the class to ask questions and tell what they liked about each personal narrative.

BOOK IT

Suggest children publish their personal narratives as books. Have them make a neat, clean final copy and staple it into a construction paper cover. Have them write the title and their names on the cover. They may wish to illustrate their stories by drawing pictures or adding photographs from home. Display the books on a table where other children can read them.

ACT IT OUT

Some children may wish to act out their personal narratives. Have them read their stories to classmates and then ask classmates to play the different characters. Encourage them to wear costumes and use simple props. Remind them to speak clearly.

First, my mom and dad helped me pack. We packed everything in my room. Then Mom and Dad packed things in other rooms. There were boxes all over the house. I helped and so did my brother. Dad let me put the tape on the boxes.

One day the moving men came. They packed all the boxes and furniture in a big truck. Then they took everything to the new house.

I love my new room. I've already met some kids. I know I'm going to have lots of friends at my new school!

RUBRIC FOR PERSONAL NARRATIVE

4
- Clearly focused on something that the writer experienced.
- Written from the author's point of view and includes author's reaction(s).
- Has a clear beginning, middle, and end.
- The sequence of events is clear.
- Contains few errors in grammar/usage/mechanics/spelling.

3
- Focused on something that the writer experienced.
- Written from the author's point of view; may include author's reaction(s).
- May have a recognizable beginning, middle, and end.
- The sequence of events is generally clear.
- May contain errors in grammar/usage/mechanics/spelling.

2
- May be focused on something that the writer experienced.
- May be written from the author's point of view; may not include author's reaction(s).
- May have a recognizable beginning, middle, and end.
- The sequence of events may be unclear.
- May contain errors in grammar/usage/mechanics/spelling that do not interfere with understanding.

1
- May not be focused on the writer's experience.
- May not be written from the author's point of view and may not include author's reaction(s).
- May not have a clear beginning, middle, and end.
- The sequence of events may be unclear.
- May contain substantial errors in grammar/usage/mechanics/spelling that interfere with understanding.

ASSESSMENT OPPORTUNITIES

SELF–ASSESSMENT Have children complete the Self-Assessment Checklist on page 52. Encourage them to share their responses orally during teacher conferences.

PORTFOLIO ASSESSMENT If children choose to include their personal narratives in their portfolios, encourage them also to consider including their prewriting lists, story maps, drafts, and Self-Assessment Checklists.

PEER EVALUATION Have children use the Peer Evaluation Checklist on page 44.

TEACHER PRIMARY TRAIT ASSESSMENT Use the Teacher Evaluation Checklist on page 53 to evaluate children's personal narratives. You may want to share your comments during teacher conferences.

RUBRIC FOR PERSONAL NARRATIVES The form-specific rubric will help you evaluate children's writing. Use the information in the rubric during teacher conferences to help children identify ways they can improve their writing.

BENCHMARK PAPERS You may want to use the Benchmark Papers on pages 54–57 along with the rubric to evaluate children's writing.

Folk Tale

OBJECTIVES

★ RECOGNIZE the characteristics of a folk tale.

★ RESPOND to a model folk tale retold by a published author.

★ PLAN, WRITE, and REVISE a folk tale.

★ USE a story chart to organize ideas.

1 Begin the Lesson

Ask children to recall a favorite folk tale, such as "The Three Little Pigs." As they retell the story, record the names of characters, where and when the story takes place, what the problem is, and how it is solved. You may want to use a story chart like the one on page 66 of the Big Book of Writing Models to record their ideas. See the following example.

Title: The Three Little Pigs

Characters
The three little pigs, wolf
Setting
A countryside long ago
Problem
Wolf tries to break into each pig's house to eat the pig. He blew in the first two houses because they were made of straw and sticks.
Ending
Wolf gets burned when he goes down the third pig's chimney because he can't blow in the brick house.

Read the chart and help children understand that when writers retell a very old story that has no known author, it is called a folk tale.

2 Discuss a Writer's Model

MEET THE WRITER Point out the small photo of the book cover on page 18 of the Big Book. Introduce Elphinstone Dayrell, and explain that he retold the African folk tale "Why the Sun and Moon Live in the Sky."

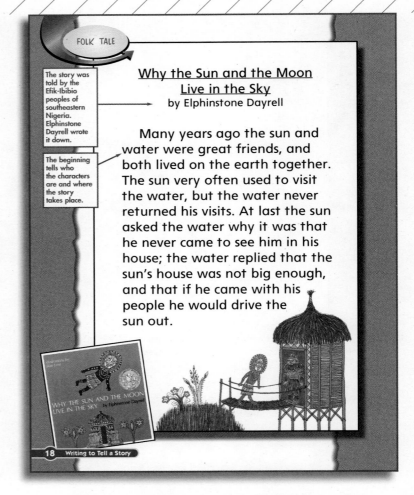

FOLK TALE

The story was told by the Efik-Ibibio peoples of southeastern Nigeria. Elphinstone Dayrell wrote it down.

The beginning tells who the characters are and where the story takes place.

Why the Sun and the Moon Live in the Sky
by Elphinstone Dayrell

Many years ago the sun and water were great friends, and both lived on the earth together. The sun very often used to visit the water, but the water never returned his visits. At last the sun asked the water why it was that he never came to see him in his house; the water replied that the sun's house was not big enough, and that if he came with his people he would drive the sun out.

18   Writing to Tell a Story

TALK ABOUT THE MODEL Read the folk tale on Big Book pages 18–24 to children. Use the callouts to help children understand the characteristics of a folk tale as well as who first told the story, who the characters are, where the story takes place, what the problem is, what the characters do, and how the story ends. Invite children to compare this information with the information they listed about "The Three Little Pigs."

Ask children to consider the following questions.

* *Could this story happen in real life? Why or why not?*

* *What problem do the characters have?*

* *What does this folk tale try to explain?*

Guide children to see that the characters in folk tales can be animals or objects that talk and act like people. The characters usually have one big problem to solve, with other small problems to face along the way.

* **A continuation of this lesson follows on page 70.**

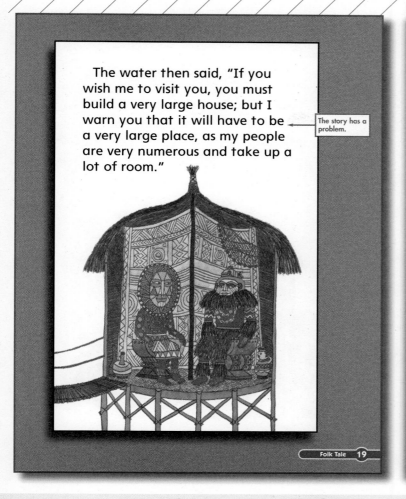

The water then said, "If you wish me to visit you, you must build a very large house; but I warn you that it will have to be a very large place, as my people are very numerous and take up a lot of room."

The story has a problem.

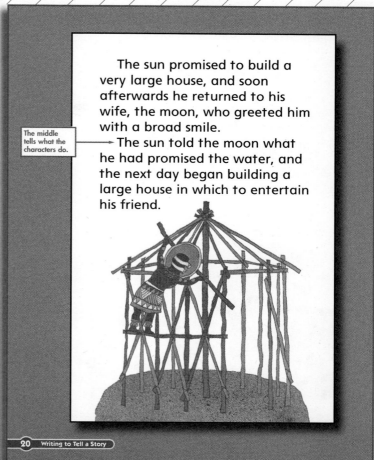

The sun promised to build a very large house, and soon afterwards he returned to his wife, the moon, who greeted him with a broad smile.

The middle tells what the characters do.

The sun told the moon what he had promised the water, and the next day began building a large house in which to entertain his friend.

Meeting Individual Needs

Mini Lesson

Characters and Setting

Introduce To expand children's understanding of character and setting, introduce yourself as a favorite folk tale character, provide clues, and have volunteers guess your name as well as where and when you lived. Then invite volunteers to take a turn. Explain that in the beginnings of stories writers usually name the characters and describe the setting where the story action takes place.

Model Read aloud the first paragraph of "Why the Sun and the Moon Live in the Sky" on page 18 of the Big Book. Have volunteers write on the board the names of the two main characters—the sun and the water—and explain how the setting is important to the problem in this story. *(The sun's house is not big enough.)*

Summarize/Apply Explain that writers of folk tales include make-believe characters and interesting settings that can be described in the beginning of the story. Remind children to describe their characters and settings as they write their folk tales.

WRITER'S BLOCK

Problem
Children have difficulty choosing a new setting for their stories.

Solution
Children can think about their characters and events and choose a place the characters might usually be found or a familiar place such as their home, school, or other gathering place.

ESL STRATEGY

Children may wish to choose folk tales from their countries of origin. They can use puppets or other props with partners to retell the folk tales before planning new versions.

HOME–SCHOOL CONNECTION

Have children share their folk tales with family members. Then they can look for other folk tales to share together.

WRITING ACROSS THE CURRICULUM

Science Children can solve science-related problems using the same problem-solution relationships they worked with when they planned their folk tales.

When it was completed, he asked the water to come and visit him.

When the water arrived, one of his people called out to the sun, and asked him whether it would be safe for the water to enter, and the sun answered, "Yes, tell my friend to come in."

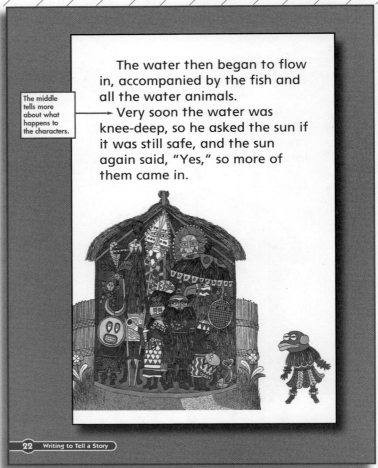

The middle tells more about what happens to the characters.

The water then began to flow in, accompanied by the fish and all the water animals.

Very soon the water was knee-deep, so he asked the sun if it was still safe, and the sun again said, "Yes," so more of them came in.

Folk Tale (CONTINUED)

3 WRITE AND CONFER

INDEPENDENT WRITING As children write their own folk tales, display Elphinstone Dayrell's model as an example.

MAKE A PLAN Have children brainstorm topics by thinking about favorite folk tales they have read or heard. Record their ideas on the board or on chart paper. Once children choose a folk tale, suggest they change the characters, setting, problem, and ending. They can use a story chart to help them organize their stories. (See page 39.)

WRITE IT DOWN As children write their drafts, remind them to begin by telling who the characters are and where the story takes place. Next, they should tell the problem the characters have. The middle tells what happens to the characters and what they do. The end tells how the problem is solved.

LOOK IT OVER Have children look for ways to improve their writing. Ask them to decide if there are enough details. Remind them to look back at their charts to see if they included everything they had planned. Then they can check for mistakes in spelling, punctuation, capital letters, and language.

TEACHER CONFERENCE If children have difficulty seeing ways to improve their folk tales, ask questions such as the following.

- *Does your folk tale introduce the characters and setting in the beginning?*

- *Where is the problem told?*

- *Did you end your folk tale in a surprising or interesting way?*

PEER CONFERENCE Have partners read their folk tales to one another. Ask them to guess which folk tales their stories are based on. Encourage them to make comments or ask questions about the characters, setting, and problem, and to tell if the story is told in an order that makes sense.

SHARE YOUR WORK Remind children that folk tales are meant to be shared with others. Ask them how they might want to publish their stories. If desired, suggest they paint or draw posters for their folk tales to display as they read aloud their stories. Children might also work in small groups to tape record their folk tales. Some children may wish to add sound effects, such as animal noises.

When the water was level with the top of a man's head, the water said to the sun, "Do you want more of my people to come?"

And the sun and the moon both answered, "Yes," not knowing any better, so the water's people flowed on, until the sun and the moon had to perch themselves on top of the roof.

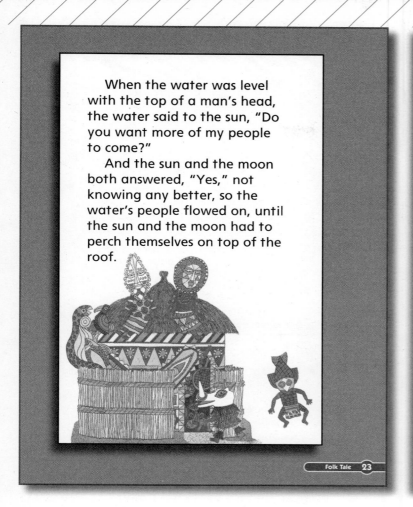

Again the water addressed the sun. He received the same answer so more of his people rushed in.

The water very soon overflowed the top of the roof, and the sun and moon were forced to go up into the sky, where they have remained ever since.

The end tells how the problem is solved.

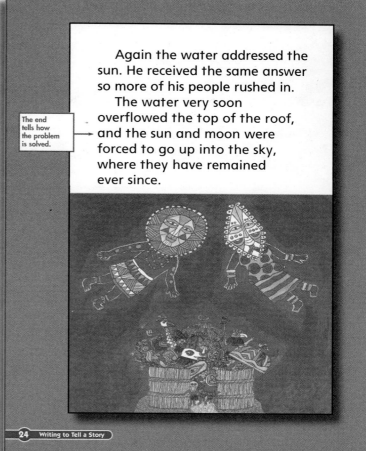

ASSESSMENT OPPORTUNITIES

SELF-ASSESSMENT Have children complete the Self-Assessment Checklist on page 42.

PEER EVALUATION Have children use the Peer Evaluation Checklist on page 44.

TEACHER HOLISTIC ASSESSMENT Use the Teacher Evaluation Checklist on page 43 to evaluate children's folk tales.

Writer's Workshop Planner

Realistic Story

WRITING PROCESS STAGE	MINILESSONS			
	Writer's Craft; Grammar, Usage, Mechanics, Spelling	Writing Across the Curriculum	Meeting Individual Needs	Assessment
Prewriting pp. 80–81 (1–2 days)	Plot, page 81	Art, page 81	Writer's Block ESL Strategy Home-School Connection	• Teacher and Peer Conferencing, page 81
Drafting pp. 82–83 (2–3 days)	Planning a Composition Using a Story Map, page 83	Science, page 83	Writer's Block ESL Strategy Home-School Connection	• Self-Assessment Checklist, page 74 • Peer Evaluation Checklist, page 44 • Teacher Evaluation Checklist, page 75 • Teacher and Peer Conferencing, page 82
Revising pp. 84–85 (1–2 days)	Sequencing Events by Cutting and Pasting Sentences, page 85	Social Studies, page 85	Writer's Block ESL Strategy Home-School Connection	• Self-Assessment Checklist, page 74 • Peer Evaluation Checklist, page 44 • Teacher Evaluation Checklist, page 75 • Teacher and Peer Conferencing, page 84
Editing & Proofreading pp. 86–87 (1–2 days)	Capitalization—Names, page 87	Language Arts, page 87	Writer's Block ESL Strategy Home-School Connection	• Self-Assessment Checklist, page 74 • Peer Evaluation Checklist, page 44 • Teacher Evaluation Checklist, page 75 • Teacher and Peer Conferencing, page 86
Publishing pp. 88–89 (1 day)				• Benchmark Papers, pages 76–79 • Rubric, page 89 • Portfolio, page 89

Suggestions for Planning Each Day

- Whole Class Meeting/Minilesson (5–10 minutes)
- Independent Writing/Teacher-Student Conferences (30–40 minutes)
- Peer Conferences (5–10 minutes)
- Group Share (5–10 minutes)

Connecting Multiple Intelligences
With the Stages of the Writing Process

Linguistic

Prewriting — Read through your journal or literature log to find ideas for your story.

Revising — Use a thesaurus to find interesting words to add or to replace others.

Logical-Mathematical

Prewriting — Think about different problems and solutions for your story. Pick the one that works best.

Publishing — Divide your story into short chapters and number them.

Spatial

Revising — Draw your story like a comic strip. Add speech balloons for dialogue.

Publishing — Videotape your story and present it to the class.

Bodily-Kinesthetic

Prewriting — Act out the story events with classmates to put them in the right order.

Publishing — Dress as a news anchor to present your realistic story.

Environmental (Naturalist)

Prewriting — Make the outdoors the setting for your story.

Revising — Change your story setting to a different outdoor scene.

Writing a Realistic Story

Interpersonal

Drafting — Work in a small group to change real story facts into believable fiction.

Revising, Editing and Proofreading — Work with a partner to find ways to make your story better.

Intrapersonal

Prewriting — Consider your characters' feelings about what happens to them in the story.

Revising — Use yourself as the main character. Change events to make your wishes real in the story.

Musical

Prewriting — Include music or a musical event in your story.

Publishing — Add sound effects to heighten the effect of your story.

Assessment Options

In this complete-process lesson, a variety of assessment tools are provided, specific to the realistic story form. Annotated benchmark papers, corresponding to a 4-point evaluation rubric, are included to help you better rate children's papers. Self-Assessment, Peer, and Teacher Checklists will help make Teacher and Peer Conferences more productive and useful to children.

- Benchmark Papers, pages 76–79
- Evaluation Rubric, page 89
- Teacher and Peer Conferencing, pages 81, 82, 84, 86
- Self-Assessment Checklist, page 74
- Peer Evaluation Checklist, page 44
- Teacher Evaluation Checklist, page 75
- Portfolio Assessment, page 89

Self-Assessment Checklist
Writing a Realistic Story

Name of Writer _____

Date _____

Type of Writing _____

Use this checklist when you are revising, or editing and proofreading a **realistic story**.

	YES	NO	Ways to Make My Writing Better
Is my story about something that could really happen?	❏	❏	
Did I give enough information about the story characters?	❏	❏	
Is there anything I should add to or take out of my story?	❏	❏	
Do the story characters have a problem to solve?	❏	❏	
Is my story written in complete sentences?	❏	❏	
Have I spelled words correctly?	❏	❏	
Did I use punctuation marks and capital letters correctly?	❏	❏	

Teacher Evaluation Checklist
Writing a Realistic Story

Name of Writer _____

Date _____

Writing Mode _____

Use this checklist when you are evaluating a child's **realistic story**.

	YES	NO	Recommendations to Child
Is the story about events that could happen in real life?	❑	❑	
Are the characters clearly introduced in the story beginning?	❑	❑	
Is the problem the characters are faced with well developed in the middle of the story?	❑	❑	
Does the story ending tell how the problem was solved?	❑	❑	
Does the writer adhere to the conventions of			
grammar?	❑	❑	
usage?	❑	❑	
spelling?	❑	❑	
punctuation?	❑	❑	
capitalization?	❑	❑	
Is the story legible?	❑	❑	
Was the work done neatly?	❑	❑	

Benchmark Paper 1

Writing a Realistic Story

Begin the first word in a sentence with a capital letter.

one day a dog went to skool. he came in the door and went evrywhere in evry room. All the kids pionted and yelld The dog went to the kaffteria. he wanted some food. Then he went in a nuther room. The lady gave him some soda and chips. he said thank you and went ow side.

Check your spelling.

Can dogs really say, "Thank you"?

Your story needs a problem to solve.

Rating Point 1: Undeveloped Realistic Story

The events in the story are somewhat plausible. The story has little detail and no evidence of a problem to solve. There is a rough beginning, middle, and end. There are numerous errors in spelling, grammar, and mechanics.

Benchmark Paper 2
Writing a Realistic Story

At a Party

This is a good topic for a story.

Katie was going to have a party. She told all her frends to cum at 1:00 o'clock. but they didnot come. Katie was sad. She didnt know what to do. She askd herself should she cal them. Then she went to bed. The next day she felt bad. But then her friends came. It was a surpise. They were behind the cawch. they brought her some cake.

What is the problem in the story?

Can you tell more about the party?

Tell how Katie felt at the end.

Rating Point 2: Partially Developed Realistic Story
The story focuses on plausible events and includes some detail. There is a problem, but it is not developed. There is a recognizable, but brief, beginning, middle, and end. There are errors in grammar, spelling, and mechanics.

Writing a Realistic Story

Lost Teeth

Leah had to go to the dentist office to get her teeth pulled because her big teeth were behind her baby teeth. Leah was afraid it would hurt and she would cry.

She didn't want to go but she didn't want anymore babby teeth. All of her friends had there big teeth. The dentist gave Leah headfones to put on. Then he put some music on for her to listen to. The music was nice. It made her feel better. Leah does not know how it was dun because she went to sleep. When it was over, everything was fine. It didn't hurt at all. But the best part of all was the tooth fairy came to her house.

> Spell this "headphones."

> What happened then?

> You don't need this word.

> Leah was very brave.

Rating Point 3: Adequately Developed Realistic Story
The story focuses on plausible events and includes a problem to be solved. The topic is good but detail and dialogue would make it more interesting. There is a recognizable beginning, middle, and end. There are a few spelling, usage, and mechanics errors.

Benchmark Paper 4
Writing a Realistic Story

The Big Move

One day Henry's dad came home and said, "Guess what everybody? We're moving to Texas." Henry couldn't believe it. "Where's Texas?" said his little sister Anna. His dad had a new job and they were moving in one month.

Texas was far away. They drove and drove. Henry already missed his friends. When they got to the new house everything was different. There was no one to play with. He didn't want to play with his sister and the TV wasn't hooked up so he couldn't play video games. "This is a terrible place," thought Henry.

Just then the doorbell rang. It was the lady who lived next door. When she saw Henry she said, "I know a boy who is just about your age. Come with me." Henry went with the lady to a house across the street. A boy with brown hair and glasses came to the door. "Henry, this is James," she said. "James, this is Henry." James said, "hey, do you like to skateboard?" Henry said, "yes I used to skateboard everyday." "Come on, said James, let's go find my friends and go to the skateboard park." When Henry went home to get his skateboard he told his mom Texas might be ok after all.

Good beginning sentence.

Dialogue makes the story seem real.

There is a problem and a solution.

Check your quotation marks.

Rating Point 4: Well-Developed Realistic Story
The story focuses on plausible events and makes use of detail and dialogue to make it seem real. The sequence of events is clear and there is a problem with a solution. The beginning, middle, and end are integrated. There are few errors in writing.

Realistic Story

Prewriting

OBJECTIVES

★ RECOGNIZE the characteristics of a realistic story.

★ RESPOND to a prewriting plan written by a student writer.

★ BRAINSTORM and SELECT a topic for a realistic story.

★ USE a web and story map to gather and organize ideas for a realistic story.

1 Begin the Writer's Workshop

Invite children to think of memorable events in which they encountered funny or serious problems, such as swimming in a rough ocean or acting in a play. Have volunteers briefly share their experiences. Make a web of their topics on the board. You might want to use the web on page 62 of the Big Book of Writing Models to create a graphic organizer such as the following.

Focus on one idea from the web. Remind children that this event really happened to one of them. Then invite children to add exciting details that did not happen but could have. Help children understand that a story that seems true, with made-up details that could have happened, is called a realistic story.

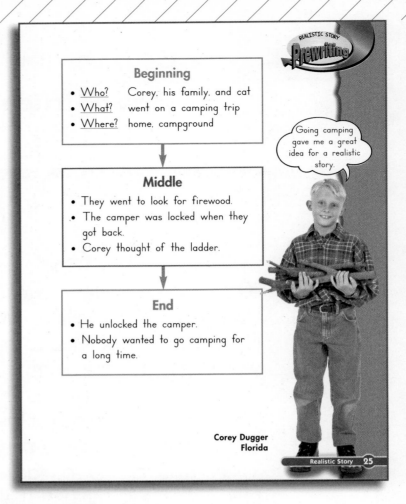

Realistic Story 25

2 Discuss a Writer's Model

MEET THE WRITER Point out the photo on page 25 of the Big Book. Introduce the writer, second grader Corey Dugger. Explain that Corey got his idea for a realistic story from a family camping trip.

Point out that Corey went through several steps to write his story. Help children realize that Corey's model will help them as they learn to write realistic stories.

BRAINSTORM Explain that the first step in writing a realistic story is to select a topic based on a real event. Elicit different ways to find a topic, such as brainstorming, reading journals or logs, talking to family members, looking at family photos, or talking with classmates.

SELECT A TOPIC Children can make webs of possible topics (see page 100), and then discuss them with partners. Encourage each child to pick an interesting event that has a clear-cut problem that can be solved.

DESIGN A PLAN Focus children's attention on Corey's story map on page 25 of the Big Book. Help them understand that Corey used the map to organize the events of his story in the order that they happened. Ask questions like the following.

- *What information will Corey give in the beginning of his story?*

- *What is the problem in his story? How is it solved?*

- *How does everyone feel at the end?*

3 Prewrite and Confer

INDEPENDENT WRITING Give children blank story maps or charts (see pages 36 and 39). Remind them to use a real event as a starting point, name characters who are real or who seem real, and use a place that is or seems real. They should also give the characters a problem to solve and think of an ending that did or could have happened in real life.

TEACHER CONFERENCE Use questions like the following to help children think about their story plans.

- *What is the main idea of your story?*

- *Did you list events in an order that can really happen?*

- *Is the problem something that could have happened in real life? How is the problem solved?*

PEER CONFERENCE Have partners share their story maps or charts.

- *Suggest that they ask each other which details really happened.*

- *Have them talk about details that could be added to make the stories seem more realistic.*

- *Ask partners to help each other make sure their story maps or charts are complete.*

Meeting Individual Needs

Plot

Introduce On the board write the words *Who?, Where?, What happens?,* and *How does it end?* Choose a favorite storybook and have children answer the questions about the book. Point out that they just explained the plot of the story. Tell children that the plot is what happens to the main characters in a story.

Model Have children review Corey's story map. Ask volunteers to name details in the map that answer the questions on the board. Help children see that Corey uses the story map to plan the plot of the story he will write.

Summarize/Apply Have children work in pairs to use their story maps to share the plot of the stories they will write. Partners should make sure they can identify *who, where, what happens,* and *how it ends*.

WRITER'S BLOCK

Problem	Solution
Children can't figure out how to solve the problem in their stories.	Have children think of different endings that are funny, surprising, or happy and then brainstorm solutions to the problem that would lead to the kind of ending chosen.

ESL STRATEGY

Encourage children to draw pictures or act out their stories with partners to help them write details for their maps or charts.

HOME–SCHOOL CONNECTION

Ask children to share their story maps or charts with their families. Encourage them to talk about realistic ideas that could have happened and consider adding these to their story maps or charts.

WRITING ACROSS THE CURRICULUM

Art Display a work of art, a photograph, or a poster that depicts people in realistic situations. Encourage children to describe what's going on in the picture using a story map.

Realistic Story

Drafting

OBJECTIVES

★ **IDENTIFY** the characteristics of a realistic story in a first draft of a student model.

★ **FOLLOW** a writing plan to write a first draft of a realistic story.

 Continue the Writer's Workshop

Invite children to imagine they are going to act in a play. Ask them what they'd need to get started. Elicit that they'd need things like costumes, props, and most importantly, a script that tells them what to say and do.

Explain that as writers, they also need to have a plan before beginning to write a story. They'll need their story maps or charts and their story ideas, pencils, and paper.

 Discuss a Writer's Model

Read aloud Corey's first draft on pages 26–27 of the Big Book of Writing Models. Point out the colored lines with arrows, and explain how they show the beginning, middle, and end of Corey's story. Refer children back to Corey's story map and help them understand how he followed his plan to include all the information in order.

IDENTIFY CHARACTERISTICS OF A REALISTIC STORY Review with children the following characteristics of a realistic story.

- *Uses a real event or something that happened to the writer as the starting point*

- *Has a beginning that introduces the characters and setting*

- *Has a middle that describes a problem and tells what happens in order*

- *Has an end that tells how the problem is solved*

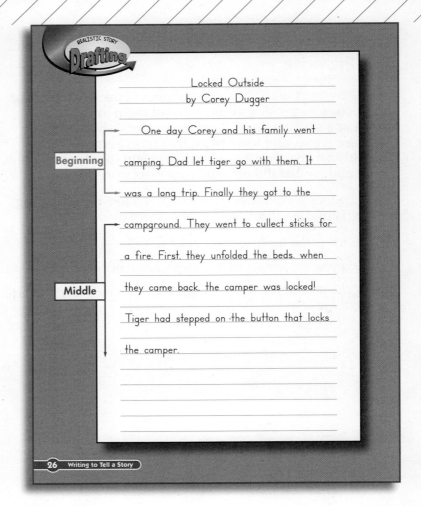

Locked Outside
by Corey Dugger

Beginning — One day Corey and his family went camping. Dad let tiger go with them. It was a long trip. Finally they got to the

Middle — campground. They went to cullect sticks for a fire. First, they unfolded the beds. when they came back. the camper was locked! Tiger had stepped on the button that locks the camper.

26 Writing to Tell a Story

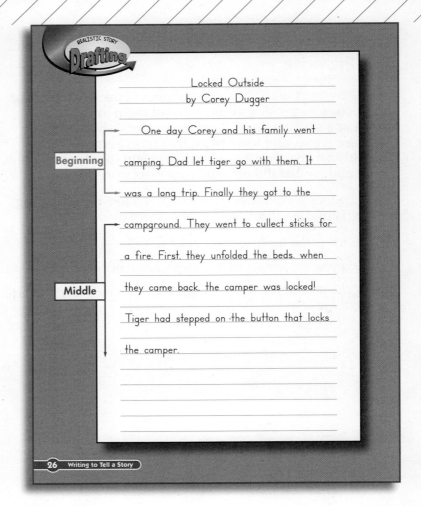 **Draft and Confer**

THINK LIKE A WRITER As children write their drafts, have them ask themselves questions like the following.

- *What is my story about?*

- *How can I make my story sound real to my readers?*

- *What do I have to remember about writing a realistic story?*

INDEPENDENT WRITING Have children follow their story maps or charts as they write. Remind them that this is the time to get their ideas on paper and not to worry about spelling and punctuation. Suggest they keep their drafts and story plans in their portfolios.

TEACHER CONFERENCE If children need help writing their drafts, ask questions like the following.

- *Did you include everything from your map or chart?*

- *Have you let your readers know what happens in the beginning, middle, and end of your story?*

- *Did you clearly tell how everything works out?*

- *Could the events in the story really happen?*

PEER CONFERENCE Have partners read their drafts to each other. Then writers can ask listeners questions.

- *Do you know who my characters are?*

- *Does my problem sound like it can really happen?*

- *Does the order of my story make sense?*

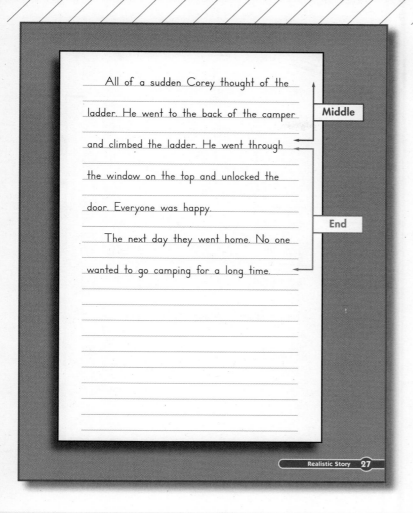

All of a sudden Corey thought of the ladder. He went to the back of the camper and climbed the ladder. He went through the window on the top and unlocked the door. Everyone was happy.

Middle

The next day they went home. No one wanted to go camping for a long time.

End

Realistic Story 27

Planning a Composition Using a Story Map

Introduce Ask children to name different kinds of maps, such as road maps, zoo maps, or Web site maps. Explain that maps are tools that help people see where they want to go. Tell children that story maps are tools that writers use to help them write their first drafts.

Model Have children compare Corey's story map to his first draft. Ask questions like the following to guide the discussion.

> *What information did Corey tell at the beginning of his story? Where can you find that on his story map?*
>
> *Does the middle of Corey's story use all of the ideas in his story map, or does he include more in the draft?*
>
> *Is the end of Corey's story different or the same as on the story map?*

Summarize/Apply Remind children to use their story maps or charts to help them know where they are going as they write. Afterwards, have children decide if they followed their original plan or if the changes they made as they drafted made their writing better.

WRITER'S BLOCK

Problem	Solution
Children write their story events in random order.	Have children number each sentence in chronological order. Then have children go back and rearrange the sentences to reflect the correct order.

ESL STRATEGY

Children can draw a three-panel comic strip showing the beginning, middle, and end of their stories. Then they can work with English-proficient partners to add captions.

HOME–SCHOOL CONNECTION

As children share their drafts with family members, encourage them to talk about other ways that the story problem could be solved.

WRITING ACROSS THE CURRICULUM

Science When children write in science journals, learning logs, or observation logs, remind them to record the events from an experiment in order.

On March 3, the orange slice was juicy and wet.
On March 6, the slice was beginning to look dry.
On March 10, the orange slice was all dried up.
We decided that the water in the orange slice evaporated into the air.

Realistic Story

Revising

OBJECTIVES

- ★ **ANALYZE a model to understand how a student writer revised his writing.**
- ★ **REVISE a first draft of a realistic story to add more details.**
- ★ **CUT and PASTE sentences to show the correct sequence of events.**

1 Continue the Writer's Workshop

Remind children that writers often revisit their writing with "fresh eyes" to make changes. Review on page 28 of the Big Book of Writing Models the special marks writers use to add and move information. In addition, review the symbol for making a capital letter lowercase. (If desired, make copies of the blackline master on page 30 of this Teacher Resource Guide for children.)

2 Discuss a Writer's Model

Read the excerpt of Corey's revised draft on page 28 of the Big Book. When you get to the end of the page, point out the torn paper border and help children understand that this is just a part of Corey's story.

Ask children to look at the marks Corey used to show what he added, changed, or moved. Use the callouts to explain why Corey made the changes he did. Encourage children to explain how his changes improved his realistic story.

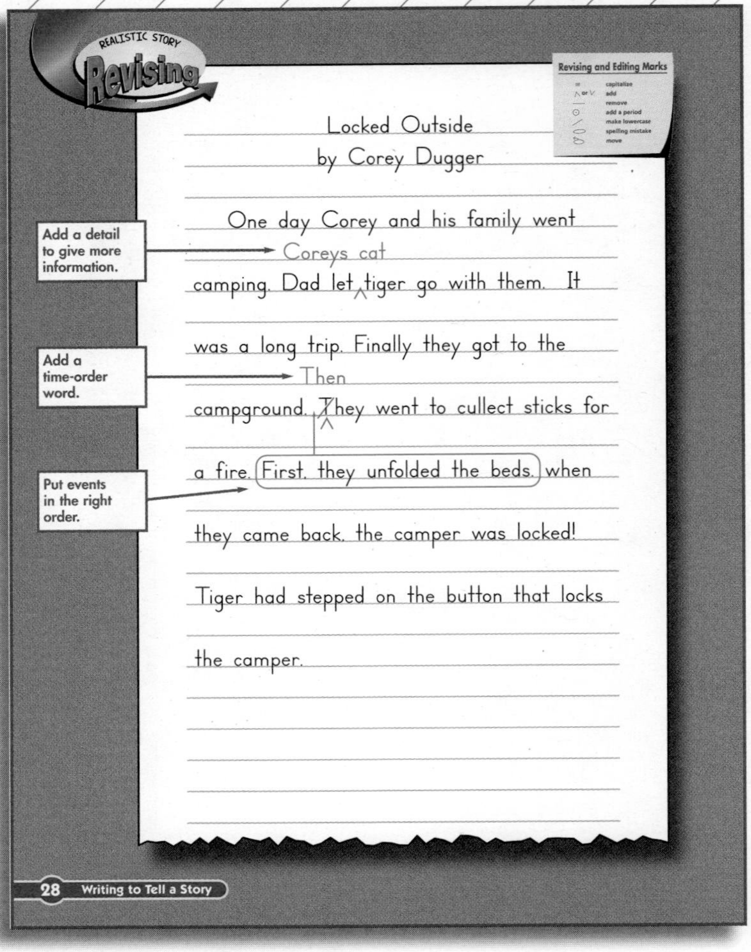
Realistic Story
Revising
Revising and Editing Marks
capitalize
add
remove
add a period
make lowercase
spelling mistake
move
Locked Outside
by Corey Dugger
Add a detail to give more information.
Add a time-order word.
Put events in the right order.
One day Corey and his family went camping. Dad let Coreys cat tiger go with them. It was a long trip. Finally they got to the campground. Then They went to cullect sticks for a fire. First, they unfolded the beds. when they came back. the camper was locked! Tiger had stepped on the button that locks the camper.
28 Writing to Tell a Story

3 Revise and Confer

As children revise their drafts, have them keep in mind questions like the following.

- *Did I tell the events in order?*
- *Is there any information I need to move or take out?*
- *Can I add details to make my story more interesting?*

TEACHER CONFERENCE If children have difficulty seeing ways to improve their drafts, ask questions such as the following.

- *Will the reader be able to tell the beginning, middle, and end of your story?*
- *Can you add or take away any details to make the story easier to understand?*
- *Do you need to move any words to fix the sequence of events?*

PEER CONFERENCE Have partners read their drafts to each other, explain the changes they made, and ask questions such as the following.

- *Does my story sound real to you?*
- *Did I tell about a problem the characters have and how it is fixed?*
- *What details do you think are interesting?*

Mini Lesson

Sequencing Events by Cutting and Pasting Sentences

Introduce Ahead of time, use a computer's word processor to type each of the following sentences so that when printed out, they can be cut into individual sentence strips. Display the strips in the order shown.

First, I ate breakfast.

Finally, I rushed off to school.

Next, I gave my dog a hug.

Ask children if the sentences are in the right order. Invite them to show how the sentences should be ordered. *(The last sentence should be second.)*

Model Explain that writers often move words and sentences around to put them in a better order. Review Corey's revisions on Big Book page 28, and have volunteers tell what text has been moved and why. Then, use the computer to show children how the sample sentences above can be cut and pasted so that they are in the correct order.

Summarize/Apply Tell children that when they revise their drafts, they should read each sentence carefully and decide if it is placed in the right order. When using a computer, encourage them to cut and paste sentences that need to be moved.

WRITER'S BLOCK

Problem	Solution
Children have difficulty adding descriptive, vivid language to revise their drafts.	Encourage children to pantomime actions from their stories, then look for sentences where they can add words that tell more about the characters' actions.

ESL STRATEGY

Encourage children to tape-record their first drafts with English-proficient partners, then listen to the recording to decide what they like and what they want to change.

HOME–SCHOOL CONNECTION

Encourage children to share their revised stories with their families and explain why they made certain changes.

WRITING ACROSS THE CURRICULUM

Social Studies Show children how they can use the caret symbol to add information to social studies learning log entries.

> the 16th
> Abraham Lincoln was president
>   of the U.S.
>   in a log cabin
> He was born on February 12, 1809.
>   on March 4, 1861
> He became President.

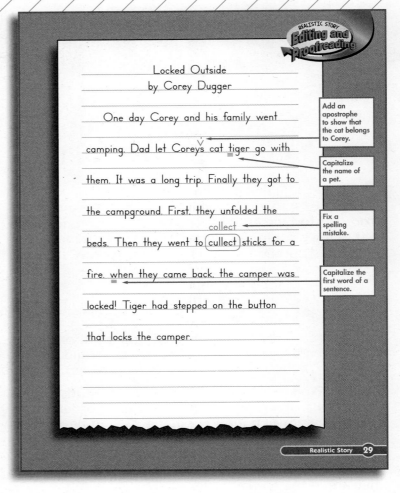

The handwritten model:

Locked Outside
by Corey Dugger

One day Corey and his family went camping. Dad let Corey's cat tiger go with them. It was a long trip. Finally they got to the campground. First, they unfolded the beds. Then they went to (cullect) sticks for a fire. when they came back, the camper was locked! Tiger had stepped on the button that locks the camper.

Callouts:
- Add an apostrophe to show that the cat belongs to Corey.
- Capitalize the name of a pet.
- Fix a spelling mistake.
- Capitalize the first word of a sentence.

Realistic Story **29**

Realistic Story

Editing and Proofreading

OBJECTIVES

★ ANALYZE a model to understand how a student writer edited and proofread his writing.

★ EDIT and PROOFREAD a draft for grammar, usage, mechanics, and spelling.

★ USE a capital letter at the beginning of proper nouns.

1 Continue the Writer's Workshop

Explain to children that writers often check their drafts several times before they publish. They check to correct mistakes in spelling, punctuation marks, and capital letters.

Review the chart of revising and editing marks on page 28 of the Big Book of Writing Models (see also page 30 in this Teacher Resource Guide), pointing out the symbols for capitalizing a letter, adding an apostrophe or other punctuation marks, and correcting a spelling mistake.

2 Discuss a Writer's Model

Review the excerpt of Corey's edited draft on page 29 of the Big Book. Invite children to look at the revising and editing marks Corey used to make corrections. Use the callouts to help children understand why he made those changes. Then ask children if they think Corey missed any mistakes.

3 Edit, Proofread, and Confer

As children edit their drafts, have them keep in mind the following questions.

- *Have I spelled words correctly?*
- *Do names and sentences begin with a capital letter?*
- *Is there a punctuation mark at the end of each sentence?*
- *Did I use an apostrophe to show that something belonged to someone?*

TEACHER CONFERENCE As children share their drafts with you, ask questions such as the following.

- *How did you check words you had trouble spelling?*
- *Does each sentence have the correct end punctuation? How can you tell?*
- *What nouns need to begin with a capital letter?*
- *Do any nouns need apostrophes to show possession?*

PEER CONFERENCE Have partners exchange drafts and read them slowly, looking for any problems the writer might have missed. Have them create a small check box to check the following.

- *Is the end punctuation correct in each sentence?*
- *Are any words misspelled?*
- *Does each sentence begin with a capital letter?*
- *Are apostrophes used correctly?*

Capitalization—Names

Introduce Remind children that nouns are words that name people, places, and things. Write these words on the board: *girl, restaurant, building*. Ask volunteers to name a specific girl, restaurant, and building, such as *Jill, Pizza King,* and *Mountain Avenue School*. Explain that nouns that name a specific person, place, or thing are called proper nouns. Important words in proper nouns begin with capital letters.

Model Have children review Corey's draft. Ask volunteers to place a self-stick note under each proper noun they find in the draft. Then have volunteers draw three lines under the first letter in each proper noun if it is not capitalized and should be.

Summarize/Apply Remind children that proper nouns, such as characters' names and names of places, should begin with a capital letter in their drafts. As children edit their drafts, they can do an "extra pass" to check for this specific element.

WRITER'S BLOCK

Problem	Solution
Children end every sentence with a period, disregarding the need for variety in end punctuation.	Have children read their stories aloud to themselves with expression. Ask them to check the end punctuation to see if it matches the tone of voice they used when reading.

ESL STRATEGY

Pair children with varying language proficiencies and have them work together to check for nouns that name specific people, places, or things.

HOME–SCHOOL CONNECTION

Invite children to share their edited drafts with their families and explain the changes they will make in their final drafts.

WRITING ACROSS THE CURRICULUM

Language Arts As children record information in their literature logs, remind them to use capital letters to begin the names of characters and specific places used in the story.

Dec. 8

<u>Alexis Goes to Australia</u>

by Elizabeth Niles

Alexis was having a bad day. She wanted to go to Australia. She didn't think she'd miss her friends at Oak Valley School.

Realistic Story

Publishing

OBJECTIVE

★ PUBLISH a realistic story.

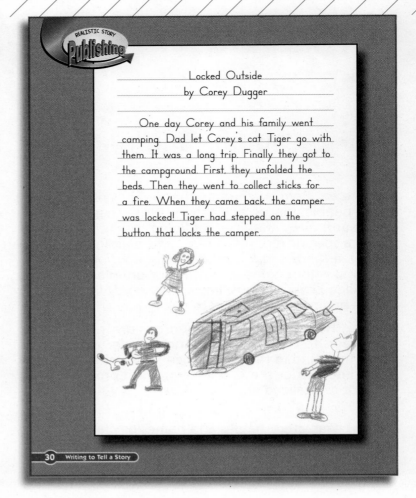

Locked Outside
by Corey Dugger

One day Corey and his family went camping. Dad let Corey's cat Tiger go with them. It was a long trip. Finally they got to the campground. First, they unfolded the beds. Then they went to collect sticks for a fire. When they came back, the camper was locked! Tiger had stepped on the button that locks the camper.

1 End the Writer's Workshop

Explain that children are ready for the last step of the writing process—publishing. When writers publish their work, they share it with other people, so they want it to be the best it can be.

2 Discuss a Writer's Model

Have children look at Corey's final draft on pages 30–31 of the Big Book of Writing Models. Encourage them to compare it with the first draft and discuss what has changed. Invite volunteers to comment on how Corey displayed it.

3 Publish and Celebrate

Brainstorm different ways children might publish their writing. Use the publishing suggestions to the right as a guide. Discuss the steps for each option. Then give children some time to decide which one they will use or allow them to come up with their own ideas. Provide materials as needed.

Set aside a special time for a publishing celebration during which children can read, display, or perform their realistic stories. You may wish to add to the celebration by placing a notice in the school newspaper or on a prominent school bulletin board.

Publishing Ideas

CLASS BOOK

Have children compile their neat final copies into a class book titled *Our Amazing Stories*. Encourage children to create a table of contents for the book.

PUPPET SHOW

Provide materials so children can make paper bag puppets or stick puppets of their characters. Have them narrate their stories as one or two classmates use puppets to act out the events.

PUBLISH ON-LINE

Invite children to publish their stories on the Internet. One web site to consider is **www.kidnews.com**. Preview the web site ahead of time so you are familiar with its content and procedures.

88

All of a sudden Corey thought of the ladder. He went to the back of the camper and climbed the ladder. He went through the window on the top and unlocked the door. Everyone was happy.

The next day they went home. No one wanted to go camping for a long time.

Realistic Story 31

ASSESSMENT OPPORTUNITIES

SELF-ASSESSMENT Have children complete the Self-Assessment Checklist on page 74. Encourage them to share their responses orally during teacher conferences.

PORTFOLIO ASSESSMENT If children choose to include their realistic stories in their portfolios, encourage them also to consider including their prewriting idea webs, story maps or charts, drafts, and Self-Assessment Checklists.

PEER EVALUATION Have children use the Peer Evaluation Checklist on page 44.

TEACHER PRIMARY–TRAIT ASSESSMENT Use the Teacher Evaluation Checklist on page 75 to evaluate children's realistic stories. You may want to share your comments during teacher conferences.

RUBRIC FOR REALISTIC STORIES The form-specific rubric will help you evaluate children's writing. Use the information in it during teacher conferences to help children identify ways they can improve their writing.

BENCHMARK PAPERS You may want to use the Benchmark Papers on pages 76–79 along with the rubric to evaluate children's writing.

RUBRIC FOR REALISTIC STORY

4
- Clearly focused on plausible events.
- Includes substantial detail that makes the story seem real.
- The story problem is clearly developed and solved.
- Has a clear, well-integrated beginning, middle, and end.
- Contains few errors in grammar, usage, mechanics, or spelling.

3
- Focused on plausible events.
- May include detail that makes the story seem real.
- The story problem may not be clearly developed and solved.
- May have a recognizable beginning, middle, and end.
- May contain errors in grammar, usage, mechanics, or spelling that do not interfere with understanding.

2
- May not focus on plausible events.
- May not include detail that makes the story seem real.
- The story problem may be unclear and unresolved.
- May have a recognizable beginning, middle, and end.
- May contain errors in grammar, usage, mechanics, or spelling that do not interfere with understanding.

1
- May not be focused on plausible events.
- May not include any detail that makes the story seem real.
- May not include a story problem.
- May not have a clear beginning, middle, and end.
- May contain substantial errors in grammar, usage, mechanics, or spelling that interfere with understanding.

Fantasy

OBJECTIVES

★ RECOGNIZE the characteristics of a fantasy.

★ RESPOND to a model fantasy written by a student.

★ PLAN, WRITE, and REVISE a fantasy.

★ USE a story chart or map to plan a fantasy.

 Begin the Lesson

Help children complete a two-column chart labeled *Real* and *Make-Believe*. In column one, record descriptions of real-life people, places, and things. Then have children suggest ways to change the information into make-believe. Record these ideas in column two. See the example below. Then explain that children's make-believe ideas can be used to write a make-believe story called a fantasy.

Real	Make-Believe
1. a rabbit—hops on the grass	1. a rabbit—hops over tall buildings
2. a boy—walks to school	2. a boy—flies to school
3. a house—made of bricks	3. a house—made of marshmallows

2 Discuss a Writer's Model

MEET THE WRITER Show children the picture of second grader Sasha Marie Negron on page 32 of the Big Book of Writing Models and read her quote aloud. Invite volunteers to suggest why they think Sasha likes to write fantasies. Help children understand that Sasha uses her own ideas to write make-believe stories.

Sasha Marie Negron
Pennsylvania

TALK ABOUT THE MODEL Have children follow along as you read aloud Sasha's story on Big Book pages 32–34. Then use the callouts to help children identify and understand the characteristics of a fantasy. Discuss the characters, setting, and problem.

• *How do you know this story is a fantasy?*

• *What is real and what is make-believe?*

• *Why do you think the writer uses real animals and places in her story?*

Help children understand that a fantasy can include both real and imaginary parts. Explain that writing about a real animal doing imaginary things can make a fantasy more interesting. Remind children that all stories should be well organized and easy to follow. Invite volunteers to identify the beginning, middle, and end of Sasha's story.

• **A continuation of this lesson follows on page 92.**

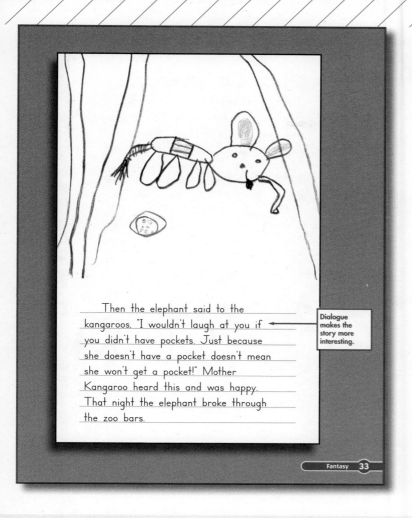

Then the elephant said to the kangaroos, "I wouldn't laugh at you if you didn't have pockets. Just because she doesn't have a pocket doesn't mean she won't get a pocket!" Mother Kangaroo heard this and was happy. That night the elephant broke through the zoo bars.

Dialogue makes the story more interesting.

Fantasy 33

WRITER'S BLOCK

Problem

Children overuse words and do not include vivid details in their prewriting plans and stories.

Solution

Display lists of descriptive verbs, adjectives, and adverbs that children can use. Explain how to use these words in sentences. Children can then refer to the lists as they write.

ESL STRATEGY

Have children tell their fantasy stories through a series of drawings. Then have partners help them write captions to describe what is happening in each picture.

HOME–SCHOOL CONNECTION

Encourage children to discuss their prewriting charts or maps and their stories with family members. Family members can suggest additional make-believe elements to include in the stories.

WRITING ACROSS THE CURRICULUM

Science Children can use a two-column chart to clarify real versus make-believe information that they have learned about different science topics.

Real	Make-Believe
1. Rainbows form when sunlight passes through raindrops.	1. Mr. Rainbow lives on a cloud and paints rainbows.
2. The colors of a rainbow are red, orange, yellow, green, blue, and violet.	2. There is a pot of gold at the end of each rainbow.

Identifying Form: Real vs. Make-Believe

Introduce Tell children the following story.

Last week, I traveled in a rocket to the moon. On the way there, we stopped to drink milk at the Milky Way. We stayed on the moon all day, but then our rocket wouldn't start. I had to ride on a shooting star to get home.

Ask children if this story is real or make-believe. Encourage them to share reasons for their answers. Help children understand that even though some of the details might seem real, the story could not happen, so it is make-believe.

Model Have children review the fantasy on pages 32–34 of the Big Book. Have them tell which details are real and which ones are make-believe. Invite them to suggest other make-believe details that could be added to the story. Explain that anything can happen in a make-believe story because you use your imagination to make up the events.

Summarize/Apply Suggest that children reread their fantasies and underline all the parts that are make-believe. If needed, encourage them to add more make-believe details.

Fantasy (CONTINUED)

3 WRITE AND CONFER

INDEPENDENT WRITING Have children write their fantasies. Encourage them to refer to the student model as they plan and write.

MAKE A PLAN Have children brainstorm story topics. Suggest they think of favorite dreams, family outings, and secret wishes or use the Real or Make-Believe chart on page 37 to generate a list of possible topics. Encourage them to pick the idea they like most.

Then have them use story maps or charts, such as the ones on Big Book pages 63 and 66, to plan their stories. (See also pages 36 and 39 in this Teacher Resource Guide for blackline masters.) Have children name who the characters are, where and when the story takes place, what the problem is, and how everything works out.

WRITE IT DOWN Have children use their maps or charts to help them write fantasies that have clear beginnings, middles, and ends. Suggest they picture in their minds the events that happen and how the characters look and act, as they write about them. Help children use the correct form when they include dialogue. They can look back at the student model for help.

LOOK IT OVER Have children reread their stories. Ask them to look for ways to improve the stories, such as by adding imaginary details or dialogue, deleting information that is not important, and correcting capitalization and spelling errors.

TEACHER CONFERENCE To help children find ways to improve their stories, ask questions such as the following.

- *How did your map or chart help you to write your story?*

- *What parts of your story are make-believe and what parts are realistic?*

- *Did you use colorful words and details to tell about the characters and setting?*

- *What problem are your characters trying to solve? How do they solve it?*

PEER CONFERENCE Have children read their stories to partners. Encourage partners to close their eyes and picture what is being said. Have them suggest details that could be added, deleted, or rearranged to make the story more interesting and clear. Remind them to give helpful advice and positive comments.

> The characters are make-believe.
>
> The characters solve the problem.
>
> He ran to the Pocket Person's house. The elephant picked up the Pocket Person and started back to the zoo. The zookeeper saw the elephant coming and opened the gate. The Pocket Person saw Mother Kangaroo and her baby. He saw she didn't have a pocket, so he gave her one. Mother Kangaroo was very happy.
>
> 34   Writing to Tell a Story

SHARE YOUR WORK After children revise their stories, have them write a clean, final copy. Children can illustrate their stories and bind the pages to make books. Invite them to read their stories aloud as classmates act out the parts. Children might also enjoy making stick puppets that they can use to perform their stories.

ASSESSMENT OPPORTUNITIES

SELF-ASSESSMENT Have children complete the Self-Assessment Checklist on page 42.

PEER EVALUATION Have children use the Peer Evaluation Checklist on page 44.

TEACHER HOLISTIC ASSESSMENT Use the Teacher Evaluation Checklist on page 43 to evaluate children's fantasies.

Imagine That: Writing to Describe

Contents

RESOURCES

TEACHING PLANS

Writing to Describe — Unit Planner

WRITING FORM	MINILESSONS Basic Skills/ Writing Process/ Writer's Craft	Grammar, Usage, Mechanics, Spelling	Writing Across the Curriculum	Meeting Individual Needs	Assessment
Lesson 1 SHAPE POEM pp. 110–111 (3–4 days)	• Alliteration, 111		• Math, 111	• Writer's Block, 111 • ESL Strategy, 111 • Home-School Connection, 111	• Self-Assessment Checklist, 104 • Teacher Evaluation Checklist, 105 • Peer Evaluation Checklist, 106 • Teacher and Peer Conferencing, 111
Lesson 2 DESCRIPTION OF AN EVENT pp. 112–113 (3–4 days)	• Details: Sensory Words, 113		• Science, 113	• Writer's Block, 113 • ESL Strategy, 113 • Home-School Connection, 113	• Self-Assessment Checklist, 104 • Teacher Evaluation Checklist, 105 • Peer Evaluation Checklist, 106 • Teacher and Peer Conferencing, 113
Lesson 3 DESCRIPTION OF A PERSON pp. 122–131 (6–10 days)	• Planning a Composition Using a Word Web, 123 • Using Precise/Vivid Verbs, 125 • Using Precise/Vivid Adjectives, 127	• Apostrophes— in Contractions, 129	• Health, 123 • Language Arts, 125 • Science, 127 • Social Studies, 129	• Writer's Block, 123, 125, 127, 129 • ESL Strategy, 123, 125, 127, 129 • Home-School Connection, 123, 125, 127, 129	• Rubric, 131 • Benchmark Papers, 118–121 • Self-Assessment Checklist, 116 • Teacher Evaluation Checklist, 117 • Peer Evaluation Checklist, 106 • Portfolio, 131 • Teacher and Peer Conferencing, 123, 125, 126, 128
Lesson 4 FREE-VERSE POEM pp. 132–133 (3–4 days)	• Adding Descriptive Details to Support Main Idea, 133		• Language Arts, 133	• Writer's Block, 133 • ESL Strategy, 133 • Home-School Connection, 133	• Self-Assessment Checklist, 104 • Teacher Evaluation Checklist, 105 • Peer Evaluation Checklist, 106 • Teacher and Peer Conferencing, 133
Lesson 5 COMPARISON pp. 134–136 (3–4 days)	• Using a Journal to Get Ideas, 135		• Art, 135	• Writer's Block, 135 • ESL Strategy, 135 • Home-School Connection, 135	• Self-Assessment Checklist, 104 • Teacher Evaluation Checklist, 105 • Peer Evaluation Checklist, 106 • Teacher and Peer Conferencing, 136

Making the Reading-Writing Connection
Writing to Describe

You may want to add the following books to your classroom library. Each category of books represents one form of writing children will be introduced to in *Writing to Describe*. The books serve as models for good writing and are valuable resources to use throughout each lesson. The suggested titles offer reading opportunities for children of varying reading abilities and are labeled as follows.

 Easy—books with a readability that is below second-grade level, but with content of interest to second graders

 Average—books with an average readability level that can be read independently by most second-grade students

 Challenging—books with above-average readability for more proficient students or those that can be read aloud to students

Use literature to introduce a writing form, as a model of successful writing, to enhance minilessons, to focus on grammar and usage, and to expand each lesson.

SHAPE POEM	DESCRIPTION OF AN EVENT	DESCRIPTION OF A PERSON
Winter Eyes by Douglas Florian. Greenwillow, 1999. Poems and shape poems about winter and winter activities are included in this collection.	**Just Grandma and Me** by Mercer Mayer. Golden Books, 1983. Many humorous things happen to Little Critter and his grandma as they spend the day at the beach.	**Riding the Ferry With Captain Cruz** by Alice K. Flanagan. Children's Press, 1997. Ride along with Captain Cruz on the Staten Island ferry and see how he commands the boat and crew.
In the Swim by Douglas Florian. Harcourt Brace, 1997. Twenty-one poems feature strange and fascinating underwater creatures. Several shape poems are included.	**Hill of Fire** by Thomas P. Lewis. HarperTrophy, 1985. This is a story about the eruption of Paricutin, a volcano in Mexico, and how it affected the people who lived near it.	**Annie's Gifts (Feeling Good)** by Angela Shelf Medearis. Just Us Books, 1997. Everyone in the family has a musical talent, except Annie. She eventually discovers that she has her own special gifts.
Insectlopedia by Douglas Florian. Harcourt Brace, 1998. Twenty-one short poems feature insects. Some of the poems are in the shape of the bug about which they tell.	**Man on the Moon** by Anastasia Suen. Viking Children's Books, 1997. The astronauts on the Apollo 11 in 1969 became the first people to land and walk on the moon.	**Amazing Grace** by Mary Hoffman. Dial Books for Young Readers, 1991. A young African-American girl discovers that she can be anything she wants to be—including Peter Pan.

FREE-VERSE POEM	COMPARISON
Soap Soup and Other Verses by Karla Kuskin. HarperTrophy, 1992. A collection of poems about ordinary and not-so-ordinary things that kids can relate to. Some free-verse poems are included.	**Big and Little** by Steve Jenkins. Houghton Mifflin, 1996. The sizes of animals from all over the world are compared to each other.
Sky Scrape/City Scrape: Poems of City Life Selected by Jane Yolen. Boyds Mills Press, 1996. An anthology of poems that tell the sights, sounds, and energy of the city.	**Stellaluna** by Janell Cannon. Harcourt Brace, 1993. A baby bat named Stellaluna learns how birds and bats are both alike and different.
Til All the Stars Have Fallen: A Collection of Poems for Children by David Booth. Puffin, 1994. A collection of poems for children that includes a wide range of free-verse poems, both short and long.	**Snakes** by Patricia Demuth. Price Stern Sloan, 1993. Snakes are long and short but have no arms or legs. Comparisons of many snakes are included in this colorful, science topic book.

The Classroom Writing Center
Writing to Describe

As children begin to engage in different kinds of descriptive writing, you may want to make some additions to your writing center. Here are some ideas.

◆ Introduce the use of a thesaurus for young children.

◆ Help children create a word wall with words that focus on each of the five senses. Children can refer to the word wall when writing.

SEE	TOUCH	TASTE	SMELL	HEAR
cloudy	chilly	nutty	fresh	hiss
beautiful	hot	salty	rotten	gurgle
colorful	soft	sour	smoky	splash
gigantic	sticky	sweet	pleasant	roar
tiny	rough	buttery	sweet	crash

◆ After sharing a poem at the beginning of the week, display the poem on chart paper or poster board. In the space around the poem, let children write responses telling what they think of the poem.

◆ Establish a Poetry Corner in your classroom library or writing center. Display plenty of poetry books and posters.

◆ Add multi-colored pens, colored pencils, glitter sticks, ink pads, stamps, and other craft items to your writing center's supplies. Provide computer software that lets children draw.

The Stages of the Writing Process

Consider using the following activities to further engage children as they learn about various forms of descriptive writing.

A Prewriting Activity for Poetry Develop a picture file of objects, toys, foods, animals, plants, nature, and weather scenes for the writing center. Children can describe pictures to one another as a way to choose a subject and to brainstorm describing words.

A Drafting Activity for a Description of an Event Display a white board with dry erase markers. Label it "Special Events." Have children take turns using the board to draft a description of a special event.

A Publishing Activity for Poetry Post a list of ways children can publish their poems. See the example to the right for ideas.

Different Ways to Publish a Poem
- Create a dance to go with your poem.
- Get a group of classmates to recite your poem.
- Paint a poetry poster.
- Add sound effects or music.
- Make a class poetry book.
- Make a puppet who can recite your poem.

Graphic Organizers

The following blackline masters can help children with parts of the lessons in this unit. Make copies for the writing center and transparencies for use with an overhead projector. Display a completed example of each organizer if desired.

Blackline Master	Purpose	Writing Form
Poetry Web, page 98	Prewriting: using descriptive language	Poetry and other descriptive writing
Description Map, page 99	Designing a Plan: beginning-middle-end map	Description of an Event or Person, Comparison
Web, page 100	Prewriting: web diagram	Description of a Person or Event, Poetry
Venn Diagram, page 101	Prewriting: Venn diagram	Comparison

Create a Bulletin Board

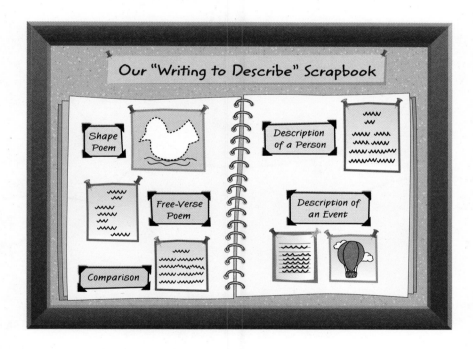

◆ Set up a bulletin-board display that resembles two open pages of a scrapbook. The title of the display is *Our "Writing to Describe" Scrapbook.*

◆ Post labels for each form of writing: Shape Poem, Description of an Event, Description of a Person, Free-Verse Poem, and Comparison. Include a published example of each writing form.

◆ Use the bulletin board to introduce *Writing to Describe.* As children publish their own writing, replace the samples with children's work. Change the writing often so each child's writing can be showcased. Encourage children to include pictures and photos with their writing for the scrapbook display.

Name _____ **Date** _____

Poetry Web

Write words that tell about your topic.

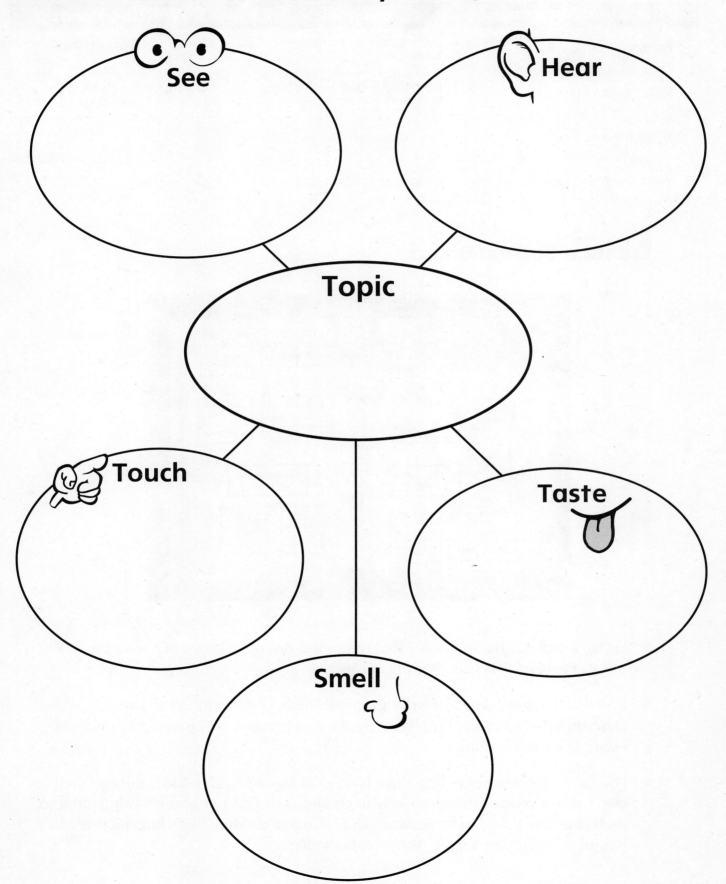

Description Map

Use this page to plan your description.

Topic: _____

Beginning

↓

Middle

↓

End

Web

Write your topic in the middle. Then write words that describe your topic.

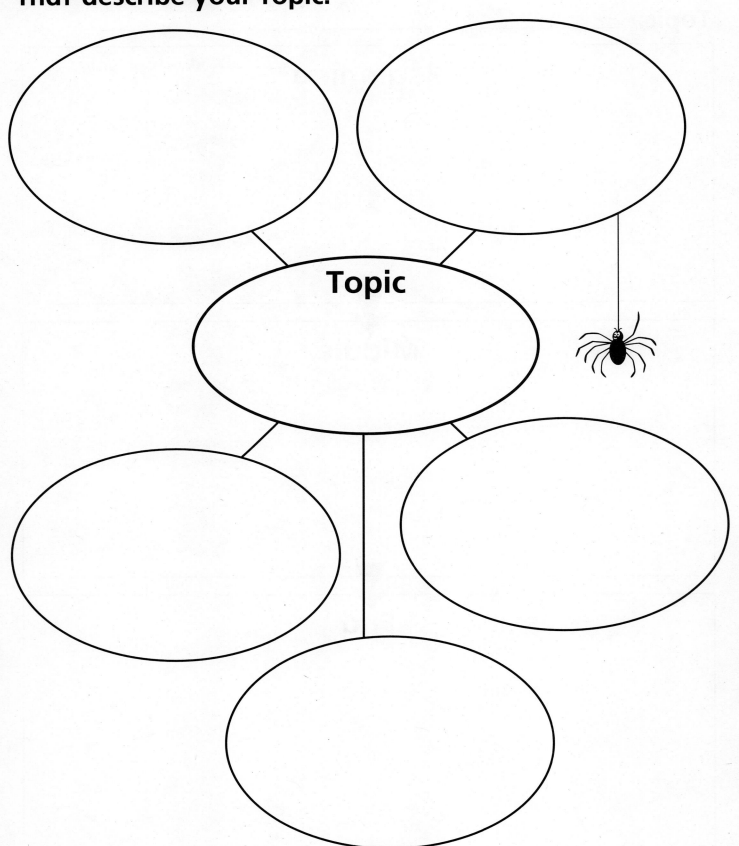

Topic

Venn Diagram

Write ideas about two things that are alike.

Topic: _____   **Topic:** _____

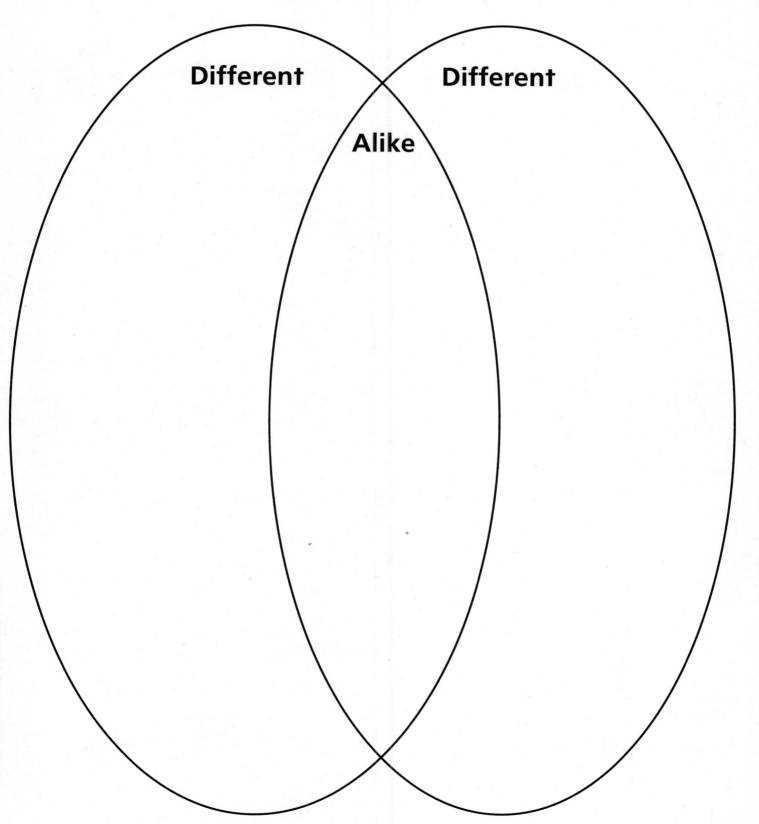

Connecting Multiple Intelligences
Writing to Describe

The following activities focus on specific prewriting and publishing ideas for children who demonstrate intelligence in different ways: talent and skill with words (linguistic), with numbers (logical-mathematical), with pictures (spatial), with movement (bodily-kinesthetic), with people (interpersonal), with self (intrapersonal), with music (musical), and/or with nature (environmental or naturalist).

Linguistic
Prewriting — Create lists of describing words grouped by sense to use when writing.
Publishing — Read your description without naming the person or event. Ask your audience to guess.

Logical-Mathematical
Prewriting — Sketch several simple shapes before choosing one to write about in a poem.
Publishing — In your comparison, plan to include details that tell about size and shape.

Spatial
Prewriting — Look at pictures of two subjects you are comparing.
Publishing — Show a model of the shape you are describing as you share your shape poem.

Bodily-Kinesthetic
Prewriting — Use a favorite sport or game activity as a topic for a poem or description.
Publishing — Turn your free-verse poem into a jump rope chant.

Writing to Describe

Environmental (Naturalist)
Prewriting — Choose an outdoor vacation as a topic for a free-verse poem or description of an event.
Publishing — Make a frame using twigs, shells, leaves, and feathers to display a poem or description.

Intrapersonal
Prewriting — Spend quiet time observing, drawing pictures, or listing words that describe the person you want to write about.
Publishing — Create a poem poster to display for others to read.

Interpersonal
Prewriting — Interview classmates who attended the event you will write about.
Publishing — Ask a partner to help you share your comparison of two subjects.

Musical
Prewriting — Plan to describe a person who loves music or an event that included music.
Publishing — Sing the words of your poem or play music as you read it.

Evaluating Student Writing
Writing to Describe

The Write Direction offers a variety of assessment options. The following are short descriptions of the assessment opportunities available in this unit. Just select the assessment option that works best for you.

Types of Assessment	Complete-Process Writing Lessons	Short-Process Writing Lessons
Rubric Specific characteristics of a writing form are used to develop a 4-point scale for evaluating children's writing (4–Well Developed, 3–Adequately Developed, 2–Partially Developed, 1–Undeveloped). Children's writing is compared with the characteristics to determine a rating point.	• Description of a Person, page 131	
Benchmark Papers Annotated and scored student writing models are provided as benchmarks for evaluating children's writing. Children's published writing can be compared with these models for assessment.	• Description of a Person, pages 118–121	
Checklists Self-Assessment, Teacher, and Peer Evaluation Checklists help children refine their descriptive writing at each writing process stage.	• Self-Assessment Checklist for Description of a Person, page 116 • Teacher Evaluation Checklist for Description of a Person, page 117 • Peer Evaluation Checklist, page 106	• Self-Assessment Checklist, page 104 • Teacher Evaluation Checklist, page 105 • Peer Evaluation Checklist, page 106
Portfolio Assessment Children's work generated throughout the writing process may be used in creating a portfolio illustrating their progress as writers. Strategies and tips for assessment using a portfolio appear in each lesson. Suggested pieces for a portfolio include completed writing and works-in-progress, logs, journals, and checklists.	• Description of a Person, page 131	
Teacher and Peer Conferencing Throughout each lesson in this unit, there are opportunities to interact with children, informally questioning them about their progress and concerns. Children also have opportunities to interact with one another to ask questions, share ideas, and react to their partner's writing.	• Description of a Person, pages 123, 125, 126, 128	• Shape Poem, page 111 • Description of an Event, page 112 • Free-Verse Poem, page 133 • Comparison, page 136

Self-Assessment Checklist
Writing to Describe

Name of Writer _____

Date _____

Type of Writing _____

Use this checklist when you are revising, or editing and proofreading a
- **shape poem**
- **description of an event**
- **free-verse poem**
- **comparison**

	YES	NO	Ways to Make My Writing Better
Is it clear what my writing is about?	☐	☐	
Is there anything I should add to or take out of my writing?	☐	☐	
Could I use more description to make my writing more interesting?	☐	☐	
Have I used and spelled words correctly?	☐	☐	
Should I change any punctuation marks or capitalization?	☐	☐	

Teacher Evaluation Checklist
Writing to Describe

Name of Writer _____

Date _____

Writing Mode _____

Use this checklist when you are evaluating a child's
- **shape poem**
- **description of an event**
- **free-verse poem**
- **comparison**

	YES	NO	Recommendations to Child
Is the topic appropriate for this writing assignment?	☐	☐	
Is the writing focused on the topic?	☐	☐	
Does the writing include detailed descriptions?	☐	☐	
Do these descriptions include vivid or colorful language?	☐	☐	
Does the writing have a clear, well-developed structure?	☐	☐	
Does the writer adhere to the conventions of			
grammar?	☐	☐	
usage?	☐	☐	
spelling?	☐	☐	
punctuation?	☐	☐	
capitalization?	☐	☐	
Is the handwriting legible?	☐	☐	
Was the work done neatly?	☐	☐	

Peer Evaluation Checklist
Writing to Describe

Name of Writer _____

Name of Writing Partner _____

Conference Date _____

Type of Writing _____

Use this checklist during revising or editing and proofreading conferences for a
- **shape poem**
- **description of an event**
- **free-verse poem**
- **comparison**

	What My Writing Partner Said	Ways to Make My Writing Better
What did you like best about my writing?		
Did the words I used help you see and feel what I was writing about?		
Is there anything missing from my writing?		
Is there anything I should take out of my writing?		

Home Letter

Dear Family,

For the next few weeks your child will be learning about writing to describe. This kind of writing allows your child to use the five senses to discover "picture" words that can be used to describe a special event, tell about a person, and write a comparison. Your child will also learn to choose words to write a shape poem and a free-verse poem.

You can encourage your child to use his or her five senses to describe things. Try these activities at home.

1 On your next road trip or while waiting in line, play games that involve describing things such as "I Spy" or "Twenty Questions."

2 After reading a picture book together, go back and have your child "read the pictures" by telling what is happening in each illustration.

3 Read a poem a day. Look for books with action rhymes and fingerplays. Your child will enjoy learning these.

4 After your child draws or paints a picture, ask him or her to describe it to you before showing it. Close your eyes as your child describes. Then open your eyes to see if the description was accurate.

5 Here are some books that you and your child will enjoy.

◆ *Come On, Rain* by Karen Hesse. Illustrated by Jon J. Muth. Scholastic Trade, 1999. Gray clouds roll across a purple sky as rain approaches. This event calls for a little girl to gather her neighborhood friends for a romp in the rain.

◆ *April Bubbles Chocolate: An ABC of Poetry* by Lee Bennett Hopkins et al. Simon and Schuster, 1994. This collection of poems with themes from A to Z is perfect for family read-alouds.

Sincerely,

Carta para el hogar

Estimada familia,

Durante las próximas semanas su hijo/a va a estudiar la escritura para describir. Este tipo de escritura le permitirá a su hijo/a usar sus cinco sentidos para descubrir palabras "visuales" que se pueden usar para describir un acontecimiento especial, para hablar de una persona y para escribir una comparación. Su hijo/a también aprenderá a elegir palabras para escribir un poema con un formato especial y poemas de versos libres.

Pueden animar a su hijo/a a usar sus cinco sentidos para describir cosas. Intenten estas actividades en casa.

1 En el próximo viaje que den o mientras hacen una cola, jueguen juegos que requieran la descripción de cosas, tales como "Soy espía" o "20 preguntas".

2 Luego de leer juntos un libro ilustrado, pídanle a su hijo/a que "lea las ilustraciones", o sea, que diga qué pasa en cada ilustración.

3 Traten de leer un poema diario. Busquen libros con rimas de acción y representaciones teatrales con los dedos. A su hijo/a le encantarán estas cosas.

4 Cuando su hijo/a haya dibujado o coloreado un dibujo, pídanle que lo describa antes de mostrárselos. Cierren los ojos mientras su hijo/a lo describe. Después, abran los ojos para ver si la descripción fue exacta.

5 He aquí algunos libros que su hijo/a y ustedes pueden disfrutar.
- ◆ *Come On, Rain* por Karen Hesse. Ilustrado por Jon J. Muth. Scholastic Trade, 1999. Nubes grises se desplazan en un cielo morado a medida que se aproxima la lluvia. Este acontecimiento impulsa a una niña a reunir a sus amigos para darse un paseo por la lluvia.
- ◆ *April Bubbles Chocolate: An ABC of Poetry* por Lee Bennett Hopkins y otros. Simon and Schuster, 1994. Esta colección de poemas con temas de la A a la Z es perfecto para la lectura familiar en voz alta.

Sinceramente,

IMAGINE THAT:

Writing to Describe

Writing to Describe

Introduction

Invite children to go on an imaginary trip with you. Use the following prompts or ideas of your own to encourage children to respond.

★ **Imagine you are a deep-sea diver and are going down, down, down to the bottom of the ocean. What do you see? How do you feel?**

★ **Now you are standing in a crowd and watching a circus parade. What do you see passing by? What do you hear? What do you feel?**

★ **Picture yourself visiting a chocolate factory. What do you see and smell? Have you tasted anything yummy?**

★ **Oh no! You have come face-to-face with a bearded giant who has bad manners. What do you see and hear? Do you smell or feel anything?**

Point out to children that many of the words they used to tell about things on their imaginary journey are the same kinds of words writers use to help readers "see" the people, animals, things, and events they are writing about. When writers do this, they are writing to describe.

Explain to children that over the next weeks they will be writing to describe special people they know and events they think their classmates will enjoy reading about. They will also become poets and try their hand at writing shape poems and free-verse poems. Last of all they will write comparisons to tell how two different but similar things are alike.

Point out to children that when they describe something in writing they will use their five senses to choose the right words to help their readers see, hear, feel, smell, or taste whatever it is they are writing about.

Shape Poem

Lindamichelle Baron

OBJECTIVES

★ RECOGNIZE the characteristics of a shape poem.

★ RESPOND to a model shape poem written by a published author.

★ PLAN, WRITE, and REVISE a shape poem.

★ USE creative language, such as alliteration, in a shape poem.

1 Begin the Lesson

Ask children to name shapes or objects that remind them of something special, such as a favorite toy, game, or activity. Have them choose one shape. Make a web to brainstorm ideas about the shape. Explain that writers use ideas like theirs to write poems that look like the objects being described and that are called *shape poems.*

2 Discuss a Writer's Model

MEET THE WRITER Focus on the poem on page 35 of the Big Book of Writing Models and introduce the author, Lindamichelle Baron. Explain that she is the author of many poems, including a book of poems called *The Sun Is On: Poetry and Ideas.* She is also a former New York City teacher and believes that poetry is a great way to enjoy language and learn about reading and writing.

TALK ABOUT THE MODEL Have children read the poem's title and look at the poem's shape. Discuss what the poem might be about. Read the poem aloud. Use the callouts to point out the colorful words, the use of alliteration (the repetition of initial sounds in words), and how the words form the shape of a ballerina twirling around on her toes. Discuss whether the poem is free-verse or rhymed verse.

• *What does this poem describe?*

• *How does reading the poem make you feel?*

• *Why do you think the author used this shape?*

• *What words make a nice sound?*

3 Write and Confer

INDEPENDENT WRITING Have children create their own shape poems, using the model as a guide.

MAKE A PLAN Have children think of an object or something they like to do and choose a shape that stands for this one thing. Then have children make idea webs like the following (see page 98).

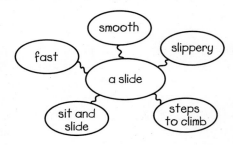

WRITE IT DOWN Have children draw their shapes. Then they can use their web ideas to write their poems around or inside the shapes. Encourage children to use colorful words and alliteration.

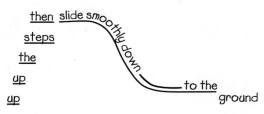

LOOK IT OVER Have children look for ways to improve their poems by adding or replacing describing words to make the poems more interesting. Suggest they read aloud their poems to listen for words and rhythm.

TEACHER CONFERENCE As children work on their shape poems, ask questions like the following.

- *Why did you choose this shape for your poem?*
- *How do the words of your poem tell about the shape?*
- *What will readers like best about your poem?*

PEER CONFERENCE Have partners tell what they see when they read each other's poems. Remind children to talk about possible word changes or adding groups of words that begin with the same letter.

SHARE YOUR WORK After children neatly copy their poems onto drawing paper, suggest they use colored pencils or crayons to make their poems visually interesting. Display the poems in a hallway "poetry gallery."

ASSESSMENT OPPORTUNITIES

SELF-ASSESSMENT Have children complete the Self-Assessment Checklist on page 104.

PEER EVALUATION Have children use the Peer Evaluation Checklist on page 106.

TEACHER HOLISTIC ASSESSMENT Use the Teacher Evaluation Checklist on page 105 to evaluate children's shape poems.

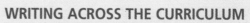

Meeting Individual Needs

Alliteration

Introduce Say the following tongue twister aloud.

Sally sells seashells by the seashore.

Ask children what letter sound they hear repeated *(s)*. Explain that the repeating *s* sound makes the sentence fun to hear and read. Help children understand that when a writer uses a group of words that begin with the same sound, it is called *alliteration*. Invite children to share tongue twisters that they have heard.

Model Reread "On My Toes" and have children identify the sound that is repeated (/t/). Ask volunteers to read aloud the poem in a way suggested by the size of the words and shape the words form. Then ask children to think of groups of words beginning with the same sound that could describe the actions of a dancer, such as *tip-tippity tapping toes* or *little legs lift and leap*.

Summarize/Apply Encourage children to look for ways to use alliteration in their shape poems. Suggest they think of words they can repeat and synonyms they might use to form a group of words with the same beginning sound, such as changing *busy dancing toes* to *tippy tippy toes*.

 WRITER'S BLOCK

Problem

Children have trouble using alliteration in their shape poems.

Solution

Ask children to select key words from their web. Write each word. Then help them list related words with the same beginning sounds. Children can refer to the lists when writing.

ESL STRATEGY

Help children draw and name simple objects. Invite them to talk about and pantomime actions suggested by the objects as you write the corresponding words. Guide children in using the words to write poems along the outlines of the drawings.

HOME–SCHOOL CONNECTION

Invite children to share their shape poems with family members. Suggest they work together to create a shape poem about an object in their home.

WRITING ACROSS THE CURRICULUM

Math Encourage children to use the concept of shape poems to draw and define shapes they learn about in math class.

Description of an Event

OBJECTIVES

★ RECOGNIZE the characteristics of a description of an event.

★ RESPOND to a model description of an event written by a student.

★ PLAN, WRITE, and REVISE a description of an event.

★ USE a description map to organize information.

1 Begin the Lesson

Invite children to brainstorm details about a recent school event. Have them tell what the event was, where it took place, who was there, and what happened. Write children's details in a description map like the one below. Explain that the map's details can be used to write a description of the event.

Event:	Puppet Show

Beginning:	The fourth grade gave a puppet show on Tuesday at 2:00 in the gym

Middle:	Stick puppets were fairy tale characters.

End:	Everyone cheered and clapped. We thought the show was great.

2 Discuss a Writer's Model

MEET THE WRITER Show page 36 of the Big Book of Writing Models and introduce the writer, Rolando Ortega, a second grader. Ask a volunteer to read aloud Rolando's comment. Explain that Rolando wrote about the parade because it was an event he enjoyed.

TALK ABOUT THE MODEL Read aloud "The Parade." Use the callouts to guide children through the model. Then have them find sentences that tell the name of the event, where and when it took place, who was there, and what happened. Ask questions such as:

- *What did Rolando see (hear, feel) at the parade?*

- *What happened before (after) the parade started?*

The event being described is named at the beginning.

The writer tells where things took place.

The Parade
by Rolando Ortega

My family went to see the 4th of July parade. We went early to get a good place to sit. We brought chairs and a picnic lunch. We sat right at the edge of the street. It was hot.

I wrote about the parade because there was so much to see and hear.

36 Writing to Describe

Rolando Ortega
California

- *What does the writer tell you in the beginning of his description?*

- *What words help you see the parade in your mind?*

3 Write and Confer

INDEPENDENT WRITING Invite children to write their own descriptions using Rolando's as a model.

MAKE A PLAN Suggest children think of a family outing, school assembly, or class trip to describe. Their journals may contain ideas. Provide description maps for children to use to plan their writing (see page 99).

WRITE IT DOWN Have children follow their maps. Encourage them to picture their events as they write. Remind them to begin with a sentence that names the event. Then they can tell exactly how things looked, sounded, felt, tasted, and smelled.

LOOK IT OVER Have children decide what to add or change to make their writing more interesting and clear.

TEACHER CONFERENCE Ask questions to help children improve their writing.

- *What sentence names the event?*

- *What happened first (next, last)?*

- *What describing words help readers "see" the event?*

PEER CONFERENCE As partners share their writing, suggest they close their eyes to picture the events.

SHARE YOUR WORK Have children publish their descriptions in a class newsletter titled *Special Events*.

Finally, the parade started. A big band went by. The music was very loud. I marched in place with them. Then we saw colorful floats. One looked like a giant flag. Everyone waved at us. I liked the end of the parade the best. There were five clowns. They tumbled down the street. I hope we go to the parade again next year!

The writer tells what happened.

Events are told in order.

A precise verb describes how the clowns moved.

Description of an Event 37

SELF-ASSESSMENT Have children complete the Self-Assessment Checklist on page 104.

PEER EVALUATION Have children use the Peer Evaluation Checklist on page 106.

TEACHER HOLISTIC ASSESSMENT Use the Teacher Evaluation Checklist on page 105 to evaluate each child's description of an event.

Meeting Individual Needs

Details: Sensory Words

Introduce Have children imagine a bowl of fresh-popped popcorn or the smell of cookies baking in the oven. Invite them to brainstorm words that describe what they feel, hear, smell, and taste. List the words on the board or chart paper. Help children understand that writers use words like these to create pictures for readers. These details help readers see, hear, feel, taste, or smell what is being described. These words are called sensory words.

Model Have children find words in Rolando's description on pages 36–37 of the Big Book that help them see, hear, and feel the event. Encourage children to think of other sensory words that could be used to describe a parade.

Summarize/Apply Have children look for words in their descriptions that help their readers see, hear, touch, smell, or taste the event they are describing. Encourage children to add details like these to make their descriptions interesting.

 WRITER'S BLOCK

Problem
Children write descriptions that do not include vivid details.

Solution
Have children circle words that name a person, place, or thing. Ask them to think of describing words that tell about each naming word.

ESL STRATEGY
Help children create bilingual lists of words that tell about the sights and sounds of the events and the feelings they had. Children can choose words from the lists as they write their descriptions.

HOME–SCHOOL CONNECTION
If the event described was a family outing, have families look at photos to remember details about it.

WRITING ACROSS THE CURRICULUM
Science Have children use sensory words to describe what happened in the beginning, middle, and end of science experiments. They could also use a description map to record their observations.

Writer's Workshop Planner

Description of a Person

WRITING PROCESS STAGE	MINILESSONS			
	Writer's Craft; Grammar, Usage, Mechanics, Spelling	Writing Across the Curriculum	Meeting Individual Needs	Assessment
Prewriting pp. 122–123 (1–2 days)	Planning a Composition Using a Word Web, page 123	Health, page 123	📦 Writer's Block ⓔ ESL Strategy 🏠 Home-School Connection	• Teacher and Peer Conferencing, page 123
Drafting pp. 124–125 (2–3 days)	Using Precise/Vivid Verbs, page 125	Language Arts, page 125	📦 Writer's Block ⓔ ESL Strategy 🏠 Home-School Connection	• Self-Assessment Checklist, page 116 • Peer Evaluation Checklist, page 106 • Teacher Evaluation Checklist, page 117 • Teacher and Peer Conferencing, page 125
Revising pp. 126–127 (1–2 days)	Using Precise/Vivid Adjectives, page 127	Science, page 127	📦 Writer's Block ⓔ ESL Strategy 🏠 Home-School Connection	• Self-Assessment Checklist, page 116 • Peer Evaluation Checklist, page 106 • Teacher Evaluation Checklist, page 117 • Teacher and Peer Conferencing, page 126
Editing & Proofreading pp. 128–129 (1–2 days)	Apostrophes—in Contractions, page 129	Social Studies, page 129	📦 Writer's Block ⓔ ESL Strategy 🏠 Home-School Connection	• Self-Assessment Checklist, page 116 • Peer Evaluation Checklist, page 106 • Teacher Evaluation Checklist, page 117 • Teacher and Peer Conferencing, page 128
Publishing pp. 130–131 (1 day)				• Benchmark Papers, pages 118–121 • Rubric, page 131 • Portfolio, page 131

Suggestions for Planning Each Day

- Whole Class Meeting/Minilesson (5–10 minutes)
- Independent Writing/Teacher-Student Conferences (30–40 minutes)
- Peer Conferences (5–10 minutes)
- Group Share (5–10 minutes)

Connecting Multiple Intelligences
With the Stages of the Writing Process

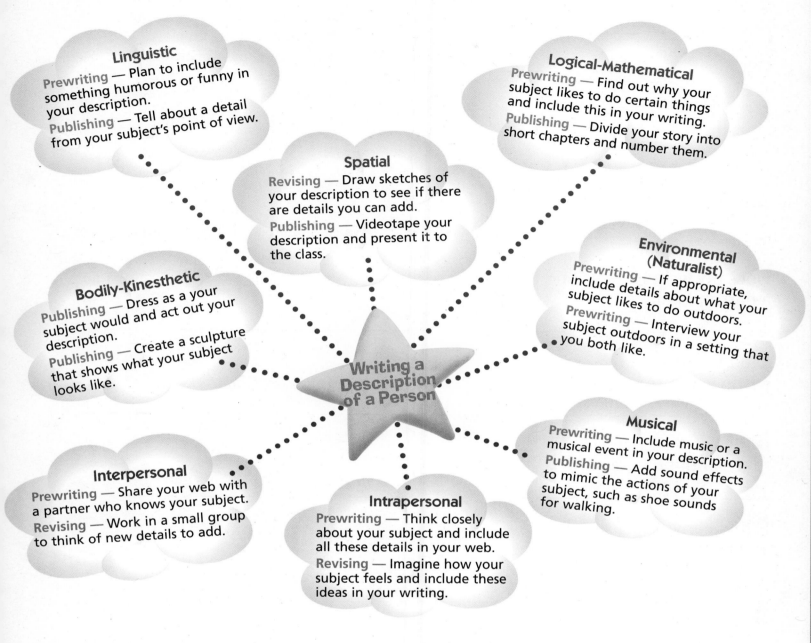

Linguistic
Prewriting — Plan to include something humorous or funny in your description.
Publishing — Tell about a detail from your subject's point of view.

Logical-Mathematical
Prewriting — Find out why your subject likes to do certain things and include this in your writing.
Publishing — Divide your story into short chapters and number them.

Spatial
Revising — Draw sketches of your description to see if there are details you can add.
Publishing — Videotape your description and present it to the class.

Bodily-Kinesthetic
Publishing — Dress as a your subject would and act out your description.
Publishing — Create a sculpture that shows what your subject looks like.

Environmental (Naturalist)
Prewriting — If appropriate, include details about what your subject likes to do outdoors.
Prewriting — Interview your subject outdoors in a setting that you both like.

Writing a Description of a Person

Interpersonal
Prewriting — Share your web with a partner who knows your subject.
Revising — Work in a small group to think of new details to add.

Intrapersonal
Prewriting — Think closely about your subject and include all these details in your web.
Revising — Imagine how your subject feels and include these ideas in your writing.

Musical
Prewriting — Include music or a musical event in your description.
Publishing — Add sound effects to mimic the actions of your subject, such as shoe sounds for walking.

Assessment Options

In this complete-process lesson, a variety of assessment tools are provided, specific to the description of a person form. Annotated benchmark papers, corresponding to a 4-point evaluation rubric, are included to help you better rate children's papers. Self-Assessment, Peer, and Teacher Checklists will help make Teacher and Peer Conferences more productive and useful to children.

- Benchmark Papers, pages 118–121
- Evaluation Rubric, page 131
- Teacher and Peer Conferencing, pages 123, 125, 126, 128

- Self-Assessment Checklist, page 116
- Peer Evaluation Checklist, page 106

- Teacher Evaluation Checklist, page 117
- Portfolio Assessment, page 131

Self-Assessment Checklist
Writing a Description of a Person

Name of Writer _____

Date _____

Type of Writing _____

Use this checklist when you are revising, or editing and proofreading a **description of a person**.

	YES	NO	Ways to Make My Writing Better
Does my writing focus on a person I know?	☐	☐	
Did I tell whom I'm writing about?	☐	☐	
Did I use describing words to tell about the person?	☐	☐	
Is there anything I should add to or take out of my writing?	☐	☐	
Did I use complete sentences?	☐	☐	
Have I spelled words correctly?	☐	☐	
Did I use punctuation marks and capital letters correctly?	☐	☐	

Teacher Evaluation Checklist
Writing a Description of a Person

Name of Writer _____

Date _____

Writing Mode _____

Use this checklist when you are evaluating a child's **description of a person.**

	YES	NO	Recommendations to Child
Is the writing focused on a real person?	☐	☐	
Is it clear who the writer is describing?	☐	☐	
Are adjectives used to describe the person?	☐	☐	
Are vivid verbs used to tell how the person moves or acts?	☐	☐	
Does the writer adhere to the conventions of			
grammar?	☐	☐	
usage?	☐	☐	
spelling?	☐	☐	
punctuation?	☐	☐	
capitalization?	☐	☐	
Is the description legible?	☐	☐	
Was the work done neatly?	☐	☐	

117

Benchmark Paper 1

Writing a Description of a Person

Who is Amelia?

Capitalize the first word in a sentence.

Check your spelling.

Amelia is the funnest girl in the world. we've known each othr since three years. We like to play Mary-kate and Ashley when she crys and gets sick I try to make her feel beter.

What does Amelia look like?

Rating Point 1: Undeveloped Description of a Person
Although the description focuses on a real person, the person is not identified. It includes a brief reference to what the person likes and little about how she acts. There are numerous errors in grammar, usage, mechanics, and spelling.

Benchmark Paper 2

Writing a Description of a Person

Good job. You tell who the person is in the first sentence.

Check verb tense.

My friend is David Andrews. David plays basebal. David is tall and use to have a Babe Ruth card. Trading basebal cards and watching TV is fun to him. You can all ways find him playing basebal outside.

Watch your spelling.

Can you tell more about what David looks like?

Rating Point 2: Partially Developed Description of a Person
The description focuses on a real person who is identified. It includes details about what the person looks like and what he likes to do. There is some organization. There are some spelling and grammar errors.

Benchmark Paper 3

Writing a Description of a Person

My Friend

Haley is a special girl in my classroom. She is 8 years old. Haley is good at cheerleading. She has drity blound hair and brown eyes. Haley looks very pretty. She is one of the prettiest girls in the class. Haley always dose her best in school. Haley is my best friend.

Haley is special to me because she is very nice. Haley helps me with my wrok. She writes neatly. She makes me write my work neatly too. That's why Haley is special to me.

Good description.

How does she act?

Can you think of somewhere else this sentence could go?

Tell more about what Haley likes to do.

Rating Point 3: Adequately Developed Description of a Person

The description focuses on a real person and gives several descriptions of the person's personality and appearance and what she likes to do. The organization is generally clear and the description ends with a concluding sentence. There are a few spelling errors, mainly transposed letters.

Benchmark Paper 4
Writing a Description of a Person

My Mother

Good opening sentence.

Let's talk about my mother! She has straight black hair and she dresses very well.

My mom lives in New York City and she works in Chinatown with her new friends and her old friends.

My mom likes to take me to places like the beach. She also takes me to buy things for me when she has the money.

My mom is honest because she never lies. She cares about how I'm doing in school. She is loving because she loves me and she is kind because she buys me candy when I behave well

She likes to listen to music and is saving her money so that we can go to the Dominican Republic.

Truly, my mom is great.

Your description includes a lot of information and good details.

Add a comma.

Rating Point 4: Well-Developed Description of a Person
This description is well organized and includes details about what the person looks like, how she acts, and what she likes. The writer includes a good opening sentence and conclusion. There are minor errors in spelling and punctuation.

Description of a Person

Prewriting

OBJECTIVES

★ **RECOGNIZE** the characteristics of a description of a person.

★ **RESPOND** to a prewriting plan written by a student writer.

★ **BRAINSTORM** and **SELECT** a person to describe in writing.

★ **USE** a web to organize words and phrases that describe a person.

1 Begin the Writer's Workshop

Invite children to name people whom they admire. Zero in on one person and create a web to record children's ideas about that person. The web might look like the following.

Lead children to understand that the words in the web describe the person whose name is in the middle. Introduce the idea that when writers tell what a person is like, they use interesting details to create a clear picture for their readers who may have never met the person.

Anahndi Maragh
Florida

2 Discuss a Writer's Model

MEET THE WRITER Display page 38 of the Big Book of Writing Models. Tell children that second grader Anahndi Maragh created this web to write a description of her mom. Invite a volunteer to read aloud her quote. Talk about why Anahndi chose to write about her mother and the kinds of details she recorded in her web.

BRAINSTORM Work with children to create a list of groups of people on the board. The list might include classmates, adults at school, family members, television and movie stars, athletes, and so on. Invite children to give examples of real people for each group.

SELECT A TOPIC Children can look at the ideas on the board to create "top three" lists of people they would like to describe. Then prompt children to narrow their choices to focus on one subject they know really well.

DESIGN A PLAN Explain that the purpose of Anahndi's web is to help her list and remember characteristics about the person she will describe. The following questions may help children.

- *What words tell what Anahndi's mom looks like and how she acts?*
- *What things does Anahndi's mom like?*
- *What is she good at doing?*
- *What do you think is Anahndi's favorite thing about her Mom?*

3 Prewrite and Confer

INDEPENDENT WRITING Have children create their own webs (see page 100). Remind them that the name of the person is written in the center of the web and words that tell what the person is like are written around it.

TEACHER CONFERENCE Meet with children to talk about their webs. You might use questions such as the following.

- *Why did you select this person to describe?*
- *Do you know enough information about this person? How could you find out more details?*
- *How do you feel about this person?*

PEER CONFERENCE Pair children of varying abilities to share their webs with each other. Remind them of the following guidelines.

- *Be a good listener. Let the reader finish reading before giving your comments.*
- *Tell what you like best about the details the writer included.*
- *If you know the person being described, offer ideas that tell about the person.*

Meeting Individual Needs

Mini Lesson

Planning a Composition Using a Word Web

Introduce Show children a picture of a spider web. Discuss how the web is built. *(tightly woven, everything held together, and so on)* Lead children to compare the web to the ones they have made for writing, pointing out that just as a spider web is structured and organized, a web helps children organize their ideas for writing.

Model Have children take another look at Anahndi's web on Big Book page 38. Ask them to suggest other ways that Anahndi could have organized it. Model creating a different type of web such as the one shown.

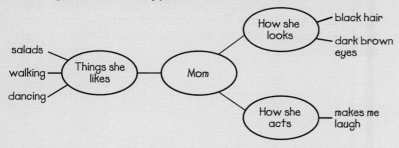

Summarize/Apply Invite children to revisit their webs to see if a different way of organizing their information would work better for them. Encourage them to experiment with different forms of organization. Help children understand how making a web is one way to plan and organize their writing.

 WRITER'S BLOCK

Problem	Solution
Children have difficulty choosing one person to write about.	Suggest they share their "top three" lists with writing partners and talk about their choices. This will help them recognize the person they can most easily describe.

ESL STRATEGY

Children can draw pictures on their webs to illustrate their ideas. Classmates can help label the pictures.

HOME–SCHOOL CONNECTION

Invite children to take their webs home and share them with their families. Family members can help add more descriptive words and phrases.

WRITING ACROSS THE CURRICULUM

Health Remind children that webs can be used to compile information about many kinds of topics, including health and nutrition.

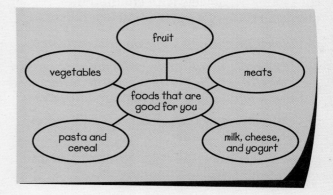

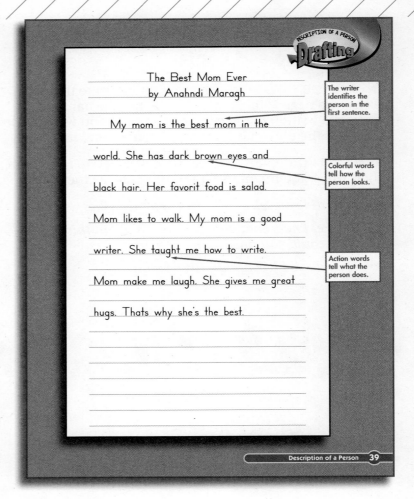

The Best Mom Ever
by Anahndi Maragh

My mom is the best mom in the

world. She has dark brown eyes and

black hair. Her favorit food is salad.

Mom likes to walk. My mom is a good

writer. She taught me how to write.

Mom make me laugh. She gives me great

hugs. Thats why she's the best.

The writer identifies the person in the first sentence.

Colorful words tell how the person looks.

Action words tell what the person does.

Description of a Person **39**

Description of a Person

Drafting

OBJECTIVES

★ **IDENTIFY** the characteristics of a description of a person in a first draft of a student model.

★ **FOLLOW** a writing plan to write a first draft of a description of a person.

 Continue the Writer's Workshop

Ask children to name the types of things they would plan to take with them for a day at the beach, such as sunglasses, sunscreen, swimsuit, towel, cooler with drinks, and a hat.

Tell children that writers plan in much the same way. Discuss items they will need to write their descriptions, such as pencils, paper, their webs, good lighting, a quiet place, and so on.

2 Discuss a Writer's Model

Point to the words and have children read with you "The Best Mom Ever" on page 39 of the Big Book of Writing Models. Have children give a "thumbs up" sign when they hear words that Anahndi included from her web.

Ask a volunteer to find the sentence that tells who the description is about. Explain that the first sentence tells this. Have a volunteer find a sentence in which Anahndi tells how she feels about her mom. Point out how the writer ends her description with this sentence.

IDENTIFY CHARACTERISTICS OF A DESCRIPTION OF A PERSON Review with children the characteristics of a description of a person.

- *Identifies the person in the first sentence*

- *Uses exact words to describe how the person looks, to tell the person's favorite things, and to tell what the person likes and dislikes*

- *Describes how the person acts and moves using action words*

- *Shares personal feelings about the person*

3 Draft and Confer

THINK LIKE A WRITER Remind children to ask themselves questions like the following as they write.

- *Who am I writing about?*

- *Why did I choose this person to write about?*

- *What do I know about this person?*

INDEPENDENT WRITING Suggest children use their webs as guides. Remind them that they are working on drafts and should not be concerned with punctuation and spelling. Have them keep their drafts and webs in their portfolios.

TEACHER CONFERENCE During conferences, ask questions like the following.

- *Which sentence tells who you are writing about?*
- *Did you use all the details from your web? Is there anything else that you could add?*
- *Why will your readers have a clear picture of this person?*
- *What makes the person special and different from other people?*

PEER CONFERENCE Have partners read each other's drafts. Writers can ask listeners questions like the following.

- *What did you like best about my description?*
- *Did I use words that clearly tell you what this person is like?*
- *Did I give enough details so you feel like you know the person?*

Meeting Individual Needs

Mini Lesson

Using Precise/ Vivid Verbs

Introduce Close a book abruptly. Say: *I closed the book. I slammed the book shut.* Ask children which verb, *closed* or *slammed*, gives a clearer idea. Explain that *slammed* is a more exact verb. It gives a clearer picture in the reader's mind.

Model Invite volunteers to point to the action words in Anahndi's first draft on Big Book page 39. Then write on the board *walk/stroll* and *laugh/giggle* along with other word pairs, such as *talk/chatter, ran/jogged,* and *look/stare*. Discuss which verb in each pair paints a better picture in their minds. You might have children "act out" the verbs to understand the differences between them.

Summarize/Apply Remind children to use exact verbs when they are describing how a person acts and moves. Ask them to review their drafts to see if there are verbs they can change to ones that will give better pictures for their readers.

WRITER'S BLOCK

Problem

Children forget to identify the subject in the first sentence.

Solution

Ask children to show where they tell who the description is about. Encourage them to include this information at the beginning.

ESL STRATEGY

Let children work with partners, a teacher's aide, or a parent volunteer. Have them first use words from their webs to tell about the person, then encourage them to ask for help in writing their drafts.

HOME–SCHOOL CONNECTION

Invite children to read their drafts to family members, skipping the sentence in which the person is identified. See if family members can guess the person.

WRITING ACROSS THE CURRICULUM

Language Arts Have children use descriptive writing to tell about characters in books they have read so classmates can picture them clearly in their minds.

Nate, the Great

Nate the Great is a curious, young detective. He has moppy, blonde hair. When Nate has on his plaid detective hat, you know he is on a case.

Revising

OBJECTIVES

★ ANALYZE a model to understand how a student writer revised her writing.

★ REVISE a first draft of a description of a person to elaborate with more details and add variety.

★ USE colorful, vivid adjectives to describe a person.

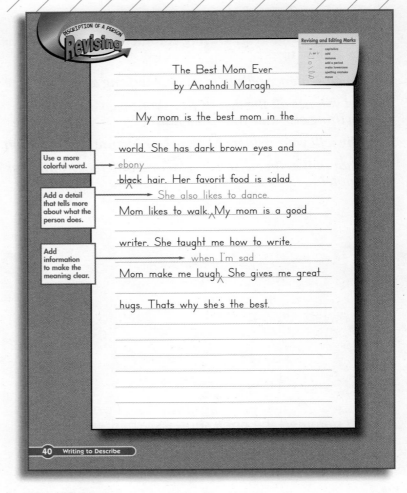

Revising

The Best Mom Ever
by Anahndi Maragh

My mom is the best mom in the

world. She has dark brown eyes and

ebony
~~black~~ hair. Her favorit food is salad.

She also likes to dance.
Mom likes to walk. My mom is a good

writer. She taught me how to write.

when I'm sad
Mom make me laugh. She gives me great

hugs. Thats why she's the best.

Use a more colorful word.

Add a detail that tells more about what the person does.

Add information to make the meaning clear.

1 Continue the Writer's Workshop

Remind children that once writers get their ideas on paper, they can change or add words to make the writing clearer and easier to understand. Let children know that it is OK to mark up a first draft using carets and drawing lines through words to add ideas and make changes.

2 Discuss a Writer's Model

Read Anahndi's revised draft of "The Best Mom Ever" found on page 40 of the Big Book of Writing Models. Encourage volunteers to identify the revising and editing marks Anahndi used and the changes she made.

Using the callouts as a guide, discuss how this draft compares to the one on page 39 of the Big Book. Ask children if they like the changes Anahndi made or if they would have made other changes. Which change makes the writing more colorful?

3 Revise and Confer

Have children consider these questions as they revise their drafts.

- *Does my first sentence identify the person I am describing?*

- *Did I describe the person with colorful words that create a clear picture for my readers?*

- *Did I use action words to tell how the person acts and moves?*

- *Did I tell how I feel about this person?*

TEACHER CONFERENCE To help children improve their drafts, you might use the following questions.

- *How did you introduce your person?*

- *Do you think you included enough details to tell what the person is like? What else could you add?*

- *How does this person make you feel? Have you shared your feelings with your readers?*

PEER CONFERENCE Have partners read each other's drafts. Readers can complete the statements below to offer encouragement and helpful suggestions to writers.

- *My favorite sentence was _____.*

- *I loved the way you described his/her _____.*

- *I would change the word _____ to _____.*

Using Precise/Vivid Adjectives

Introduce   Discuss children's favorite lunch foods. Then write the following sentences on the board.

I enjoy eating a nice ham sandwich with great lettuce, tomato, and mustard.

I enjoy eating a tasty ham sandwich with crunchy lettuce, juicy tomato, and spicy brown mustard.

Ask children which sentence gives them a better idea of your favorite lunch. Have them name the words that make one description better than the other. Identify these words as adjectives.

Model   Display Anahndi's description of her mom on Big Book page 40. As you read it aloud, point out how the writer changed the adjective *black* to *ebony* to paint a clearer picture. Then write adjective pairs on the board, such as *nice/friendly* and *tall/towering*. Ask children which adjective in each pair paints a better picture. Also show how two adjectives together tell more than one, for example, *brown eyes* and *dark brown eyes*.

Summarize/Apply   Discuss how choosing just the right adjectives for a description will make the person "come alive" for the reader. Then suggest that children check their drafts and decide where they might add or change adjectives.

WRITER'S BLOCK

Problem	Solution
Children do not include many descriptive words.	Have children underline the descriptive words they have used. Set a goal of five underlines, encouraging children to add more words if they are short of the goal.

ESL STRATEGY

Have children keep lists of descriptive words in their writing journals or learning logs. As they revise their work, they can look at their lists to find new words to use. Children can add to their lists throughout the year, drawing illustrations to spark their thinking.

HOME–SCHOOL CONNECTION

Explain that reading aloud to an audience can help writers pinpoint problems they may not have noticed before. Invite children to read their descriptions aloud to their families. Encourage them to ask if the descriptions "sound right."

WRITING ACROSS THE CURRICULUM

Science   Encourage children to use adjectives as they describe observations and recollections.

One day the fuzzy green caterpillar found just the right twig to make his cozy home.

He made an amazing chrysalis and hid himself inside.

Soon the caterpillar will turn into a lively, colorful butterfly.

Description of a Person

Editing and Proofreading

OBJECTIVES

★ ANALYZE a model to understand how a student writer edited and proofread her writing.

★ EDIT and PROOFREAD a draft for grammar, usage, mechanics, and spelling.

★ USE apostrophes in contractions.

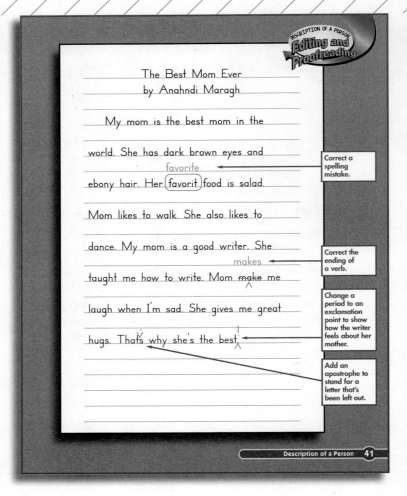

The Best Mom Ever
by Anahndi Maragh

My mom is the best mom in the world. She has dark brown eyes and ebony hair. Her ~~favorit~~ favorite food is salad.

Mom likes to walk. She also likes to dance. My mom is a good writer. She taught me how to write. Mom make makes me laugh when I'm sad. She gives me great hugs. That's why she's the best!

Correct a spelling mistake.

Correct the ending of a verb.

Change a period to an exclamation point to show how the writer feels about her mother.

Add an apostrophe to stand for a letter that's been left out.

Description of a Person 41

1 Continue the Writer's Workshop

Remind children that the next step in their writing is for them to go back and check their descriptions for mistakes in spelling, language, punctuation, and capital letters.

Review the chart of revising and editing marks (see also the blackline master on page 30), pointing out the symbols for correcting a spelling mistake, crossing out an error, and inserting something (both upward and downward facing carets).

2 Discuss a Writer's Model

Read Anandhi's edited description of her mother on page 41 of the Big Book of Writing Models. Refer to the callouts as you discuss Anahndi's changes and the revising and editing marks she used to show the changes. Have children tell how Anahndi's changes improved her work. Ask them if they think Anahndi missed any errors.

3 Edit, Proofread, and Confer

Tell children to think about the following questions as they edit their drafts.

- *Are there any misspelled words?*
- *Do my sentences end with the right punctuation?*
- *Do my verbs end correctly?*
- *Have I used apostrophes in all contractions?*

TEACHER CONFERENCE Ask these or similar questions as students confer with you about their drafts.

- *Are there any words that you are unsure of? How can you find out if the words are spelled correctly?*
- *Have you checked for capital letters and correct punctuation marks?*
- *Do all your action words agree with their naming words?*

PEER CONFERENCE Invite partners to read each other's drafts. Suggest they ask themselves the questions below.

- *Does every sentence have the right end punctuation?*
- *Is an apostrophe used to stand for a letter left out in a contraction?*
- *Do all verbs have the right ending?*
- *Are all words spelled correctly?*

128

Apostrophes—in Contractions

Introduce Ask children if they have ever had a substitute teacher. Explain that a substitute teacher stands in for the regular teacher. Point out that in some words, apostrophes are like substitute teachers. They stand in for letters.

Model Create letter cards for the letters *d, d, n, o, o, t, i,* and *s* and an apostrophe card. Distribute the cards and have volunteers create the words *do not*. Then select another child to replace the *o* in *not* with the apostrophe card to create the contraction *don't*. Repeat with *did not, is not*, and other high-frequency contractions.

Summarize/Apply Ask a volunteer to explain why apostrophes are used in contractions. Point out that contractions are often used in writing. Have children revisit their writing to check the spelling of contractions or to consider replacing two words with a contraction.

WRITER'S BLOCK

Problem	Solution
Children forget to write end punctuation at the ends of sentences.	Invite children to read their drafts aloud. Tell them when they come to the end of one complete idea, they should stop and look for a punctuation mark.

ESL STRATEGY

Select just one thing for children to check their writing for. You might, for example, have children check only for end punctuation.

HOME–SCHOOL CONNECTION

Encourage children to share and compare their first drafts and their edited drafts with their families.

WRITING ACROSS THE CURRICULUM

Social Studies Remind children to capitalize the names of people, titles, and months in their writing.

> Abraham Lincoln and George Washington were famous presidents. George Washington was the first President of the United States. Abraham Lincoln was the 16th. We celebrate their birthdays every year in February.

Description of a Person

Publishing

OBJECTIVE

★ PUBLISH a description of a person.

1 End the Writer's Workshop

Ask children to recall the last thing they do after they've written, revised, and edited a piece of writing. Lead children to understand that the final step, publishing, involves sharing their best work with others.

2 Discuss a Writer's Model

Invite children to read Anahndi's final draft on page 42 of the Big Book of Writing Models. Talk about her neat writing and corrected mistakes. Discuss how the picture helps illustrate the description of her mom.

3 Publish and Celebrate

Invite children to suggest ways they would like to publish and share their descriptions. Use the Publishing Ideas to the right as a springboard to prompt children's thinking. If desired, allow children to choose how they wish to present their final drafts. Provide materials as needed.

Children may enjoy using a decorated Author's Chair in the classroom. Authors can take turns sitting in the chair reading their descriptions. You might have children who wrote about family members read on day one, children who wrote about television stars read on day two, and so on.

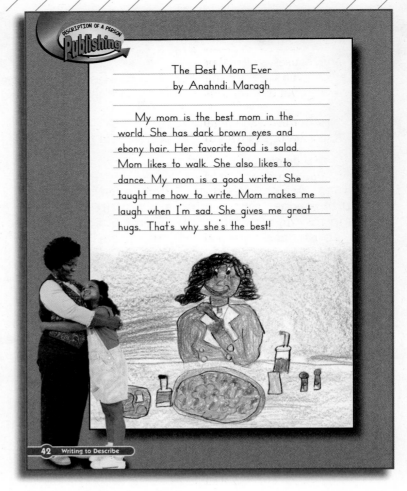

Publishing Ideas

OUR BIOGRAPHY BOOK

Have children find photos or pictures of the people they wrote about. Create two-page layouts with photos on the left pages and descriptions on the right. Compile the pages into a class book titled *Our Biography Book*.

GUESS WHO?

Compile the descriptions into a class book. For each paper, cover up the name of the person being described with a strip of paper with the words *Guess Who?* written on it. Use a piece of tape to attach the strip to the page in such a way that it can be lifted to reveal the name. When children read the book they can check to see if their guesses are correct by lifting the strip to reveal the name.

WHO AM I?

Have children dress and act like the people they wrote about. Invite classmates to guess who is being portrayed. Give the class three guesses. If no one guesses correctly, children can read their descriptions to the class.

RUBRIC FOR DESCRIPTION OF A PERSON

4
- Clearly focuses on a real person.
- Begins with a sentence that identifies the person.
- Includes vivid descriptions of what the person looks like and likes to do.
- Has a well-developed organization.
- Contains few errors in grammar, usage, mechanics, or spelling.

3
- Focuses on a real person.
- Includes a sentence that identifies the person.
- Includes several descriptions of what the person looks like and likes to do.
- Has a clear organization.
- May contain minor errors in grammar, usage, mechanics, or spelling.

2
- May focus on a real person.
- May include a sentence that identifies the person.
- May include several descriptions of what the person looks like and likes to do.
- May have minimal organization.
- May contain errors in grammar, usage, mechanics, or spelling that do not interfere with understanding.

1
- May not focus on a real person.
- May not include a sentence that identifies the person.
- May not include descriptions of what the person looks like and likes to do.
- May have little or no organization.
- May contain substantial errors in grammar, usage, mechanics, or spelling that interfere with understanding.

ASSESSMENT OPPORTUNITIES

SELF-ASSESSMENT Have children complete the Self-Assessment Checklist on page 116. Encourage them to share their responses orally during teacher conferences.

PORTFOLIO ASSESSMENT If children choose to include the final drafts of their description of a person in their portfolios, encourage them also to consider including their prewriting lists, webs, drafts, and Self-Assessment Checklists.

PEER EVALUATION Have children use the Peer Evaluation Checklist on page 106.

TEACHER PRIMARY–TRAIT ASSESSMENT Use the Teacher Evaluation Checklist on page 117 to evaluate children's descriptions. You may want to share your comments during teacher conferences.

RUBRIC FOR DESCRIPTION OF A PERSON The form-specific rubric will help you evaluate children's writing. Use the information in the rubric during teacher conferences to help you assist children in identifying ways they can improve their writing.

BENCHMARK PAPERS You may want to use the Benchmark Papers on pages 118–121 along with the rubric to evaluate children's writing.

Free-Verse Poem

OBJECTIVES

★ **RECOGNIZE** the characteristics of a free-verse poem.

★ **RESPOND** to a model free-verse poem written by a student.

★ **PLAN, WRITE,** and **REVISE** a free-verse poem.

★ **USE** descriptive words in a free-verse poem.

1 Begin the Lesson

Tell children to picture your school at recess. Invite them to describe what they "see." As children brainstorm words and phrases, write them on the board, one per line.

> **Recess**
> Big and noisy,
> shouts of joy,
> lots of laughter,
> children everywhere.
> They are racing all around,
> playing games of tag,
> sliding to the ground,
> swinging to the sky,
> kicking rubber balls,
> having lots of fun!

Explain that they have just written a free-verse poem. Read the poem together.

2 Building Background

MEET THE WRITER Introduce second-grader Brandon Sparks and his poem about his dog on page 43 of the Big Book of Writing Models. Read what Brandon says about his writing.

TALK ABOUT THE MODEL Use the callouts to help children identify the features of a free-verse poem. Help them understand that a free-verse poem says a lot in a few words.

- *How does the writer feel about his dog? How do you know?*

- *What words help you "see" the writer's dog?*

Brandon Sparks
Kentucky

- *Does the writer use rhyming words?*

- *Does Brandon's title go with the poem? Why do you think so?*

Point out how the writer uses similes (comparisons with *like* or *as*) to describe his dog. Talk about how the words flow freely and have rhythm. Explain that not all poems have words that rhyme.

3 Write and Confer

INDEPENDENT WRITING Have children write their own free-verse poems, using "My Dog" as a model.

MAKE A PLAN As children brainstorm topics, encourage them to write about something that really matters to them. Suggest they look in their journals for ideas. After children choose their topics, have them write details in a list or web. (See pages 6 and 98.) Encourage them to express their thoughts and feelings.

WRITE IT DOWN Have children use ideas from their lists or webs to write their free-verse poems. Remind them to skip lines so they have space to make changes. Encourage them to express their feelings clearly using colorful words and similes. Remind them to include a title.

LOOK IT OVER Have children read their poems aloud to decide if the words sound right. Suggest that they listen for the rhythm of the words and change any part that isn't clear or doesn't fit.

TEACHER CONFERENCE As children write their free-verse poems, ask questions such as the following.

- *When you read your poem aloud, does it sound right?*
- *Why did you choose this title?*
- *What words help your reader "see" your subject?*

PEER CONFERENCE As children read their poems to partners, remind them to tell what they like and ask questions about what they don't understand.

SHARE YOUR WORK Have a poetry reading. Invite children to use rhythm instruments and bells to play the rhythm of their poems as they read. Children can also copy their poems onto posterboard and illustrate them. Display the poetry posters for all to enjoy.

ASSESSMENT OPPORTUNITIES

SELF-ASSESSMENT Have children complete the Self-Assessment Checklist on page 104.

PEER EVALUATION Have children use the Peer Evaluation Checklist on page 106.

TEACHER HOLISTIC ASSESSMENT Use the Teacher Evaluation Checklist on page 105 to evaluate children's free-verse poems.

Meeting Individual Needs

Mini Lesson

Adding Descriptive Details to Support Main Idea

Introduce Have volunteers use one sentence to tell what their poem is about. Explain that the *main idea* is what a story or poem is about. Lead children to see that writers carefully choose their details, or small important pieces of information, to describe or tell about their main idea. Then readers can picture the writers' ideas in their minds.

Model Reread Brandon's poem on Big Book page 43. Have volunteers name details Brandon included that let them know exactly what his dog is like.

Summarize/Apply To help children choose their words carefully, have them ask themselves the following questions.

- *Does my poem include enough details to help my reader picture what I'm writing about?*
- *What details can I change to give a better picture of my main idea?*

WRITER'S BLOCK

Problem	Solution
Children have difficulty using descriptive language, such as similes.	Guide children through a tactile experience by having them squeeze, smell, and play with clay, dry leaves, flavored gelatin, cooked noodles, dough, and so on. Invite children to describe what they are experiencing as you record their ideas.

ESL STRATEGY

Help children create lists of descriptive words and phrases about their topics. Invite them to dictate their poems to you using some of these words and phrases.

HOME–SCHOOL CONNECTION

Suggest that children and family members write a free-verse poem together. Then they can give the poem as a gift to another family member.

WRITING ACROSS THE CURRICULUM

Language Arts To help children think of similes, create a word wall of frequently used similes and have children complete them in different ways.

> as funny as _____
> silly like a _____
> as smooth as _____
> bumpy like a _____
> as sweet as _____

Comparison

OBJECTIVES

★ **RECOGNIZE** the characteristics of a comparison.

★ **RESPOND** to a model comparison written by a published author.

★ **PLAN, WRITE,** and **REVISE** a comparison.

★ **USE** a Venn diagram to organize information.

1 Begin the Lesson

Ask volunteers to name their favorite sport. Then ask children if they think soccer is more like football or baseball. After comparing the three sports, use a Venn diagram (see page 67 of the Big Book of Writing Models) to record children's ideas about how two of the sports are alike. An example is provided below.

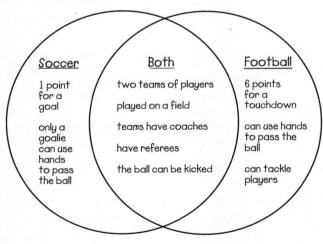

Soccer	Both	Football
1 point for a goal	two teams of players	6 points for a touchdown
only a goalie can use hands to pass the ball	played on a field	can use hands to pass the ball
	teams have coaches	
	have referees	can tackle players
	the ball can be kicked	

Help children understand that the middle part of a Venn diagram shows how two things are alike, and the outer sections show how two things are different. Explain that when a writer describes how two things are alike, it's called a comparison.

2 Discuss a Writer's Model

MEET THE WRITER Point out the photo of the *Ranger Rick* magazine cover on page 44 of the Big Book. Explain that a writer named Elizabeth Schleichert wrote a comparison for *Ranger Rick* that tells how seals and sea lions are alike.

COMPARISON

The writer chose two animals to compare.

"Seals and Sea Lions"
by Elizabeth Schleichert

The first sentence tells that the animals are alike.

Seals and sea lions are part of the same animal group. A long time ago seals and sea lions lived on land and walked on legs. Then their legs slowly changed. Their feet became flippers.

Ranger Rick
SUPER SCOOPERS

44   Writing to Describe

TALK ABOUT THE MODEL Read aloud "Seals and Sea Lions." Use the callouts to help children understand that the title identifies the two animals and the first sentence explains how seals and sea lions are alike. The next sentences give details that tell more about how the animals are alike. These details are facts, not opinions. Clue words like *both, all, same,* and *alike* signal comparisons.

Help children think about the comparison with questions like the following.

- *What two things does the writer tell you in both the title and the first sentence?*

- *Does the comparison tell how the two animals are alike, or how they are different?*

- *What are some interesting facts and details about how the animals are alike?*

- *Does the writer use words like* all *and* same *to tell how the animals are alike?*

- **A continuation of this lesson follows on page 136.**

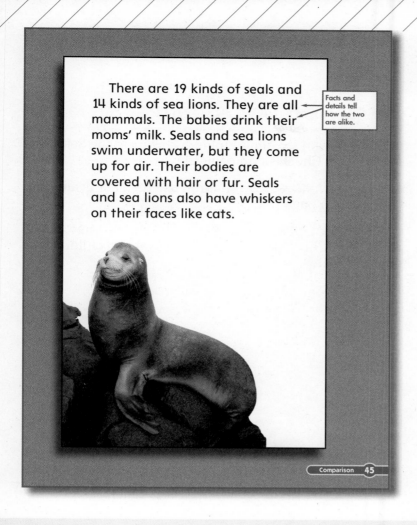

There are 19 kinds of seals and 14 kinds of sea lions. They are all mammals. The babies drink their moms' milk. Seals and sea lions swim underwater, but they come up for air. Their bodies are covered with hair or fur. Seals and sea lions also have whiskers on their faces like cats.

 Facts and details tell how the two are alike.

Comparison 45

WRITER'S BLOCK

Problem

Children have difficulty thinking of two things to compare.

Solution

Guide children in brainstorming topics that interest them, such as favorite games, TV shows, pets, story characters, places to visit, or foods. Then help them choose one topic and two examples to compare.

ESL STRATEGY

Help children whose native language is not English to understand what "comparing" means. Have them work with pairs of objects or pictures and talk about how the items are alike.

HOME–SCHOOL CONNECTION

Children's families may be able to offer topics to write about, such as two family pets, two favorite dinner foods, two places where they've lived, two places they like to visit, and so on. Family members can then help suggest details.

WRITING ACROSS THE CURRICULUM

Art Suggest that children use Venn diagrams to compare two paintings, photos, posters, sculptures, or other art forms.

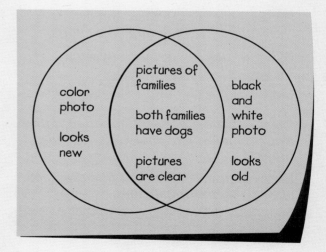

Using a Journal to Get Ideas

Introduce Invite children to share the kinds of writing they've done in their journals. Explain that a journal is a good place to look for writing topics since journals often contain facts, memories, feelings, drawings, doodles, and ideas about interesting events and activities.

Model Ask children why they think Elizabeth Schleichert, the author of "Seals and Sea Lions," chose the topic she did for her comparison. Elicit that she may have always liked the two animals and decided then to write about them, or perhaps she read a book about the animals, saw them on TV or at a zoo, or wrote about them in her journal.

Summarize/Apply Encourage children to search through their journal entries to look for ideas to write about. You may wish to have them search for two people, places, animals, things, or experiences that they could write about in a comparison.

Comparison (CONTINUED)

3 Write and Confer

INDEPENDENT WRITING Children can write their own comparisons using Elizabeth Schleichert's model on Big Book pages 44–45 as a guide.

MAKE A PLAN Suggest that children brainstorm topics by looking through their journals, talking with partners, or looking at photographs or pictures. Record children's ideas on the board.

Once children pick two similar subjects, have them write facts about each subject in a Venn diagram (see page 101). Encourage children to use reference sources if needed.

WRITE IT DOWN Remind children to start with a sentence that names their subjects and tells how they are alike. Then they can use facts from the middle part of their Venn diagrams to write sentences that tell more details about the subjects. Have children add a title.

LOOK IT OVER Suggest that children read aloud their comparisons. Ask them to make sure their comparisons tell how two things are alike, and use words such as *both* or *same*. Then have them check their writing for spelling, punctuation, capital letters, and grammar.

TEACHER CONFERENCE To help children improve their comparisons, ask questions like the following.

- *Does your first sentence name the two subjects you are comparing and explain how they are alike?*
- *Do you have enough facts and details about each subject? How do you know that?*
- *Will your title interest your readers?*

PEER CONFERENCE Have partners read their comparisons to each other.

- *Suggest that children ask questions if they want to know more about one or both subjects.*
- *Have children tell the most interesting part of each other's comparisons.*
- *Encourage children to offer suggestions for improvement.*

SHARE YOUR WORK Tell children they can learn from each other's comparisons. You may want to suggest they make mobiles to illustrate their comparisons. Another idea would be to compile their comparisons into a class spiral notebook with different categories, such as Animals, Places, or Things We Like. They can use colored tabs to separate each section.

ASSESSMENT OPPORTUNITIES

SELF-ASSESSMENT Have children complete the Self-Assessment Checklist on page 104.

PEER EVALUATION Have children use the Peer Evaluation Checklist on page 106.

TEACHER HOLISTIC ASSESSMENT Use the Teacher Evaluation Checklist on page 105 to evaluate children's comparisons.

Just the Facts: Writing to Inform

Contents

Writing to Inform — Unit Planner

WRITING FORM	MINILESSONS				
	Basic Skills/ Writing Process/ Writer's Craft	Grammar, Usage, Mechanics, Spelling	Writing Across the Curriculum	Meeting Individual Needs	Assessment
Lesson 1 INSTRUCTIONS pp. 154–155 (3–4 days)	• Choosing a Topic, 155		• Math, 155	• Writer's Block, 155 • ESL Strategy, 155 • Home-School Connection, 155	• Self-Assessment Checklist, 148 • Teacher Evaluation Checklist, 149 • Peer Evaluation Checklist, 150 • Teacher and Peer Conferencing, 155
Lesson 2 INVITATION pp. 156–157 (3–4 days)		• Capitalization—Letter Parts, 157	• Social Studies, 157	• Writer's Block, 157 • ESL Strategy, 157 • Home-School Connection, 157	• Self-Assessment Checklist, 148 • Teacher Evaluation Checklist, 149 • Peer Evaluation Checklist, 150 • Teacher and Peer Conferencing, 157
Lesson 3 FRIENDLY LETTER pp. 158–159 (3–4 days)		• Commas—in Letter Parts, 159	• Social Studies, 159	• Writer's Block, 159 • ESL Strategy, 159 • Home-School Connection, 159	• Self-Assessment Checklist, 148 • Teacher Evaluation Checklist, 149 • Peer Evaluation Checklist, 150 • Teacher and Peer Conferencing, 158–159
Lesson 4 BOOK REPORT pp. 160–161 (3–4 days)		• Capitalization—Titles of Books, 161	• Science, 161	• Writer's Block, 161 • ESL Strategy, 161 • Home-School Connection, 161	• Self-Assessment Checklist, 148 • Teacher Evaluation Checklist, 149 • Peer Evaluation Checklist, 150 • Teacher and Peer Conferencing, 160
Lesson 5 REPORT pp. 170–179 (8–11 days)	• Card Catalog, 171 • Varying the Beginning of Sentences, 175	• Skipping Lines When Writing a Draft, 173 • Subject-Verb Agreement, 177	• Science, 171 • Science, 173 • Social Studies, 175 • Physical Education/ Math, 177	• Writer's Block, 171, 173, 175, 177 • ESL Strategy, 171, 173, 175, 177 • Home-School Connection, 171, 173, 175, 177	• Rubric, 179 • Benchmark Papers, 166–169 • Self-Assessment Checklist, 164 • Teacher Evaluation Checklist, 165 • Peer Evaluation Checklist,150 • Portfolio, 179 • Teacher and Peer Conferencing, 171, 172, 174, 176

Making the Reading-Writing Connection
Writing to Inform

You may want to add the following books to your classroom library. Each category of books represents one form of writing children will be introduced to in *Writing to Inform*. The books serve as models for good writing and are valuable resources to use throughout each lesson. The suggested titles offer reading opportunities for children of varying reading abilities and are labeled as follows.

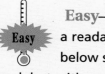

Easy—books with a readability that is below second-grade level, but with content of interest to second graders

Average—books with an average readability level that can be read independently by most second-grade students

Challenging—books with above-average readability for more proficient students or those that can be read aloud to students

Use literature to introduce a writing form, as a model of successful writing, to enhance minilessons, to focus on grammar and usage, and to expand each lesson.

INSTRUCTIONS

Hiccups for Elephant
by James Preller. Cartwheel Books, 1995. Cute instructions for curing hiccups are given to Elephant by his friends, who are annoyed by the noise he makes.

Bruno the Baker
by Lars Klinting. Henry Holt and Co., 1997. Bruno, the beaver, and his friend, Felix, bake a cake for Bruno's birthday party. A recipe is included at the end of the book.

Pig and Crow
by Kay Chorao. Henry Holt and Co., 2000. Pig feels very lonely. Crow trades "magic" items to make Pig feel better. Crow writes step-by-step instructions for Pig on how to care for a magic egg.

INVITATION

Dog and Cat Make a Splash
by Kate Spohn. Viking Children's Books, 1997. There are four short stories in this book starring Cat and Dog. In one, they put on a magic show and make invitations for their friends.

Messages in the Mailbox
by Loreen Leedy. Holiday House, 1994. Different kinds of letters are illustrated by Leedy to help kids realize they need to send a letter to get a letter in return.

Young Cam Jansen and the Dinosaur Game
by David A. Adler. Viking Children's Books, 1996. Cam Jansen is invited to a party. She solves a mystery when someone doesn't play the games fairly.

FRIENDLY LETTER

Arthur's Pen Pal
by Lillian Hoban. Econo-Clad Books, 1999. Arthur learns there's more to little sisters and pen pals when he writes to his pen pal.

Zack's Alligator
by Shirley Mozelle. HarperTrophy, 1995. Zack's uncle sends him a package and a letter. The package contains an alligator key chain that becomes life-size when watered.

Pinky and Rex Go to Camp
by James Howe. Aladdin Paperbacks, 1999. Pinky doesn't want to go to camp, so he writes to a newspaper columnist for advice.

BOOK REPORT

Author's Day
by Daniel Pinkwater. Aladdin, 1997. Hilarious misadventures occur when a school prepares for and hosts an Author's Day.

Ivy Green, Cootie Queen
by Joan Holub. Troll, 1998. Ivy Green prepares a book report on bacteria but is teased by classmates. She finally triumphs over her fears as she gives another book report.

How to Write Terrific Book Reports
by Elizabeth James and Carol Barkin. William Morrow & Co., 1998. A book that tells all about how to write book reports. It includes sample book reports.

REPORT

My Town
by William Wegman. Hyperion Press, 1998. The cartoon character Chip can't find a topic for his report until he goes looking in town for ideas.

The Magic School Bus and the Electric Field Trip
by Joanna Cole. Scholastic, 1995. Ms. Frizzle and her class take a trip through the electric wires. The students write reports on what they learn.

Tornado Alert
by Franklyn M. Branley. HarperTrophy, 1990. The author tells where, how, and when tornadoes develop and how to keep safe during one.

The Classroom Writing Center
Writing to Inform

Try to enhance your classroom writing center to focus on *Writing to Inform.* Here are some suggestions you may want to consider.

◆ Create a Message Board near your writing center. Use the board to inform children about what they will engage in that day. Write the message as a set of instructions, an invitation, or a friendly letter.

◆ Outfit your writing center with fancy paper, stickers, and stamps, so children can make stationery for invitations and friendly letters.

◆ Include software at your computer station that allows children to make greeting cards.

◆ Create a class message board or a writing wall where children can write and post messages to tell about favorite books they've read.

◆ Gather books relating to themes children are interested in as they choose topics for their reports. Keep these books in special crates. Also make available audio books on tapes for the listening station.

The Stages of the Writing Process

Consider trying some or all of the following ideas as children engage in various writing activities for informative writing.

A Prewriting Activity for Instructions
Have small groups list ideas about things they know how to do well. After choosing one idea, suggest they pantomime or do the steps. Then they can write the steps in a list to plan their writing. Group members can work on a draft together or independently.

A Drafting Idea for Letter Writing and Book Report
Write children's names on slips of paper. Have each child draw a name. Children can then draft a friendly letter to the child whose name they've drawn to tell about a favorite book they have read, or they can draft an invitation inviting the child to read a book with them. Ask them to include the title and author's name and tell a few details about the book. Children can deliver their letters or invitations.

A Publishing Activity for a Report
Encourage children to publish their reports by sharing them orally. They can tell important facts about their subject and show pictures or examples. Make a chart to help them. See the example to the right.

How to Give an Oral Report.
First, name your topic.
Next, tell facts about it.
Then, have pictures or examples to show.
Last, tell how you feel about what you have learned.

Graphic Organizers

The following blackline masters can help children with parts of the lessons in this unit. Make copies for use in the writing center and transparencies to use with an overhead projector. Display a completed example of each organizer if desired.

Blackline Master	Purpose	Writing Form
Instructions, page 142	Designing a Plan: organizing information	Instructions
Friendly Letter, page 143	Designing a Plan: organizing information	Friendly Letter, Invitation
KWL Chart, page 144	Prewriting: KWL chart	Report and other informative writing forms
Book Report, page 145	Designing a Plan: organizing information	Book Report

Create a Bulletin Board

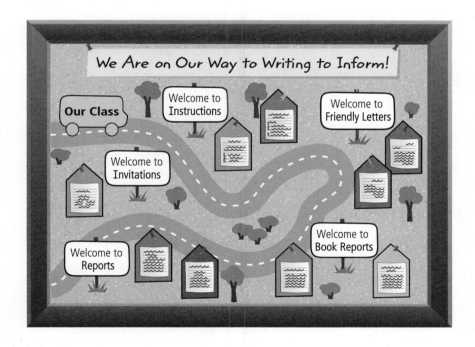

◆ Create a display that features a winding road traveling through five small writing towns. Label each town with *Welcome to* followed by the name of the writing form: Instructions, Invitations, Friendly Letters, Book Reports, and Reports.

◆ In each town, display a published sample of the writing form affixed to house-shaped paper. A school bus labeled *Our Class* sits at the beginning of the road.

◆ Use the board to introduce the five forms of writing children will learn about in this unit.

◆ Gradually, replace the samples on the board with samples of children's own writing. With each new lesson have a volunteer move the school bus along the road to show what children will learn next.

Instructions

Use the lines below to help you write instructions.

_____

What you need:

_____

_____

_____

What you do:

1. _____

2. _____

3. _____

4. _____

5. _____

Friendly Letter

Use the lines below to help you write a friendly letter.

Date _____

Dear _____,

_____

_____

_____

_____

_____

_____

_____

Closing _____

Signature _____

KWL Chart

In the first column, write what you know about your topic. In the second column, write what you'd like to know about it. After finding out about your topic, write what you learned in the third column.

What I Know	What I Want to Know	What I Learned

Name _____ Date _____

Book Report

Write about a book you've read.

Title	
Author	
Characters	
Setting	
What Happens	
Favorite Part	

Connecting Multiple Intelligences
Writing to Inform

The following activities focus on specific prewriting and publishing ideas for children who demonstrate intelligence in different ways: talent and skill with words (linguistic), with numbers (logical-mathematical), with pictures (spatial), with movement (bodily-kinesthetic), with people (interpersonal), with self (intrapersonal), with music (musical), and/or with nature (environmental or naturalist).

Linguistic
Prewriting — Make a list of ideas you want to write about in a letter.
Publishing — Give your instructions to a small group who can do the activity with you.

Spatial
Prewriting — Draw favorite scenes from a book as part of a plan for writing a book report.
Publishing — Turn your report or instructions into a multi-page booklet with drawings.

Logical-Mathematical
Prewriting — Write instructions for a game that uses counting or adding.
Publishing — Design an invitation that organizes information on separate lines telling who, what, when, where, and why.

Bodily-Kinesthetic
Prewriting/Drafting — Practice the steps of your instructions before writing them.
Publishing — Cover a box with pictures of characters, setting, and story scenes to tell about a book.

Writing to Inform

Environmental (Naturalist)
Prewriting — Plan a report or how-to instructions about a nature theme you are interested in.
Publishing — Decorate letter stationery with feathers and leaves.

Intrapersonal
Prewriting — Create a list of favorite things to choose a topic for a report.
Publishing — Send a friendly letter to a book author telling why you liked the book.

Interpersonal
Prewriting — Interview several people who know about the topic of your report.
Publishing — Develop a penpal system with children in another grade or school.

Musical
Prewriting — Write instructions to teach others a dance, a musical game, or how to play an instrument.
Publishing — Tape record yourself singing your friendly letter. Mail the tape.

Evaluating Student Writing
Writing to Inform

The Write Direction offers a variety of assessment options. The following are short descriptions of the assessment opportunities available in this unit. Just select the assessment option that works best for you.

Types of Assessment	Complete-Process Writing Lessons	Short-Process Writing Lessons
Rubric Specific characteristics of a writing form are used to develop a 4-point scale for evaluating children's writing (4–Well Developed, 3–Adequately Developed, 2–Partially Developed, 1–Undeveloped). Children's writing is compared with the characteristics to determine a rating point.	• Report, page 179	
Benchmark Papers Annotated and scored student writing models are provided as benchmarks for evaluating children's writing. Children's published writing can be compared with these models for assessment.	• Report, pages 166–169	
Checklists Self-Assessment, Teacher, and Peer Evaluation Checklists help children refine their informative writing at each writing process stage.	• Self-Assessment Checklist for Report, page 164 • Teacher Evaluation Checklist for Report, page 165 • Peer Evaluation Checklist, page 150	• Self-Assessment Checklist, page 148 • Teacher Evaluation Checklist, page 149 • Peer Evaluation Checklist, page 150
Portfolio Assessment Children's work generated throughout the writing process may be used in creating a portfolio illustrating their progress as writers. Strategies and tips for assessment using a portfolio appear in each lesson. Suggested pieces for a portfolio include completed writing and works-in-progress, logs, journals, and checklists.	• Report, page 179	
Teacher and Peer Conferencing Throughout each lesson in this unit, there are opportunities to interact with children, informally questioning them about their progress and concerns. Children also have opportunities to interact with each other to ask questions, share ideas, and react to each other's writing.	• Report, pages 171, 172, 174, 176	• Instructions, page 155 • Invitation, page 157 • Friendly Letter, pages 158–159 • Book Report, page 160

Self-Assessment Checklist
Writing to Inform

Name of Writer _____

Date _____

Type of Writing _____

Use this checklist when you are revising, or editing and proofreading
- **instructions**
- **an invitation**
- **a friendly letter**
- **a book report**

	YES	NO	Ways to Make My Writing Better
Is it clear what my writing is about?	☐	☐	
Is there anything I should add to or take out of my writing?	☐	☐	
Could I give more information about my topic?	☐	☐	
Did I write in complete sentences?	☐	☐	
Have I spelled words correctly?	☐	☐	
Did I use punctuation marks and capital letters correctly?	☐	☐	

Teacher Evaluation Checklist
Writing to Inform

Name of Writer _____

Date _____

Writing Mode _____

Use this checklist when you are evaluating a child's
- **instructions**
- **invitation**
- **friendly letter**
- **book report**

	YES	NO	Recommendations to Child
Is the topic appropriate for this writing assignment?	☐	☐	
Is the writing focused on the topic?	☐	☐	
Does the writing include facts and details that support the focus? Is this information well organized?	☐ ☐	☐ ☐	
Does the writing have a clear, well-developed structure?	☐	☐	
Does the writer adhere to the conventions of			
grammar?	☐	☐	
usage?	☐	☐	
spelling?	☐	☐	
punctuation?	☐	☐	
capitalization?	☐	☐	
Is the handwriting legible?	☐	☐	
Was the work done neatly?	☐	☐	

Peer Evaluation Checklist

Writing to Inform

Name of Writer _____

Name of Writing Partner _____

Conference Date _____

Type of Writing _____

Use this checklist during revising or editing and proofreading conferences for
- **instructions**
- **an invitation**
- **a friendly letter**
- **a book report**
- **a report**

	What My Writing Partner Said	Ways to Make My Writing Better
What did you like best about my writing?		
Are there any facts missing from my writing?		
Did I include facts that do not belong?		
Does my writing make sense to you?		

150

Home Letter

Dear Family,

When you share instructions for making a craft project or a recipe, you usually write them down. When you correspond with a friend or relative, you call or write a letter. When you prepare a report for your workplace, you write it for others to read. These are all examples of writing to inform.

In the next few weeks, your child will be learning how to write instructions, an invitation, a friendly letter, a book report, and a report on a topic that he or she chooses.

Here are some ways to help your child use writing to inform.

1 Let your child watch as you write instructions like recipes. Create a family message board to leave instructions or notes to one another.

2 Ask your child to explain how to play the game they are engaged in. Following their instructions, play the game with your child.

3 Provide materials for your child to make colorful stationery to write letters. Help them address the envelopes. If you have a computer, your child can send an invitation or letter electronically.

4 Discover books you can read together that give information.
- *Kids Create! Art & Craft Experiences for 3- to 9- Year-Olds* by Laurie Carlson. Illustrated by Loretta T. Braren. Williamson Publishing, 1990. There are more than 150 craft and art activities with easy-to-follow instructions for your child.
- *Crinkleroot's Nature Almanac* by Jim Arnosky. Simon & Schuster, 1999. The woodsman, Crinkleroot, walks children through the seasons explaining the changes in animals and plants. Facts are accurate and pictures are labeled.

Sincerely,

Carta para el hogar

Estimada familia,

Cuando uno intercambia instrucciones para un trabajo de artesanía o una receta de cocina, casi siempre las escribe. Cuando uno se comunica con un amigo o pariente, uno lo llama o le escribe una carta. Cuando uno prepara un informe en el trabajo, lo escribe para que otros lo lean. Estos son todos ejemplos de la escritura para informar.

En las próximas semanas, su hijo/a va a aprender a escribir instrucciones tales como una invitación, una carta amistosa, una reseña de un libro y un informe sobre un tema que él o ella seleccione.

He aquí algunas sugerencias que le pueden servir a su hijo/a a la hora de escribir para informar.

1 Permitan que su hijo/a los observe cuando estén escribiendo instrucciones, tales como una receta. Creen un tablero de avisos para dejarse instrucciones o notas mutuamente.

2 Pidan a su hijo/a que les explique cómo jugar un juego favorito. Siguiendo sus instrucciones, jueguen el juego con su hijo/a.

3 Tengan a mano materiales para que su hijo/a haga sus membretes propios en hojas de papel para escribir cartas. Ayúdenlo a poner la dirección en el sobre. Si tienen computadora, su hijo/a puede enviar la invitación o carta electrónicamente.

4 Descubran libros que contienen información que puedan leer juntos.
◆ ***Kids Create! Art and Craft Experiences for 3-to-9-Year-Olds*** por Laurie Carlson. Ilustrado por Loretta T. Braren. Williamson Publishing, 1990. Hay más de 150 actividades manuales y de arte con instrucciones fáciles para su hijo/a.
◆ ***Crinkleroot's Nature Almanac*** por Jim Arnosky. Simon and Schuster, 1999. El montañés Crinkleroot, repasa con los niños las estaciones del año explicándoles los cambios en animales y plantas. Los datos son correctos y las ilustraciones vienen acompañadas de textos.

Sinceramente,

JUST THE FACTS:

Writing to Inform

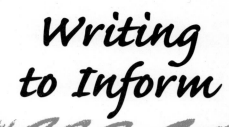

Writing to Inform

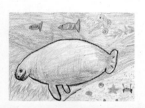

Introduction

Ask children how they would feel in each of the following situations.

★ They received a toy robot as a birthday present. The robot needs to be put together, but there are no instructions.

★ An invitation for a pizza party just came in the mail. Oh no! The invitation does not tell where to go, when the party will begin, and who the invitation is from.

★ You spent a long time making a neat birthday card for a friend who lives far away. You just mailed the card. Oh no! You forgot to sign your name and write your return address on the envelope. Will your friend know who sent the birthday greeting?

Explain to children that they will be learning about different kinds of writing that tell readers important information. The situations you just talked about presented problems because information was missing. As you introduce each of the following kinds of informative writing, talk about why it's important to include all the important information.

★ **Instructions** include step-by-step directions telling how to do or make something.

★ An **invitation** is a written message asking someone to come to a special event or to do something.

★ A **friendly letter** is a written message to a friend or family member sharing information about what is happening in the writer's life.

★ A **book report** tells about the characters, setting, and some events from a story and may include what the writer thinks about the book.

★ A **report** tells information about one topic and includes facts that have been collected from many different places.

Instructions

★ **RECOGNIZE** the characteristics of a set of instructions.

★ **RESPOND** to a model set of instructions written by published authors.

★ **PLAN, WRITE,** and **REVISE** a set of instructions.

★ **USE** a numbered list to organize steps in order.

 Begin the Lesson

Talk with children about things they are good at doing. Choose one activity, such as making a jigsaw puzzle, and work with children to name and record the materials needed and each step in the process.

How to Make a Jigsaw Puzzle

What you need:

a colorful picture

crayons

scissors

glue

cardboard

What you do:

1. Glue the picture on cardboard and trim the sides.
2. Draw lines on the cardboard to make puzzle pieces.
3. Cut out the pieces.

Explain that when writers tell how to do something, they are writing instructions.

2 Discuss a Writer's Model

MEET THE WRITER Use page 46 of the Big Book to introduce Sarah Williamson and Zachary Williamson as sister and brother, and explain that they wrote instructions, or recipes, for a cookbook. Talk about why Sarah and Zachary might have decided to write a cookbook.

INSTRUCTIONS

The writers introduce the topic.

The writers tell what is needed.

The steps are written in order and numbered.

"Make a Breakfast Sundae"
by Sarah Williamson and
Zachary Williamson

What you need:
A small bowl of yogurt
Fruit, such as strawberries,
blueberries, or banana pieces
Granola cereal
Raisins

What you do:
1. Put some fruit on top of the yogurt.
2. Sprinkle on some granola.
3. Add some raisins.
4. Eat!

Makes one sundae.

Kids Cook!

46   Writing to Inform

Sarah Williamson
Zachary Williamson

TALK ABOUT THE MODEL Have children read "Make a Breakfast Sundae" with you. Use the callouts to point out that the title introduces the topic, the materials needed are listed, and the steps to follow are numbered and written in order.

- *What are Sarah and Zachary telling us how to make?*

- *What do we need to make a breakfast sundae?*

- *What is the first step? The second? The third? The last?*

- *How do the writers make the instructions easy for you to follow?*

Remind children that the materials and steps must be clearly written and in a step-by-step order using numbers or words, such as *first, next,* and *last*.

3 Write and Confer

INDEPENDENT WRITING Have children write their own sets of instructions using the model as a guide.

MAKE A PLAN Have children brainstorm things they like to do or make. Record their ideas. Remind them to choose a topic they know well enough to explain. Next, have them create lists of things needed and the steps involved. (See page 142.)

WRITE IT DOWN As children write, remind them to make their instructions like the model, or they can write them as a paragraph. For this form, a beginning sentence names the task. The next sentence names materials, and the remaining sentences tell each step, using time-order words.

LOOK IT OVER Have children make sure all materials are listed and steps are in order. Then they can check for spelling, punctuation, and capital letters.

TEACHER CONFERENCE If children need help seeing ways to improve their instructions, ask questions like:

- *Do you know enough about your topic to describe how to do or make it?*
- *Did you list all the materials in order?*
- *Are your steps complete and in the right order?*

PEER CONFERENCE As partners read each other's instructions, have them pantomime the steps. Encourage children to suggest ways to make the steps more clear.

SHARE YOUR WORK Laminate clean copies of children's instructions and put them in a file box for others to borrow and take home to do. Alternatively, compile the instructions in a class book titled *Look What We Can Do!*

ASSESSMENT OPPORTUNITIES

SELF-ASSESSMENT Have children complete the Self-Assessment Checklist on page 148.

PEER EVALUATION Have children use the Peer Evaluation Checklist on page 150.

TEACHER HOLISTIC ASSESSMENT Use the Teacher Evaluation Checklist on page 149 to evaluate children's instructions.

Meeting Individual Needs

Choosing a Topic

Introduce Invite children to suggest ideas for how to find a topic to write about. If needed, offer ideas such as thinking about what you know or can easily find information on, what would interest your readers, what interests you; using resources, experiences, personal journals, logs, or books you've read; and so on. Record the ideas on the board or chart paper.

Model Reread the model on page 46 of the Big Book. Ask children how they think Sarah and Zachary got the idea to write a cookbook. Elicit that they may have decided to write a cookbook because they both liked to cook and cooking was something they did well.

Summarize/Apply Encourage children to use the ideas they suggested above to come up with writing topics. You may wish to have them revisit their instructions and brainstorm simple tasks they know how to do well in categories like cooking, sports, chores, or crafts. Suggest they choose an activity from one of the categories to write a set of instructions.

WRITER'S BLOCK

Problem
Children have difficulty putting the steps in order.

Solution
Have children write the steps on slips of paper. Next, have them pantomime the steps. Then, have them arrange the steps in order and number them.

ESL STRATEGY
Children acquiring English can draw pictures to plan their writing. Then with English-proficient partners they can talk about and demonstrate each step. Their partners can help them write the steps.

HOME–SCHOOL CONNECTION
Encourage children to talk with family members about possible topics for instructions, such as special activities they've done at home.

WRITING ACROSS THE CURRICULUM
Math Children can write directions that use math skills.

<u>Directions to the classroom library</u>
1. From the classroom door, walk 5 steps straight ahead.
2. Turn left and take 8 steps.
3. Turn right and take 4 steps.

Invitation

June 28, 2002

Dear Jenniece,

    I'm having a pool party for my birthday. It will be on Saturday, July 3rd at 1:00 p.m. at the town pool. Bring a towel and your bathing suit. We are going to have a splash! Call me at 543-9876 if you can come.

Your friend,
Caitlin

The writer tells what the invitation is for.

The writer tells the date and time.

The writer tells the place.

The writer asks for a reply and gives a phone number.

I wrote this invitation to tell my friends about my party!

Caitlin Ray
Virginia

Invitation 47

OBJECTIVES

★ **RECOGNIZE** the characteristics of an invitation.

★ **RESPOND** to a model invitation written by a student.

★ **PLAN, WRITE,** and **REVISE** an invitation.

★ **USE** correct capitalization in letter parts.

1 Begin the Lesson

Invite children to describe invitations they have received or sent. Explain that when someone writes a message inviting a friend or relative to come to an event or to do something, it is called an invitation. Ask children to suppose they want to invite another class to a play they are performing. Discuss the information children would include in their invitation. Record their ideas in a chart like the following.

Who?	What?	When?	Where?	How?
To: Mr. Roberts' Class From: Ms. Cheng's class	a play "Tales of Ananzi the Spider"	May 8, 1:30 p.m.	Room 24	Tell Ms. Cheng by May 1

2 Discuss a Writer's Model

MEET THE WRITER Have children look at the invitation on page 47 of the Big Book of Writing Models and introduce the writer, Caitlin Ray, a second grader. Caitlin wrote this invitation to a friend. Ask a volunteer to read her words about why she wrote the invitation.

TALK ABOUT THE MODEL Use details in the invitation and the callouts to answer the questions *Who, What, When, Where,* and *How.* You may wish to help children identify the heading, greeting, body, closing, and signature.

- *Does the invitation make you want to go to the party?*
- *Is all the important information included?*
- *Why is Caitlin's phone number included?*

3 Write and Confer

INDEPENDENT WRITING Invite children to write their own invitations, using Caitlin's as a model.

MAKE A PLAN Let each child choose an event for an invitation. Suggest upcoming community events, birthdays, holidays, or activities they like to do with friends as writing ideas. Have children use a chart like the one in Begin the Lesson or copies of the Friendly Letter blackline master on page 143 to plan their information.

WRITE IT DOWN As children draft, remind them that all the important information should be given. Suggest they refer to the callouts in the model if needed.

LOOK IT OVER Have children read their invitations and make corrections or changes. In addition to content and spelling, suggest they check their use of capitalization and commas.

TEACHER CONFERENCE As you meet with children, ask questions to help them monitor their writing progress.

- *Does the invitation tell* Who, What, When, Where, *and* How to respond?
- *What in your invitation would make the person want to say, "Yes, I'll come!"?*

PEER CONFERENCE Suggest that children work in pairs to share their invitations. Emphasize that listeners should be able to tell *Who, What, When, Where,* and *How to respond* and tell why they would want to say "Yes."

SHARE YOUR WORK Children can display a final copy of each invitation with a drawing of the event on a bulletin board or mural. Partners or small groups could videotape each other as they read their invitations aloud.

ASSESSMENT OPPORTUNITIES

SELF-ASSESSMENT Have children complete the Self-Assessment Checklist on page 148.

PEER EVALUATION Have children use the Peer Evaluation Checklist on page 150.

TEACHER HOLISTIC ASSESSMENT Use the Teacher Evaluation Checklist on page 149 to evaluate children's invitations.

Meeting Individual Needs

Capitalization— Letter Parts

Introduce Discuss the use of capital letters to begin words that name the days of the week, months, and proper names of people and places. Have children provide examples of words that are typically capitalized.

Model Use Caitlin's letter on page 47 of the Big Book as a model for the correct use of capital letters in an invitation or friendly letter. Have children identify words that are capitalized, such as the first word in the greeting and closing. Mention, too, that in a two-word closing, such as *Your friend*, only the first word is capitalized.

Summarize/Apply Suggest that children check their own invitations for proper capitalization. If their invitations are organized like friendly letters, remind them to capitalize the first word in the greeting and closing as well as days of the week, months, and proper names of people and places.

WRITER'S BLOCK

Problem	Solution
Children may be confused about when to use commas in dates, greetings, and closings.	Suggest that children write the dates and greetings without punctuation and then go back and add the commas later. They can refer to Caitlin's model as needed.

ESL STRATEGY

Work together to create a list of the English words for the days of the week and months. Ask children to teach the class the words in their native languages.

HOME–SCHOOL CONNECTION

Have children share their invitations with family members and explain where they tell *Who, What, Where, When,* and *How to respond.*

WRITING ACROSS THE CURRICULUM

Social Studies Add to information children are learning by helping them keep a list of important dates in history. Model how to use proper capitalization and punctuation when writing dates.

Important Dates in History

What Happened	When It Happened
1. George Washington's birthday	1. February 22, 1732
2. Declaration of Independence	2. July 4, 1776

Friendly Letter

OBJECTIVES

★ **RECOGNIZE** the characteristics of a friendly letter.

★ **RESPOND** to a model of a friendly letter written by a student.

★ **PLAN, WRITE,** and **REVISE** a friendly letter.

★ **USE** language and details to recreate an experience for a reader.

1 Begin the Lesson

Have children name ways to keep in touch with friends and relatives. *(by telephone, e-mail, post cards, greeting cards, letters)* Talk about why it's fun to get letters in the mail and how it's different from e-mail and phone calls. Brainstorm reasons why people write letters. Record ideas in a web like the following.

2 Discuss a Writer's Model

MEET THE WRITER Focus on the friendly letter on pages 48–49 of the Big Book of Writing Models. Introduce the writer, second grader Christina Sanchez, who wrote this letter to tell a friend about a trip to her uncle's farm. Let a child read Christina's comments on page 48.

TALK ABOUT THE MODEL Read Christina's letter. Use the callout labels to show how she organized her letter. Note that Christina used language that is fun and friendly and descriptive details that make her letter interesting.

- *What is Christina's reason for writing to Brianna?*
- *What details make her message fun to read?*
- *How is the placement of the heading, closing, and signature different from the rest of the letter?*

FRIENDLY LETTER

Heading	May 4, 2002
Greeting	Dear Brianna,
Body	I went to my uncle's farm on Saturday. I got to ride Brandy, his horse. Brandy is brown. Before I rode him, we brushed him. Then we put on his blanket and saddle. I rode Brandy four times. The last time we went too fast and I fell off. I got dirty, but I had lots of fun! Write back soon!
Closing	Your friend,
Signature	Christina

I sent this letter to my friend. She likes horses as much as I do.

48 Writing to Inform

Christina Sanchez
Florida

3 Write and Confer

INDEPENDENT WRITING Have children recall and write a letter about a recent experience they'd like to share with a friend or relative.

MAKE A PLAN Have children choose a topic. Emphasize the importance of interesting details to help the reader picture what you are telling. You may want to suggest they use a list or copies of the blackline master on page 143 to plan their letters.

WRITE IT DOWN Remind children to use friendly language and interesting details. They can refer to Christina's letter as they draft to be sure they include all five letter parts.

LOOK IT OVER Ask children to check for spelling and punctuation errors as well as any content changes they'd like to make. Have them ask themselves:

- *Does my letter include all five parts?*
- *Is the order of events clear?*
- *Are there enough interesting details?*

TEACHER CONFERENCE As you meet with children, ask questions to help them monitor their writing.

- *Did you include all the parts of a letter?*
- *Will your reader be able to follow the order of events?*
- *Did you use capital letters and commas in your heading, greeting, and closing?*

PEER CONFERENCE As partners share their letters, have them discuss whether the letters are clear, interesting, and friendly, and if not, talk about ways to improve them. Then partners can check for spelling, capital letters, and punctuation.

SHARE YOUR WORK Invite children to draw pictures to enclose with their letters or suggest they send their letters electronically.

ASSESSMENT OPPORTUNITIES

SELF-ASSESSMENT Have children complete the Self-Assessment Checklist on page 148.

PEER EVALUATION Have children use the Peer Evaluation Checklist on page 150.

TEACHER HOLISTIC ASSESSMENT Use the Teacher Evaluation Checklist on page 149 to evaluate children's friendly letters.

Meeting Individual Needs

Commas—in Letter Parts

Introduce Have children recall the five parts of a friendly letter. Then write Christina's heading, greeting, and closing on the board, omitting any commas. Ask children what they notice about the letter parts. Explain that you will work together to write the letter parts correctly.

Model Have children compare the letter parts on the board with Christina's letter on page 48 of the Big Book. Invite volunteers to add a comma to separate the parts of a date, after the greeting, and after the closing.

Summarize/Apply Have children revisit their friendly letters and check their use of commas in the heading, greeting, and closing. Invite children to share with the class any changes they make to their letters.

 WRITER'S BLOCK

Problem	Solution
Children have difficulty making the language in their letters friendly and fun.	Remind children to think about how they would sound if they were telling a friend the story in person. Encourage them to write as they would speak.

ESL STRATEGY
Provide a highlighter marker and have second-language learners highlight the comma in the heading, greeting, and closing as you read their letters with them.

HOME–SCHOOL CONNECTION
Have each child share his or her friendly letter with a family member and point out the five parts of a friendly letter.

WRITING ACROSS THE CURRICULUM
Social Studies As children write thank-you letters, remind them to use correct capitalization and punctuation in headings, greetings, and closings.

Book Report

Sammy, Dog Detective
by Jose Turcios

The writer tells the title and author of the book.

Sammy, Dog Detective is by Colleen Stanley Bare. The book is about a dog that's a detective in a K-9 team.

The writer tells what the book is about.

Sammy the dog detective works with a policeman. Sammy had to be trained to be a good police dog. He went to detective school to learn hand signals.

The main events are described briefly.

A book report lets me tell about a book I really liked.

Jose Turcios
Virginia

OBJECTIVES

★ **RECOGNIZE** the characteristics of a book report.

★ **RESPOND** to a model book report written by a student.

★ **PLAN, WRITE,** and **REVISE** a book report.

★ **USE** interesting details to tell about a book's characters, setting, and plot.

Begin the Lesson

Ask how many children have read a book that was recommended to them by a friend. Explain that writing a book report is one way of telling others about a book you've read. Encourage children to brainstorm what should be included in a book report. Record their answers.

> Book Report
> 1. title and author
> 2. illustrator
> 3. characters and setting
> 4. what the book is about
> 5. favorite part
> 6. like or not like

Discuss a Writer's Model

MEET THE WRITER Focus on the book report on pages 50–51 of the Big Book of Writing Models and introduce the writer, second grader Jose Turcios. Invite a child to read Jose's words about why he wrote his book report.

TALK ABOUT THE MODEL Read aloud the book report. Use the callouts to point out that Jose named the title and author early in the report. Then he described the main character, setting, and plot without telling the whole story. Ask children questions like the following.

• *Does Jose's book report make you want to read the book? Why or why not?*

• *What was his favorite part?*

• *Why do you think Jose wrote about this book?*

Write and Confer

INDEPENDENT WRITING Have children brainstorm a list of books they have enjoyed in class, at home, or at the library, and then choose one to write about.

MAKE A PLAN After children choose a book, suggest that they make a chart to plan what they will write. (See page 145 for a blackline master.)

WRITE IT DOWN As children draft, encourage them to write about the most important events without telling the ending. Remind them to tell about the characters and what happens.

LOOK IT OVER Have children look over their book reports to make changes and correct errors. They can use Jose's model as a guide.

TEACHER CONFERENCE As you meet with children, ask questions to help them monitor their progress.

• *Where did you include information about the book's title and author?*

• *Have you given your reader enough details about the book without giving away the ending?*

• *Did you tell if you liked the book and why?*

PEER CONFERENCE Have small groups share their book reports. Remind them to tell what they enjoyed and ask questions about details they don't understand.

SHARE YOUR WORK Children can make book jackets and attach their final drafts to the jackets.

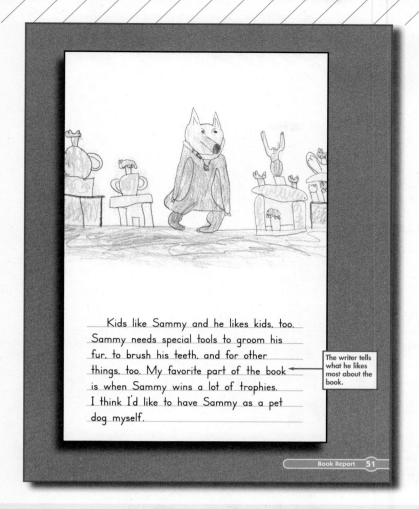

Kids like Sammy and he likes kids, too. Sammy needs special tools to groom his fur, to brush his teeth, and for other things, too. My favorite part of the book ⟵ is when Sammy wins a lot of trophies. I think I'd like to have Sammy as a pet dog myself.

The writer tells what he likes most about the book.

Book Report 51

SELF-ASSESSMENT Have children complete the Self-Assessment Checklist on page 148.

PEER EVALUATION Have children use the Peer Evaluation Checklist on page 150.

TEACHER HOLISTIC ASSESSMENT Use the Teacher Evaluation Checklist on page 149 to evaluate children's book reports.

Meeting Individual Needs

Capitalization— Titles of Books

Introduce Ask children to share the titles of the books they wrote about in their book reports. Explain that the first letter of each important word in a title of a book is capitalized, including the first word (which is always capitalized), and that the title is underlined.

Model Write *Sammy, Dog Detective* and *The Bat in the Boot* on the board. Point out the words in the titles that begin with capital letters. Explain that all of the most important words in a title as well as the first word begin with capital letters. Small unimportant words, such as *the* and *in*, do not need to be capitalized unless they are the first or last word in the title.

Summarize/Apply Invite volunteers to write on the board the title of the book described in their book report and then tell which words in the title are capitalized and why.

WRITER'S BLOCK

Problem	Solution
Children have trouble limiting the number of main events.	Suggest that children divide the book into three parts: beginning, middle, and end. Have them pick a main event from each part of the book and include those events in their book reports.

ESL STRATEGY

Pair children with proficient speakers. Partners can tell each other about their books, then write down unfamiliar words prior to writing their reports.

HOME–SCHOOL CONNECTION

To get ideas for a book report, family members can remind children about favorite books they've shared together.

WRITING ACROSS THE CURRICULUM

Science As children begin writing reports, they can keep track of reference books they use by writing a list of titles. The list will make it easy for them to find the books again in the library.

Writer's Workshop Planner

Report

WRITING PROCESS STAGE

MINILESSONS

WRITING PROCESS STAGE	Writer's Craft; Grammar, Usage, Mechanics, Spelling	Writing Across the Curriculum	Meeting Individual Needs	Assessment
Prewriting pp. 170–171 (3 days)	Card Catalog, page 171	Science, page 171	Writer's Block ESL Strategy Home-School Connection	• Teacher and Peer Conferencing, page 171
Drafting pp. 172–173 (2–3 days)	Skipping Lines When Writing a Draft, page 173	Science, page 173	Writer's Block ESL Strategy Home-School Connection	• Self-Assessment Checklist, page 164 • Peer Evaluation Checklist, page 150 • Teacher Evaluation Checklist, page 165 • Teacher and Peer Conferencing, page 172
Revising pp. 174–175 (1–2 days)	Varying the Beginning of Sentences, page 175	Social Studies, page 175	Writer's Block ESL Strategy Home-School Connection	• Self-Assessment Checklist, page 164 • Peer Evaluation Checklist, page 150 • Teacher Evaluation Checklist, page 165 • Teacher and Peer Conferencing, page 174
Editing & Proofreading pp. 176–177 (1–2 days)	Subject-Verb Agreement, page 177	Physical Education/ Math, page 177	Writer's Block ESL Strategy Home-School Connection	• Self-Assessment Checklist, page 164 • Peer Evaluation Checklist, page 150 • Teacher Evaluation Checklist, page 165 • Teacher and Peer Conferencing, page 176
Publishing pp. 178–179 (1 day)				• Benchmark Papers, pages 166–169 • Rubric, page 179 • Portfolio, page 179

Suggestions for Planning Each Day

- Whole Class Meeting/Minilesson (5–10 minutes)
- Independent Writing/Teacher-Student Conferences (30–40 minutes)
- Peer Conferences (5–10 minutes)
- Group Share (5–10 minutes)

Connecting Multiple Intelligences
With the Stages of the Writing Process

Linguistic
Revising — Check your words to see if any can be replaced with more exact or clear words.
Publishing — Present your report to a younger class.

Logical-Mathematical
Prewriting — Write your main ideas on index cards and arrange them in order.
Prewriting — Use an outline to order your ideas and to help you draft.

Spatial
Publishing — Create your report as a lift-the-flap book with questions, drawings, and answers.
Publishing — Include illustrations, charts, or graphs in your report.

Bodily-Kinesthetic
Publishing — Plan to include a demonstration as part of your report if appropriate.
Publishing — Present the report dressed as your subject—a tree, an animal, or even a kite!

Environmental (Naturalist)
Prewriting — Look around your classroom or school for a nature idea to learn more about.
Prewriting — Go outside to observe and collect data for your report.

Writing a Report

Musical
Prewriting — Choose a topic related to music, such as a composer's life or how an instrument makes sound.
Publishing — Sing your report to a favorite tune.

Interpersonal
Prewriting — Talk about possible topics with partners. Choose one everyone thinks is interesting.
Revising — Trade drafts with a partner. Note on the paper where more details are needed.

Intrapersonal
Prewriting — List ideas about things that are important to you, such as pets, sports, or hobbies.
Revising — Think about what else your reader might like to know.

Assessment Options

In this complete-process lesson, a variety of assessment tools are provided, specific to the report form. Annotated benchmark papers, corresponding to a 4-point evaluation rubric, are included to help you better rate children's papers. Self-Assessment, Peer, and Teacher Checklists will help make Teacher and Peer Conferences more productive and useful to children.

- Benchmark Papers, pages 166–169
- Evaluation Rubric, page 179
- Teacher and Peer Conferencing, pages 171, 172, 174, 176
- Self-Assessment Checklist, page 164
- Peer Evaluation Checklist, page 150
- Teacher Evaluation Checklist, page 165
- Portfolio Assessment, page 179

Self-Assessment Checklist
Writing a Report

Name of Writer _____

Date _____

Type of Writing _____

Use this checklist when you are revising, or editing and proofreading a **report**.

	YES	NO	Ways to Make My Writing Better
Does the beginning of my report tell what it is about?	☐	☐	
Did I include facts and details about my topic?	☐	☐	
Is there anything I should add to or take out of my report?	☐	☐	
Is my report written in complete sentences?	☐	☐	
Have I spelled words correctly?	☐	☐	
Did I use punctuation marks and capital letters correctly?	☐	☐	

Teacher Evaluation Checklist
Writing a Report

Name of Writer _____

Date _____

Writing Mode _____

Use this checklist when you are evaluating a child's **report**.

	YES	NO	Recommendations to Child
Is the topic clearly stated at the beginning of the report?	☐	☐	
Is the report clearly focused on the topic?	☐	☐	
Does the report include facts and details about the topic?	☐	☐	
Is the information in the report well organized?	☐	☐	
Does the closing paragraph sum up the report?	☐	☐	
Does the writer adhere to the conventions of			
grammar?	☐	☐	
usage?	☐	☐	
spelling?	☐	☐	
punctuation?	☐	☐	
capitalization?	☐	☐	
Is the report legible?	☐	☐	
Was the work done neatly?	☐	☐	

Benchmark Paper 1
Writing a Report

Manatees

Last summer I went to florda to see my grandparents. My grandmothr went with me to the dock to see some manatees. She called them see cows. I had never seen a manatee before. We wated and wated. It was hot. My grandmothr pointed to something in the water. All I cold see was a nose and wiskers. Then I saw a flipepr and it was gone. When I went back to school I read about manatees in a book. My grandmothr was right. They ARE called sea cows. Manatees are mammals. They like to live in warm water. They are big and gentle. They live in oceans and rivers. Manatees are in danger because of poluted water and moterboats. The moterboats go to fast and hit the manatees. Moterboats should go slower.

Rating Point 1: Undeveloped Report
The writing is more a narrative than a report, but it is somewhat focused on one topic. It includes some facts about the topic, but they are not organized. There are errors in grammar, usage, mechanics, and spelling.

Benchmark Paper 2

Writing a Report

Give your report a title.

Manatees are shy, gentle, large, slow mammals. They have very small hairs on there body. Baby manatees drink milk. They eat 8 hours a day. They swim in warm water. They eat up to 200 lb of hyacinths and seagrass. They are plant eaters. They have no outside ears. Manatees are endangerd mostly because of motor boats There worst enemey is a motorboat. Save the manatees. Another name for them is seacow.

Why are motorboats dangerous to manatees?

Check your punctuation (no periods at the end of several sentences).

Organize your information.
— Put sentences about what manatees look like together.
— Put sentences about what they eat together.

Rating Point 2: Partially Developed Report
This report is focused on the selected topic. It contains facts and details, but they are poorly organized. There are not enough details to explain the ending. There are errors in grammar, mechanics, and spelling.

Manatees

Manatees are gentle creatures. They eat 8 hours a day. They eat hyecinth and sea grass. They are called seacows. The baby seacow lives with his or her mother until he or she is 2 years old. They are warm-blooded and they are mammals.

Manatees are indangered of extiction. Moter boats can hurt or kill manatees. Moter boats are there worst enimes. Sometimes people are poluting the water

There are sevaral ways to help manatees. We must put up signs that say Moterboats go slow. We must stop polluting the water. We need to save the manatees.

Where do manatees live?

Check your spelling.

Your report has good information.

Don't forget to put a period at the end of a sentence.

Rating Point 3: Adequately Developed Report
The report is focused on the selected topic. It includes pertinent information that is presented in a logical order. It has a clear beginning, middle, and end. There are minor errors in grammar, usage, and spelling.

Benchmark Paper 4
Writing a Report

Manatees

Manatees are endangered animals. A manatee's habitat is the Florida east Lagoon. Manatees are mammals. Some people call them sea-cows. Back in the 1800's they were mistaken for mermaids. But what they really are is just calm, sweet, shy, curious, gental giants. Manatees look like a big gray oval with a little head and tiny round eyes. They have a long flat tail that helps them glide through the water. The usual manatee sometimes weigh about half a ton! They eat 200 lbs. of plants a day!

Manatees breathe every 3-5 minutes. When the winter comes it's time for manatees to swim to the south. The reason that the manatees head south is so the water won't get frozen and the manatees couldn't breath. The second reason is because cold weather kills them.

Manatees are in danger of extinction. In florida there are only about 1,450 manatees left. Ways we can help manatees are to drive by air boat. Another way that we can help manatees is that we can pick up trash in the water. Make signs to tell boats to slow down and that this is a manatee zone. The most important way to save them is to never ever hurt them on purpose.

Good opening sentence.

Information about the same topic is all together. (descriptions of what they look like)

You have interesting facts about manatees.

Rating Point 4: Well-Developed Report
The writer clearly focuses on the selected topic. The report includes interesting information and details that are well organized. The report has a clear beginning, middle, and end. There are minor errors in grammar, spelling, and mechanics.

Report

Prewriting

OBJECTIVES

★ RECOGNIZE the characteristics of a report.

★ RESPOND to a prewriting plan written by a student writer.

★ BRAINSTORM and SELECT a topic.

★ USE a KWL chart to organize information for a report.

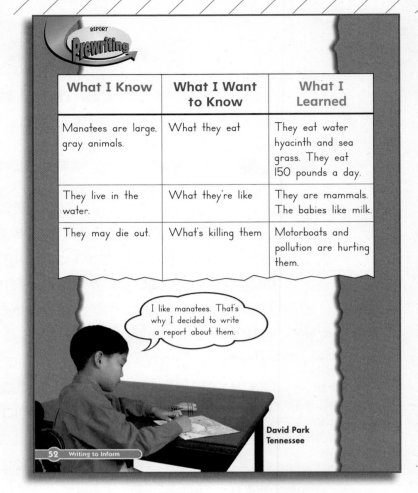

What I Know	What I Want to Know	What I Learned
Manatees are large, gray animals.	What they eat	They eat water hyacinth and sea grass. They eat 150 pounds a day.
They live in the water.	What they're like	They are mammals. The babies like milk.
They may die out.	What's killing them	Motorboats and pollution are hurting them.

> I like manatees. That's why I decided to write a report about them.

David Park
Tennessee

52   Writing to Inform

1 Begin the Lesson

Ask children to suggest things they would like to know more about, such as why the sky is blue, or what causes earthquakes. Write children's ideas in a web or list, then talk about what children could do to find out about these topics. Introduce the idea that when writers write about a topic using information they know and learn from reference sources, they are writing a report.

2 Discuss a Writer's Model

MEET THE WRITER Display page 52 of the Big Book of Writing Models. Tell children that the boy who made this chart is second grader David Park. Select a volunteer to read aloud what David says about why he chose to write about manatees. If children do not know what manatees are, you may want to show and discuss pictures so children understand the topic of David's report.

Explain that David went through many steps to write his report. Tell children that David's model will help them as they write their own reports.

BRAINSTORM To help children brainstorm topics to write about, have them copy the following sentence starter on paper: *I would like to know more about _____.* Have children think about things they wonder about, such as those discussed in the lesson opener, and write words or draw pictures to finish the sentence. Encourage children to list any ideas that come to mind.

SELECT A TOPIC Children can choose one topic from the list of ideas they have written or drawn. Suggest they select the topic they are most curious about.

DESIGN A PLAN Have children look at the excerpt of David's KWL chart on page 52 of the Big Book. Lead children to understand that David filled in the *What I Know* and *What I Want to Know* columns on his own, but that he had to look in different places to find the facts he wrote in the *What I Learned* column. Ask questions like the following to help children understand David's chart.

- *Which column do you think David filled in first?*
- *Which column do you think he filled in next? How did he get that information?*
- *What is the next step he took to complete his chart?*
- *Where could he have found information to complete the third column?*

3 Prewrite and Confer

INDEPENDENT WRITING Distribute blank KWL charts to children (see page 144). Suggest they title their charts to focus on their topics. Remind them to fill in information they know and then what they want to know. Provide reference materials for children to use. Encourage them to look in many places, such as books, magazines, tapes, videos, filmstrips, CD-ROMs, interviews, and the Internet, if available.

TEACHER CONFERENCE During your prewriting conferences, you may wish to ask the following questions to guide children.

- *How did you select your topic?*
- *What did you already know about this topic?*
- *What more do you want to find out?*
- *Where have you been looking to find answers?*
- *Are there questions that you are having trouble answering? How could you find the answers?*

PEER CONFERENCE Invite children to work in pairs to share their KWL charts. Remind them of the following peer conference guidelines.

- *Listen carefully as your partner shares his or her chart.*
- *Tell what you like about the information in the chart.*
- *Ask questions if there is a part of the chart you don't understand.*

Meeting Individual Needs

Card Catalog

Introduce Ask children to tell where they think David found the answers to his questions. Prompt children to suggest that David may have gone to the library to find books with information about manatees. Then ask children how they find books about particular topics.

Model Take children to the library and show them the card catalog or on-line database. Explain that the card or computer catalog names the books in the library. Point out that David could look for a title of a book he knows about manatees, look for the word *manatee*, or for the name of an author who writes books about animals. The cards are in alphabetical order. On a computer, just type in the title, author's name, or subject. Model how you would use the information from the card catalog or computer to find the books about manatees in your library.

Summarize/Apply Encourage children to use the card or computer catalog to find books about their topics. You might ask them to each find one resource to share with the class or in small groups.

WRITER'S BLOCK

Problem	Solution
Children cannot find the answers to the questions in their charts.	Direct children to resources with information about their topics. Children can then focus on reading to find answers rather than on searching through library materials.

ESL STRATEGY
Find reference sources that rely more on pictures than on words. Children may, for example, find it easier to locate easy-to-understand information on CD-ROMs than in print resources.

HOME–SCHOOL CONNECTION
Have children share their report topics with their families. Family members may be able to offer additional information or help children find more information at the library or on the Internet.

WRITING ACROSS THE CURRICULUM
Science A KWL chart may be used for any subject area.

Dinosaurs		
K	W	L
What I Know	What I Want to Know	What I Learned
Dinosaurs lived a long time ago. Many dinosaurs are big.	What is the biggest dinosaur? What is the smallest dinosaur?	Alamosaurus and Brachiosaurus were over 75 feet long. Compsognathus was only 3 feet long.

Drafting

OBJECTIVES

★ **RECOGNIZE** the characteristics of a report in a first draft of a student model.

★ **FOLLOW** a writing plan to write a first draft of a report.

 Continue the Writer's Workshop

Ask children what they would need to make a sand castle. Elicit that they would need items like sand, water, buckets, and digging/shaping tools. Tell children that writers also need to have specific materials ready in order to write reports. They would need their KWL charts, information resources, pencils, and paper.

 Discuss a Writer's Model

Invite the class to read David's draft on pages 53–55 of the Big Book of Writing Models. Use the callouts to talk about what David included in the beginning, middle, and end of his report. Have children compare his KWL chart and his draft. Talk about how David included details from the chart in his report.

IDENTIFY CHARACTERISTICS OF A REPORT
Point out the characteristics of a report.

- *Has a topic that the writer is curious about*
- *Uses information collected from books, encyclopedias, magazines, newspapers, CD-ROMs, and the Internet*
- *Has a beginning that identifies the topic in an interesting way*
- *Has a middle that gives facts and details about the topic*
- *Has an ending that tells how you feel about what you have learned*

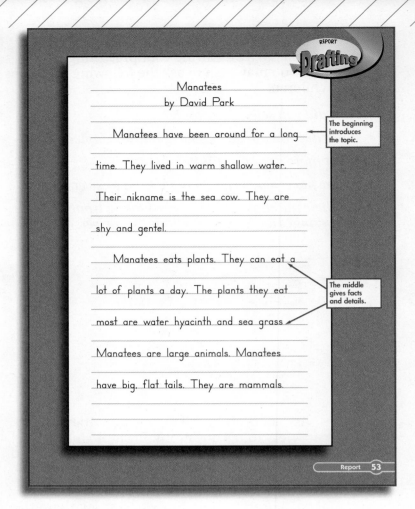

Manatees
by David Park

Manatees have been around for a long time. They lived in warm shallow water. Their nikname is the sea cow. They are shy and gentel.

Manatees eats plants. They can eat a lot of plants a day. The plants they eat most are water hyacinth and sea grass

Manatees are large animals. Manatees have big, flat tails. They are mammals.

The beginning introduces the topic.

The middle gives facts and details.

Report 53

 Draft and Confer

THINK LIKE A WRITER As children begin writing their reports, have them ask themselves these questions.

- *What is my topic? What do I want to know about it?*
- *How will I start my report? What should I tell in the middle? in the end?*

INDEPENDENT WRITING Remind children that their goal in writing the first draft is to get their ideas on paper. Using the information in their charts will help them organize their writing. They should keep their charts and drafts together in their portfolios.

TEACHER CONFERENCE As children work on their drafts, ask questions such as the following.

- *How did you start your report? Will your readers know your topic right away?*
- *How did you decide what details to include in the middle of your report?*
- *How did you end your report? Did you tell how you feel about what you learned?*

PEER CONFERENCE Pair children. Have them read each other's drafts and ask questions like the following.

- *Do you know what the topic of my report is?*
- *Did I give enough information about my topic? What else would you like to know?*
- *Can you tell how I feel about my topic?*

Manatees are warm-blooded and breathe air every few minutes. Manatees love milk. A baby manatee drinks milk. It lives with its mother for two years.

Manatees are in danger of being killed. Motorboats are their worst enemies. Manatees are also hurt by polluted water.

We can help! We can make signs. We can take care of manatees that get hurt. We can keep the water clean. I hope we can save the manatees!

The end tells how the writer feels about the topic.

Meeting Individual Needs

Mini Lesson

Skipping Lines When Writing a Draft

Introduce   Revisit David's first draft about manatees on pages 53–55 of the Big Book. Ask children what they notice about the way the draft is written. Lead children to realize that David skipped lines as he wrote.

Model   Ask children why skipping lines would be particularly helpful when writing a first draft of a report. *(The draft will be easier to read. There will be more room to cut and paste information and to make revisions and edits later.)* Copy the first paragraph of David's draft on the board or on chart paper. Invite children to make changes to his draft in the spaces between the lines, such as adding new information, replacing words, or rearranging sentences.

Summarize/Apply   As children write their drafts of reports or other kinds of writing, encourage them to skip lines. You can also show children how to double-space writing on the computer, print out the drafts, and make revisions and edits by hand in the blank spaces.

WRITER'S BLOCK

Problem	Solution
Children have trouble using the information in their KWL charts in their drafts.	Help children decide what to focus on in the beginning, middle, and end of their reports. They can then cross out facts in the charts as they write them in their reports.

ESL STRATEGY

Have children list facts about their topics. Later, they can choose several facts to record in complete sentences.

HOME–SCHOOL CONNECTION

Have children share their first drafts with their families. Family members can tell writers what they learned from the reports.

WRITING ACROSS THE CURRICULUM

Science   Encourage children to identify their topics in interesting ways.

Have you ever looked up at the sky on a dark night? If you have, then you have seen the sky's very own lights.

Report

Revising

OBJECTIVES

★ ANALYZE a model to understand how a student writer revised his writing.

★ REVISE a first draft of a report to elaborate and clarify ideas.

★ USE a catchy opening sentence to capture readers' interest.

 ## Continue the Writer's Workshop

Remind children that they have made their charts, found information for their reports, and written their drafts. Since they want their reports to be the best they can be, now is the time to reread the drafts to see if anything could be added, taken out, changed, or made clearer. Encourage children to look closely at their beginning sentences. Ask: *Is your first sentence exciting? Will it make readers want to find out more?*

 ## Discuss a Writer's Model

Have the class look at the excerpt of David's revised draft on page 56 of the Big Book of Writing Models. Explain that this shows what David decided to change when he looked at this part of his report again.

Select volunteers to point out and read the changes David made, including changing the words *a lot* to an exact number. Discuss the revisions. Ask how the changes make his report better. You may wish to have children suggest other changes David could have made to make his report even more interesting.

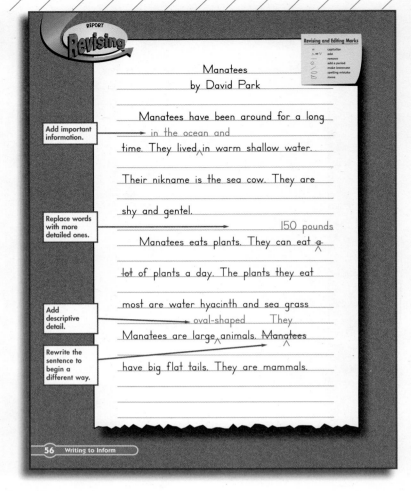

Revise and Confer

When children are revising their reports, have them consider these questions.

- *Did I begin by naming my topic?*
- *Did I present facts and details in the middle?*
- *How could I make the information easier to understand?*
- *How did I end the report? Does the ending make sense?*

TEACHER CONFERENCE Ask children questions like the following as they look again at their drafts.

- *Will your first sentence make your readers want to read on? How can you make that sentence more interesting?*
- *Have you included enough facts and details?*
- *Did you end your report by telling how you feel about the topic or what you have learned?*

PEER CONFERENCE Encourage children to discuss revisions with partners. Suggest that writers ask listeners questions like the following.

- *Why do you think my changes will make my report better? Which ideas do you like the best?*
- *Does my beginning sentence make you want to read my whole report?*
- *Can you think of any other changes I could make?*

174

Mini Lesson

Varying the Beginning of Sentences

Introduce Write the following sentences on the board: *Cheetahs are fast cats. Cheetahs have spots all over their bodies. Cheetahs live in hot, dry areas.* Ask children what they notice about the sentences. *(They all begin with the same word.)* Lead children to see that starting all the sentences the same way can make writing quite boring to read.

Model Revisit the excerpt of David's revision of his report about manatees on Big Book page 56. Ask volunteers to point out the different ways that David begins his sentences. What would this report be like if every sentence started with the word *manatees*? Invite children to suggest other ways that David could begin his sentences.

Summarize/Apply As children write, encourage them to begin their sentences in different ways. Children can focus on varied sentence beginnings as they revise.

WRITER'S BLOCK

Problem	Solution
Children may feel that the opening sentences in their reports are not very interesting.	Encourage children to write different sentences and try them out on friends. Suggest they begin their reports by naming the subjects and telling the most important or unusual fact. Another way is to ask a question: *What is . . .* or *Did you know that . . . ?*

ESL STRATEGY

Have children share their revised reports with partners who are older students. These students can model the correct usage of words and punctuation.

HOME–SCHOOL CONNECTION

Children can share their revised reports with family members and explain the changes they've made.

WRITING ACROSS THE CURRICULUM

Social Studies Remind children to vary sentence beginnings when they write about a topic in social studies.

> On July 4, 1776, the Declaration of Independence was signed. The Fourth of July now is a special day for our country. It's our country's birthday. People celebrate with parades, fireworks, picnics, and flags.

Report

Editing and Proofreading

OBJECTIVES

★ ANALYZE a model to understand how a student writer edited and proofread his writing.

★ EDIT and PROOFREAD a draft for grammar, usage, mechanics, and spelling.

★ MAKE subjects and verbs agree.

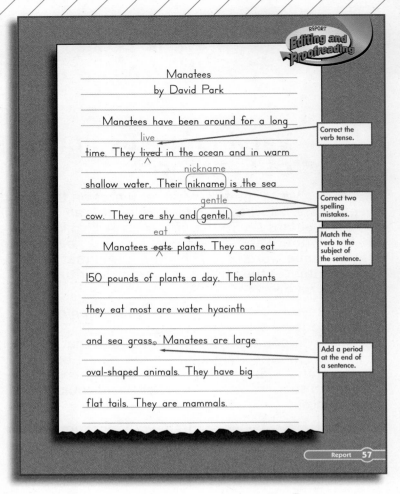

Manatees
by David Park

Manatees have been around for a long
time. They ~~lived~~ live in the ocean and in warm
shallow water. Their (nikname) nickname is the sea
cow. They are shy and (gentel.) gentle.
Manatees ~~eats~~ eat plants. They can eat
150 pounds of plants a day. The plants
they eat most are water hyacinth
and sea grass. Manatees are large
oval-shaped animals. They have big
flat tails. They are mammals.

Correct the verb tense.

Correct two spelling mistakes.

Match the verb to the subject of the sentence.

Add a period at the end of a sentence.

Report 57

1 Continue the Writer's Workshop

Remind children that after revising their writing to make it clearer and more interesting, they will want to check for missing punctuation, spelling mistakes, and words that should be changed to improve their use of language. These are the last changes to make before they write their final drafts.

Review the revising and editing marks. (See page 30 for a blackline master.) Remind children to use dictionaries and word walls to help them with spelling errors, modeling the process as needed.

2 Discuss a Writer's Model

Use the callouts to prompt discussion as you look at the excerpt of David's report during the editing and proofreading stage on page 57 of the Big Book of Writing Models. Point out the various marks that David used, such as the caret to show additions, the lineout to show words that need to be changed, and the circle to show spelling mistakes.

3 Edit, Proofread, and Confer

When children are revising their reports, have them consider these questions.

- *Did I spell all the words correctly?*
- *Did I begin every sentence with a capital letter?*
- *Did I use the correct punctuation at the end of each sentence?*
- *Do my subjects and verbs agree?*

TEACHER CONFERENCE Ask questions like the following during your conferences with children.

- *How did you make sure that your subjects and verbs agree?*
- *Did you end each sentence with the correct punctuation?*
- *What words did you have trouble spelling? How did you make sure that they are spelled correctly?*

PEER CONFERENCE Invite children to trade papers with partners. Partners can read and ask themselves these questions while looking for mistakes that may have been missed.

- *Is the handwriting neat and easy to read?*
- *Are capital letters and ending punctuation where they need to be?*
- *Are all the words spelled correctly?*

176

Subject-Verb Agreement

Introduce Write on the board or on chart paper:

My cat (run, runs) quickly.

Cheetahs (run, runs) much more quickly than my cat.

Guide children to read aloud and identify the subject in each sentence *(cat, cheetahs)*. Ask which verb fits each sentence. Point out that when the naming part of a sentence tells about one, an *s* is usually added to the verb. *Cat* means "one cat," so the verb ends in *s (runs).* When the naming part tells about more than one, the verb usually does not end with *s. Cheetahs* means "more than one cheetah," so the verb does not end with *s.*

Model Point to the first sentence in the second paragraph of David's report on page 57 of the Big Book. Ask: *What is the subject of this sentence? (manatees) Is the subject singular or plural? (plural)* Have a volunteer explain why David changed the verb as he edited. Use additional examples as needed to be sure that children understand how to make subjects and verbs agree.

Summarize/Apply Encourage children to check for subject-verb agreement in their own writing. You might have them underline subjects and verbs to "single them out" for checking.

WRITER'S BLOCK

Problem

Children are frustrated when they make mistakes as they write new drafts.

Solution

Consider having children use the computer to type and revise their drafts. They can make the changes more easily, and there will not be any eraser marks on their drafts.

ESL STRATEGY

Rather than having children search for errors to correct, you might highlight mistakes for them and discuss how to make changes so they can concentrate on fixing the errors.

HOME–SCHOOL CONNECTION

Encourage children to share their edited drafts with their families. Family members can help children use dictionaries and other reference tools to check for misspellings.

WRITING ACROSS THE CURRICULUM

Physical Education/Math Children can write log entries describing what they learned in gym, or they can write simple math word problems. Remind them to check that their subjects and verbs match.

16 ducks fly across the pond.
1 duck swims over the pond.
How many ducks in all?

Manatees
by David Park

   Manatees have been around for a long time. They live in the ocean and in warm shallow water. Their nickname is the sea cow. They are shy and gentle.
   Manatees eat plants. They can eat 150 pounds of plants a day. The plants they eat most are water hyacinth and sea grass.

58   Writing to Inform

Report

Publishing

OBJECTIVE

★ PUBLISH a report.

 End the Writer's Workshop

Praise children for the work they have done on their reports. Let them know that you want them to have the chance to share their work with their classmates. Can they think of interesting and fun ways to share their finished pieces?

 Discuss a Writer's Model

Discuss David's final draft on pages 58–60 of the Big Book of Writing Models. Compare his edited version to this clean copy. Talk about what David did to make his work ready to share, such as using neat handwriting and correct spelling and punctuation. He also added drawings to show what manatees look like.

 Publish and Celebrate

Discuss as a class how children's reports could be published. Brainstorm a list of publishing ideas on the board. Use the suggestions in Publishing Ideas to help children get started thinking of their own ideas. Give children some time to decide on ways to publish their reports, then provide materials as needed.

Schedule a specific time every day for a week for reports to be shared. You may wish to invite guests every day to hear the reports.

Publishing Ideas

MULTIMEDIA PRESENTATION

Have children add music or sound effects and pictures, photographs, maps, or other visuals to show more about their topics as they read aloud their reports. Encourage children to think of the best way to make their reports interesting for their audience. You may want to videotape each report. View the videotape as a class or share it with other classes or children's families.

RESOURCE RACK

Display the reports on a rack in your room. Children can create attractive, illustrated covers for their reports. Invite them to use classmates' reports to find information or for independent reading. As the year progresses, children can add other reports to the resource rack.

ON THE NET

Have your class place their reports on a class or school web page. Consider helping children who are ready for an extra challenge to add graphics, music, and so on to the web page. Remind children that facts should be carefully checked before they are placed on Web sites that others will read.

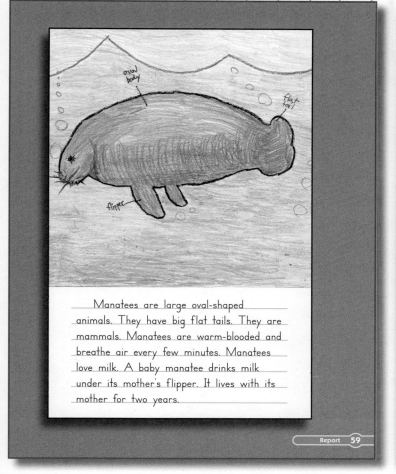

Manatees are large oval-shaped animals. They have big flat tails. They are mammals. Manatees are warm-blooded and breathe air every few minutes. Manatees love milk. A baby manatee drinks milk under its mother's flipper. It lives with its mother for two years.

Report 59

Manatees are in danger of being destroyed. Motorboats are their worst enemies. Manatees are also hurt by polluted water.

We can help! We can make signs to keep boats away. We can take care of manatees that get hurt. We can keep the water clean. I hope we can save the manatees!

60 Writing to Inform

RUBRIC FOR REPORT

4
- Clearly focuses on the selected topic.
- Clearly states the topic at the beginning of the report.
- Presents well-organized information about the topic.
- Provides a clear, complete summary at the end.
- Contains few errors in grammar/usage/mechanics/spelling.

3
- Focuses on the selected topic.
- May state the topic but not at the beginning of the report.
- May include somewhat organized information on the topic.
- May provide an incomplete summary at the end.
- May contain minor errors in grammar/usage/mechanics/spelling.

2
- Focuses somewhat on the selected topic (may include unrelated material).
- May allude to the topic at the beginning of the report.
- May include information about the topic but with little or no organization.
- May not provide a summary at the end of the report.
- May contain errors in grammar/usage/mechanics/spelling that do not interfere with understanding.

1
- May not focus on a single topic.
- Does not state or allude to the intended topic of the report.
- Includes a few facts and details about the intended topic.
- Does not provide a summary at the end of the report.
- May contain substantial errors in grammar/usage/mechanics/spelling that interfere with understanding.

ASSESSMENT OPPORTUNITIES

SELF-ASSESSMENT Have children complete the Self-Assessment Checklist on page 164. Encourage them to share their responses orally during teacher conferences.

PORTFOLIO ASSESSMENT If children choose to include their reports in their portfolios, encourage them also to consider including their KWL charts, drafts, and Self-Assessment Checklists.

PEER EVALUATION Have children use the Peer Evaluation Checklist on page 150.

TEACHER PRIMARY–TRAIT ASSESSMENT Use the Teacher Evaluation Checklist on page 165 to evaluate children's reports. You may want to share your comments during teacher conferences.

RUBRIC FOR REPORT The form-specific rubric will help you evaluate children's writing. Use the information in it during teacher conferences to help children identify ways they can improve their writing.

BENCHMARK PAPERS You may want to use the Benchmark Papers on pages 166–169 along with the rubric to evaluate children's writing.

Teacher Notes

Teacher Notes

MINILESSONS

Page numbers shown in boldface are for minilessons found in Unit 5 of the Teacher Resource Guide. Page numbers shown in lightface are for minilessons found in Units 1–4.

• **List continued on next page.**

MINILESSONS

Basic Skills

Handwriting—Cursive

Introduce On individual index cards, write each letter of the alphabet in cursive handwriting. Display the cards, one by one, and help children to identify each letter. Tell children that cursive is another form of handwriting.

Model On the board, demonstrate how to form each letter. Show how the lowercase letters connect in words and how some capital letters connect to lowercase letters in words like *Read* and *Cat*.

Summarize/Apply Give children writing paper and have them practice writing the cursive alphabet. Encourage them to use cursive handwriting in some of their writing, such as learning log entries.

Handwriting—Manuscript

Introduce Display or point to a classroom display of the alphabet that shows manuscript handwriting. Review with children each uppercase and lowercase letter. Tell children that these letters are written using manuscript handwriting.

Model On the board, model or invite volunteers to model writing letters in manuscript using their best handwriting. Then write or have other volunteers write short sentences such as *My dog's name is Fluffy*. Point out how the letters that are used more than once all look much the same and that most of the lowercase letters are similar in size, just as the uppercase letters are similar in size. Explain that this makes them easy for others to read.

Summarize/Apply For children needing extra practice with manuscript handwriting, provide paper and guidance in forming the letters. Encourage all children to use their neatest manuscript handwriting when they write for themselves and for others.

Left-to-Right Progression

Introduce Display a favorite big book story. Ask a volunteer to point to the first word on the page. Then have them point to the next words as they read the first sentence together. Point out that the words on the page are written and read from left to right.

Model Review the concepts of left and right with children. Then work with them to compose a short class story. Write the story using an overhead projector as children dictate. Verbalize that you begin on the left side of the page and move to the right as you write. Model paragraph indention as well as you demonstrate going back to the left-hand side of the page to begin a new line.

Summarize/Apply Remind children to begin their writing on the left side of the page and continue toward the right side. Suggest that children who have difficulty make a small dot at the top left of their paper. Explain that they can use the dot as a guide for where to begin.

Letters—Uppercase and Lowercase

Introduce Create a set of Bingo cards using various combinations of upper and lowercase letters, one letter per space on a card. Play a game of Bingo with children reviewing the differences between the uppercase and lowercase version of each letter.

Model Write the following sentences on the board: *Our class is going on a field trip. We will go to the Health World Museum on Monday.* Point out the use of uppercase and lowercase letters. Explain that uppercase letters are used at the beginning of each new sentence, for the first letter of all important words in titles, and at the beginning of names of people, specific places, and dates.

Summarize/Apply Have children select a piece of their own writing. Invite them to exchange papers with a partner to review one another's work. Encourage children to pay special attention to the correct use of uppercase and lowercase letters.

Basic Skills

Margins

Introduce Write a short paragraph on two different pieces of lined chart paper. On one paper, begin writing at the very top and write from one edge to the other. On the second, use standard margins. Ask children to compare the two samples. Help them see that the second paragraph is spaced correctly on the page, making the writing easy to read.

Model Introduce the term *margins* to children. Tell children that they should leave a one-inch space, or margin, at the top, sides, and bottom of their papers when they write. Using a ruler, help children measure the length of one inch on one of their fingers. Demonstrate how to use a finger to create a margin.

Summarize/Apply Remind children to use the correct margins when they write sentences on a piece of paper.

Spacing Between Words and Letters

Introduce Write the following on the board.

Tod ayismy birthd ay p arty.

Ask children what they see wrong with the sentence. If necessary, point out that the spacing between the words and letters is not correct.

Model Rewrite the sentence using the correct spacing. Explain to children that letters in the same word are written next to each other, but there should be a space left between words. Help children create this space by giving each child a craft stick. Have children draw a face on one end of the stick, then use Spacer to help them leave enough room between words in a sentence. You may wish to demonstrate for children how to use the stick for correct spacing.

Summarize/Apply Suggest that children use Spacer to help them space words in their independent writing. Remind them that letters within the same word are written without a space between them.

Spacing Between Sentences

Introduce Read aloud a few sentences from a favorite storybook as children follow along. Run the sentences together as if the ending punctuation was not present. Ask children to comment on your reading. Elicit that if the sentences did not have enough space between them, they would be hard to read.

Model Write the following sentences on the board: *The fair is coming to town. I love to see the animals! Do you think you can go?* Ask volunteers how they know where one sentence ends and the next begins. Explain that sentences end with a punctuation mark and new sentences begin with a capital letter. Writers leave space between the end punctuation and the first word of the new sentence to make the sentences easier to read. Model placing two fingers to create a space.

Summarize/Apply When writing, encourage children to place two fingers at the end of each sentence to make a space before beginning the next sentence.

Top-to-Bottom Progression

Introduce Select a familiar rhyme. Write each sentence of the rhyme on separate sentence strips. Invite volunteers to arrange the sentences in the correct order in a pocket chart. Read the finished rhyme together as a class. Point out that the sentences are arranged in order from top to bottom in the chart.

Model Create a sample paragraph. Display it on an overhead projector or write it on chart paper. Help children see that the paper is organized so that the writing begins at the top of the page and continues toward the bottom, from left to right. Point out that the heading or title also appears at the top of the page.

Summarize/Apply Remind children to begin their writing at the top of the paper and move toward the bottom, from left to right, as they continue.

Basic Skills

Writing Name, Date, and Title on Paper

Introduce Display a sample homework paper without a name, date, or title. Invite children to identify what is missing. Ask them why they think it is important to include this information on their work.

Model Use a piece of chart paper to show children how to head their independent work. Write *name, date,* and *title* in appropriate places on the paper. Next to each word, write an example of the item. Then, display the paper. Suggest children refer to this guide each time they begin a new assignment.

Summarize/Apply Invite children to look through the writing they are currently working on to check that they have included a proper heading.

Circling Spelling Errors to Be Corrected

Introduce Write these sentences on the board:

Mary picked a flowr.

What colar is your nu bike?

Guide children to identify the misspelled words *flowr, colar, and nu.* As you circle these words, point out that circling them will help a writer remember which words need to be corrected.

Model Display a draft paragraph that includes several spelling errors. Work with children to identify the misspelled words by circling them. Point out that once all errors have been found, children can easily go back and correct the misspelled words using a dictionary, word bank, or personal spelling list.

Summarize/Apply Invite children to select a current draft of their writing. Have them reread the draft and circle any misspelled words. Suggest they use a dictionary or other resource to check any words they are unsure of.

Writing Process

Brainstorming

Introduce Play a brainstorming game using a word such as *food*. Ask children to say the first word that comes to mind, such as *hungry, cookies, dinner,* and *sandwiches*. Tell children that they have been brainstorming or thinking of ideas about the subject of food.

Model Write the word *school* in the center of the board. Invite children to brainstorm ideas about school. Create a web as you record their ideas. Explain that there are no right or wrong answers in brainstorming, and that brainstorming can help a person think of writing topics, ideas for an art project, or ways to solve a problem.

Summarize/Apply Remind children that brainstorming is a great way to find writing ideas. Suggest they use brainstorming the next time they need an idea to write about.

Conducting an Interview

Introduce Ask children if they have seen someone being interviewed on a news program. Invite them to share what they saw and heard. Explain that in an interview one person asks another person questions to learn more about that person or a topic.

Model Write these questions on an index card.

1. *What is your favorite color?*
2. *What is your favorite animal?*
3. *Do you have any pets? If so, what kind?*

Invite two children to sit facing each other in front of the class. Have one child ask the partner the questions on the card. Explain that this is an example of an interview. Suggest that, in a real interview, the "reporter" would write down or tape-record what was said.

Summarize/Apply Have children write a few interview questions to ask a partner. Allow time for pairs to conduct their interviews. Then invite children to share the information they learned about their partners.

Writing Process

Conferencing—Reading Your Work to Yourself

Introduce Write these directions on the board: *Take out your math bucket. Finish your addition and coloring problems.* Tell children that if they tried to read and follow the directions, they would probably be confused. Elicit that there are mistakes in the directions. Explain that if you had read over your writing first, you would have noticed the mistakes and changed them.

Model Display a short paragraph that has some mistakes. Tell children that you have written the paragraph and are now ready to check your work. Read the paragraph aloud, identifying and correcting the errors in the writing.

Summarize/Apply Suggest that children select a piece of writing they are working on and read it to themselves to catch any mistakes.

Conferencing—How to Be a Good Listener

Introduce Provide paper, then read the following directions aloud and instruct children to follow them exactly: *Draw a square in the center of your paper. Next draw a triangle above the square. Then draw a circle in the center of the square.* Draw the figures on the board and have children check their work. Point out that in order to draw the correct picture, they had to listen carefully.

Model Guide children to list skills for being a good listener, such as *think about what the person is saying, don't interrupt, look at the person speaking.* Explain that when children are conferencing with partners, they must be good listeners.

Summarize/Apply Have children select a piece of writing and read it to a partner. Invite partners to listen and then ask questions. Remind children to be good listeners.

Conferencing—How to Make Suggestions

Introduce Make a drawing of a simple house. Tell children that you would like their help in making your drawing better. Invite them to share some suggestions on what you could do. Remind them that they should be considerate of your feelings as they share their ideas. Help them to think of ways to phrase their suggestions so that they are helpful, positive, and focused on the topic.

Model Share a first draft of a story written by a child from a previous year without identifying the writer. Ask children to imagine they are conferencing with this writer. Work with children to develop a list of suggestions that would be appropriate and helpful to the writer in improving his or her work.

Summarize/Apply Help children summarize what they have learned by working with them to make a list of things to remember when making suggestions about their partner's writing. Display the list for children to refer to.

Conferencing—Questions to Ask

Introduce Bring in a personal memento or souvenir to share with the class. Do not share any details about the item, but rather invite children to ask you questions. Help children to recognize the kinds of questions that require you to give more than a simple yes, no, or fact for an answer.

Model Write the following question words on the board: *Who, What, When, Where, How,* and *Why.* Review these question words with children and provide an example of a question using each word. Explain that asking a writer questions can help focus where the writing is unclear or provide ideas for additional information to include.

Summarize/Apply Organize the class into small groups. Display a sample writing piece and invite each group to compose a list of five questions they would ask if conferencing with a writer. Discuss each group's answers as a class.

Writing Process

Crossing Out Unwanted Words

Introduce Write the following on chart paper, speaking each word as you write: *My favorite color is blue.* Stop and tell children that you meant to write *green,* not *blue.* Ask how you might change what you wrote.

Model Rewrite the sentence three more times. On the first sentence, attempt to erase the word *blue.* Show how the paper smudges and may even tear. Scribble out *blue* in the second sentence. Point out that the big mark is messy and distracting. In the third sentence, mark a single line through *blue* and write *green* above it. Suggest that children use this method because it is neat and clearly shows the change.

Summarize/Apply Invite children to use a simple line to cross out unwanted words when they are working on a draft or revision.

Deleting Unimportant Information

Introduce Display the following directions for riding a bike and read them aloud.

> *Put your feet on the pedals. Push down on one pedal until you begin to move. Red bikes are nice. Steer by turning the handlebars as you ride.*

Ask children what the directions are for.

Model Explain that information in their writing should always be about the main, or most important, idea. Reread the directions. Ask children if each sentence tells the reader how to ride a bike. Then draw a line through the sentence *Red bikes are nice.* Tell children this sentence is not important because it does not give any information about bike riding.

Summarize/Apply Have individuals or partners review their writing. Ask them to draw a line through information that doesn't belong.

Draft and Final Copy

Introduce Write the words *draft* and *final copy* on the board. Explain that a draft is a "working copy" of a writing piece. Help children to see that writers use the drafting stage to get their ideas down on paper. The writer marks any changes on the draft copy, then recopies the piece, making all the changes. The resulting product should be neat and ready for publication. This is called a final copy.

Model Without naming the writer, display a draft and final copy of a story written by a child from a previous year. Point out any changes the writer made on the draft copy. Then read the draft and final copy aloud as children follow along. Discuss how the changes in the draft improved the writing in the final copy.

Summarize/Apply Have children select a piece of their writing that is currently in draft form. Invite them to review the draft and mark needed revisions and proofreading errors to be fixed. Then children can recopy the draft into a neat final copy.

Expanding Sentences With Adjectives

Introduce Show children a flower or picture of a flower. Then write the following sentence on the board: *I see a flower.* Ask children to comment on how well your writing describes the flower. Elicit that you did not give any details. Invite children to suggest descriptive words you could add. Write responses on the board. Explain that words describing a person, place, or thing are called adjectives.

Model Write the following on the board.

> *The boy rode a _____ bike.*
>
> *My aunt has a _____ dog.*

Invite children to make the sentences more interesting by suggesting descriptive words to fill in the blanks.

Summarize/Apply Have children work with partners to look through classroom books to find examples of descriptive words. Invite partners to list the words they find and keep the lists to refer to when writing.

Writing Process

Identifying Audience

Introduce Ask children if they have ever been to a play or concert. Tell them that as listeners or observers, they were part of the audience. Write the word *audience* on the board. Explain that the people who read their writing are also an audience. Before writers begin to write, they think about who will read their writing. Knowing their audience helps them use the right words.

Model Read aloud a paragraph from a magazine article, one in which the author writes for a specific audience, such as parents or baseball fans. Discuss how the author thought of the audience and then chose words to match the interests of that audience.

Summarize/Apply Help children list all the people or groups of people who might be the audience for their writing. Post the list for children to review and think about before they write.

Identifying Purpose

Introduce Read aloud and discuss short excerpts from a personal narrative and an informative article. Explain that each writer had a different reason for writing. One writer wanted to tell the audience a story. The other writer wanted to inform the audience. Tell children that the main reason for writing is called the purpose. Point out the main purposes for writing—to learn, to tell a story, to describe, to inform, and to persuade. Writers think about their purpose before they write so they can share their ideas in just the right way.

Model Write on the board a five-column chart with the purposes for writing as heads. Explain each purpose and write an example of a writing idea to fit in each category. Work with children to add more writing ideas for each purpose.

Summarize/Apply Display the purpose chart for children to refer to as they write independently. You may wish to have children review their past writing and identify the purpose of each piece.

Identifying Main Idea

Introduce Write the word *school* on the board. Ask children to brainstorm a list of ideas about school, such as favorite subjects, what the school building is like, or games played at recess. Explain that each idea could be a main idea about the topic of *school*. A main idea tells about a specific part of a topic. The details that tell about each main idea are written together.

Model Work with children to write two short paragraphs about two of their ideas. Introduce to children that when they write to inform, rather than write to tell a story, the main idea is often stated in the first sentence. This is the topic sentence. Point out that the remaining sentences support the main idea by adding details and important information.

Summarize/Apply Have children revisit a longer piece of writing to find the main ideas and to check that each main idea's details are grouped together.

Identifying Topic

Introduce Read aloud a science or news article. Then ask: *What was the article about?* If you had to tell what it was about in one word, what would it be? Explain that the general subject of a piece of writing is called a topic. A topic can often be described in one or two words. Tell children that when they write, they should begin with one topic and then choose one to three main ideas that can be supported with details.

Model Help children see there are many ways to find a writing topic. Work with them to develop a list of activities that are helpful in identifying topics for writing, such as reading journals or logs, looking through photographs, thinking about what they like or dislike most, or talking with partners or family members about what they think is interesting.

Summarize/Apply Invite groups to select a strategy from the list and come up with as many writing topics as they can. Encourage them to use only one or two words to describe their topics. Have groups share their ideas.

Writing Process

Inserting a Sentence by Drawing an Arrow

Introduce Display and read the following sentences: *There was a big surprise waiting for me. I couldn't believe my eyes. How did it get there?* Tell children that you forgot to add a sentence that belongs after the first sentence. Ask them to suggest how to add it.

Model Point out that when writing, you may forget to include important information or you may decide to add new information. Write the following sentence below the other display sentences: *I found a package on the table.* Show children how to circle the new sentence and draw an arrow from the sentence to the spot in the story where it belongs. Explain that this will help them remember where to include the sentence when they make their final copy.

Summarize/Apply Remind children that when drafting or revising, they can insert a new sentence by circling it and using an arrow to show its placement.

Inserting a Word or Phrase Using a Caret

Introduce Write the following sentences on the board: *My friend has a dog. He likes to play.* Tell children that you forgot to write the dog's name. Ask them for suggestions on how you could add it. Then, introduce the caret symbol to children.

Model Explain that writers use the caret to add words or phrases without rewriting the entire draft. Point out that new words can be written over the caret and then added into the next or final draft. Demonstrate this by writing a caret and *named Boo* at the end of the first sentence.

Summarize/Apply Have children review a current writing draft. Encourage them to use a caret when they want to add words or phrases to their writing.

Making a Letter Lowercase Using a Slash

Introduce Tell children that writers use special marks called revising and editing marks to make corrections in their writing. Explain that one such mark is a diagonal slash mark. It is used to show that an uppercase letter should be written as a lowercase letter. Write *D* on the board and make a slash through it to demonstrate how the mark looks.

Model Write the following sentences on the board.

> *The Ball belongs To Jim.*
> *This Book has a Ripped Cover.*

Ask volunteers to identify the mistakes in capitalization (*Ball, To, Book, Ripped, Cover*). Call on volunteers to make a slash through each capital letter as it is identified.

Summarize/Apply Remind children that the slash mark is a shortcut to help them identify capital letters that should be written as lowercase. Suggest that children use this mark as they review their own writing.

Making a Letter Uppercase Using Three Lines

Introduce Write this sentence on the board: *the book belongs to cindy.* Ask children if there are any mistakes in the sentence. Elicit that the words *The* and *Cindy* should be capitalized. Have children explain why. Introduce the idea that a writer can draw three short lines under a letter to show that the letter should be capitalized in the next or final draft.

Model Remind children that capital letters signal the beginning of a new sentence and are used to begin the names of specific people, places, and things. Explain that if a lowercase letter is used instead of an uppercase letter, draw three horizontal lines under the letter to show that it should be capitalized. Demonstrate with the example sentence.

Summarize/Apply Have children review a draft they are working on, proofread it for lowercase letters that should be capitalized, and use three short lines to mark changes needed.

189

Writing Process

Managing Time in Writer's Workshop

Introduce Role-play a child during a writer's workshop. For example, shuffle through the papers in your writing folder. Drop your papers and pick them up. Go sharpen your pencil. When you finally return to your desk, look at the clock and notice that writing time is over. Ask children to help you identify all the reasons you had no time to write.

Model Work with children to identify ways to manage time in writer's workshop. Record their ideas on chart paper. See examples below.

Sharpen your pencils at the beginning of the day.

Keep blank paper in your writing folder.

Work silently unless conferencing.

Display the list as a reference.

Summarize/Apply Remind children to use their time well. Spend a few minutes as needed before each writer's workshop reviewing time management strategies.

Publishing—Adding Illustrations

Introduce Share a picture book with children. Read the story aloud and direct children's attention to each picture. Discuss how the pictures add meaning to the story.

Model Explain that illustrations are pictures or photos that are added to writing to make it more interesting, to add meaning to words, and to make the message clearer. Display a sample paragraph and read it aloud. Have children share ideas for what kind of illustration could be added. Discuss where the illustration could be placed on the paper.

Summarize/Apply Invite children to choose a piece of writing they have completed. Ask them to review it to see if it could be improved by adding an illustration.

Publishing—About the Author

Introduce Ask children if they have ever wondered about the authors who wrote their favorite books. Invite children to share some of the kinds of information they would like to know about these authors. Record their answers on the board.

Model Read a familiar book to children that has an author biography. Turn to the biography. Show children the picture of the author, if included, and share the information about his or her life. Tell children that many books include a section about the author. Explain that this section is added so readers can understand how and why an author chose a topic for a story, as well as to help readers "connect" with the author so they are more interested in his or her books. Suggest that children consider adding such a section to the next story they write.

Summarize/Apply Invite children to write a paragraph about themselves. Provide additional examples of author biographies so children will have a model for how to write one.

Publishing—Book Dedication

Introduce Display several children's books that include dedications. Point out the dedication page. Explain that the dedication is a special message written by the author as a way to mention someone special and show the author's respect, thanks, or love for that person or group of people.

Model Organize the class into small groups. Provide each group with books that have dedications. Ask groups to find the dedications and copy them. Invite them to read their lists. Help with any difficult words. Have children share who they think the people mentioned might be to the authors, as well as which dedications they think are funny, serious, or unusual.

Summarize/Apply Invite children to think about whom they would like to dedicate their next story or book to. Then have them write a dedication. Encourage children to try writing it different ways to see which they prefer.

Writing Process

Publishing—Title Page

Introduce Display the title page of a picture book and tell children that this page is called the title page. Ask children to tell you what information they notice on this page. Elicit that the title of the book and the author's name are included. The page may also have an illustration, the name of the illustrator, and information about the company that published the book. Explain each section.

Model Demonstrate how to write a title page for a story. Ask a volunteer to name an original title. Write the title at the top of the paper. Next, add your name as the author and illustrator. Add the date, your room number, or your school's name. Review each element. Remind children that the title page is placed at the beginning of a story after the cover.

Summarize/Apply Have children practice creating title pages for stories they are currently writing. Leave your sample title page on display for children to refer to as they write.

Publishing—Making a Book

Introduce Display several student-published books in different forms. Invite children to discuss how the books were made. Explain that there are many ways to publish writing in the form of a book.

Model Set up a book-making center. Display several models, as well as visual instructions for constructing different kinds of books. Include materials, such as many colors and sizes of paper, hole punchers, cardboard, yarn, staples, and other art supplies. Using a sample story, demonstrate one way to make a book. Emphasize that the pages of the book must be placed in the correct order.

Summarize/Apply Assist children in preparing their writing for publishing. Make sure children know how to use the publishing center independently so they can create finished products with little or no assistance.

Reading Old Pieces of Writing for Revision or New Topic

Introduce Have children think about some of the stories they have written this year. Encourage them to look through their portfolios or writing folders to help them remember. Ask them if they can think of any ways to use their old pieces of writing. Explain that an "old story" can be revised into a new or better story or used to find topics for new stories.

Model Display a story that you have written and read it aloud. Work with children to brainstorm possible ways the story could be revised and improved. Then invite children to use ideas from the story to create a list of new writing topics.

Summarize/Apply Have children select a piece of writing from their portfolios or writing folders to revise or use as a springboard for ideas for new writing topics. Encourage children to list their new ideas.

Replacing an Overused Word

Introduce Read a page of dialogue from a familiar children's book, using the word *said* for every character identifier. Ask children what word they heard the most. Write the word *said* on chart paper, explaining that this word is often overused. Ask children if they can think of words that could be used instead, such as *shouted, told,* or *whispered.*

Model Work with children to create a list of other overused words, such as *very, fun, nice, good, happy, sad,* and *bad.* Invite children to help you brainstorm more interesting words for each overused word. Write the suggestions on chart paper. Display the list and encourage children to add words as they think of them. Explain that good writers try to replace overused words in their writing with more interesting, descriptive words.

Summarize/Apply Have partners work together to review current drafts to see if there are overused words that could be replaced with more interesting words.

Writing Process

Rewriting a Confused Sentence

Introduce Write the following on the board: *Read page 24 from your chair in the science book*. Invite a volunteer to read the sentence aloud and try to follow the directions. Ask children why the directions are difficult to follow. Elicit that the sentence is confusing.

Model Tell children that you wanted the person to read page 24 of the science book while sitting in his or her chair. Have them suggest ways to rewrite the sentence so that the directions are clearer, such as *Read page 24 of the science book while sitting in your chair*. When rewriting confusing sentences, children can reword them or make one sentence into two clear ones.

Summarize/Apply Have children review a current draft. Encourage them to read aloud so they hear how each sentence sounds. Suggest they rewrite sentences that sound confusing.

Setting Up Workshop Rules

Introduce Invite two children to work on a writing assignment while the rest of the class talks and gets ready for another activity. After a few minutes, discuss with the class what took place that would make it hard for the writers to concentrate.

Model Explain that writers need to be able to focus on their writing as they work. This means that everyone in the class must cooperate. Work with children to come up with rules to help make writing time go smoothly. Start off by suggesting rules such as these.

- *During writing time, be as quiet as possible and don't bother your neighbor.*
- *When you finish, put your writing in your portfolio or draw an illustration for your writing.*
- *Listen quietly as authors share their writing. Save your questions or comments for the end.*

Summarize/Apply Write children's rules on posterboard and display them. Before the next few writing sessions, take a few minutes to review the rules.

Sequencing Events Using a Story Map

Introduce Recall with children a familiar story. Write three "main idea" sentences on the board, one from the beginning, middle, and end of the story. Ask children which sentence tells about each part of the story.

Model Write *Beginning, Middle*, and *End* vertically on chart paper and work with children to create a map about the story. Explain that the beginning introduces the characters, setting, and problem. The middle tells the main events in order. The end tells how the problem is solved. As you discuss the story, fill in the parts of the story map.

Summarize/Apply Give children story maps to help them organize their writing. (See page 36.) Have them use the maps to sequence the events of their stories before they write.

Using Transition Words

Introduce Tell children a simple story, leaving out transition words: *We went on a trip. We swam in a motel pool. I was glad to see my dog*. Explain that the story is hard to follow because it tells three ideas that are not linked together.

Model Display transition words and phrases such as *The next day, Later, In the morning, After awhile, Finally*, and *Next*. Tell children good writers use words or phrases like these to make writing clearer and to help readers move from one idea to the next. Rewrite the story on the board, using underlined transitional phrases to link story events: *Last Saturday, we went on a trip. That night we swam in a motel pool. The next day I was glad to see my dog.*

Summarize/Apply Remind children to use transition words to help readers move from one idea to the next. Have children review a draft to find places where they could add transitions to make their ideas more clear.

Writing Process

Using a Portfolio

Introduce Ask children to talk about how they organize and keep track of their pictures, school supplies, and other materials at home.

Model In advance, prepare a sample writing portfolio that shows the kinds of work you want children to keep as well as how items should be organized (by date, by genre, stapled, paper clipped, and so on). For example, children might keep only their best work, or organize and keep everything related to a writing project, including writing ideas, prewriting notes, edited drafts, and final copies. Tell children that writers need to be organized, too. Display the sample portfolio, discussing the contents one item at a time. Model how to organize the papers with the newest writing on top and how to clip or staple together all the pages that relate to an individual project.

Summarize/Apply Give children folders or help them make their own. Have children decorate their portfolios and place their writing inside.

Using Revising and Editing Marks

Introduce Make a copy of page 30 and display it. Point to the revising and editing marks and explain to children that they can use these marks to make corrections and changes to their writing.

Model Write this sentence on the board, including the mistakes: *i sau a dog on the way to.* Elicit from children that *i* should be capitalized, *saw* is misspelled, and a word has been left off the end of the sentence. Use the revising and editing marks to make corrections.

Summarize/Apply Post the chart and provide copies for children to refer to. Remind children that using these marks saves time and paper. Encourage them to use the marks as they revise and edit their writing.

Using, Sharing, and Replacing Supplies

Introduce Ask children what supplies they think a writer needs, such as pencils, pens, crayons, markers, drawing paper, and lined paper. As children watch, place the supplies they mention in a writing supply center, adding other items, such as staplers and tape.

Model Tell children that everyone needs to help keep the writing center well-stocked and organized. Ask what class members can do to help. Offer suggestions like these:

- *Take only what you need.*
- *When you finish, put things back where you found them.*
- *If you take the last supply, tell the teacher.*
- *If some supplies, such as the stapler, are being used by someone else, do something else while you wait.*

Summarize/Apply Write the guidelines children suggest and display them for reference.

Writer's Craft

Dialogue

Introduce Talk with two children about the weather while the rest of the class listens. Then, explain to the class that you and the volunteers were having a conversation, or dialogue.

Model On the board, write your conversation using quotation marks. Explain that writers use dialogue to make a story more interesting and to move the events along. When writing dialogue, writers let the reader know which character is speaking by using phrases such as *asked Mark, he said,* or *said Jasmine.* Point out that these words are not spoken by the characters. Ask volunteers to underline the spoken words in your model.

Summarize/Apply Remind children that when they write dialogue, they should use quotation marks and identify the speaker with a phrase like *he said* or *she said.*

Writer's Craft

Language—Purpose and Audience

Introduce Tell children that before writers begin, they think about their purpose (why they are writing) and their audience (who will read their writing). A writer's purpose can be to learn, to tell a story, to inform, to describe, or to persuade. An audience can be formal (such as the teacher) or informal (such as a friend).

Model Read these sentences aloud: *The field trip was a blast. You have to come with us next time!* Then say these: *Our class took a field trip to the zoo. We visited the ape house where we learned about baboons.* Ask children which sentences sound like something they would say to a friend and which sound like an oral report. Discuss the differences in purpose and audience.

Summarize/Apply Have children review their current drafts to identify the purpose and audience for their writing and then decide if their language should be formal or informal.

Point of View—Third-Person

Introduce Ask a volunteer to describe a favorite story character. Write on the board any third-person pronouns the speaker uses.

Model Tell children that when writers use a person's name, or words like *he, she, her, him,* and *they,* they are telling about a character instead of letting a character speak for himself or herself. This is called using the third-person point of view. Model third-person versus first-person: *I went to the store. Mark went to the store.* Discuss the differences in the sentences.

Summarize/Apply Have children review their drafts of stories about other people or characters to see if they've used words like *he, she, him, her,* and *they* to tell the story from the characters' point of view.

Reader Interest—Writing a Conclusion

Introduce Read aloud or summarize a familiar short story with a strong ending or conclusion. Stop before the conclusion and ask children what is missing.

Model Explain that all writing needs a conclusion to let the reader know the writing is finished. In a story, the conclusion may be a solution to a problem. In nonfiction, the conclusion may tell how something ends or how the writer feels about the topic. Write this paragraph on chart paper: *Our school day begins with reading and math. We have lunch and recess. In the afternoon we learn about science.* Then have children help you write a conclusion. You might end with *At three o'clock, we go home.*

Summarize/Apply Remind children that a missing conclusion leaves the reader wondering what happened. Have children review a draft in their portfolios to see if the writing has a conclusion or if it could be revised to give it a better one.

Reader Interest—Writing a Strong Title

Introduce Read aloud the titles of a few books in the classroom library or from a bibliography of children's books. Ask children to discuss the titles, tell which books they would like to read, and explain why a title sounds interesting.

Model Explain that a good title makes readers want to read a piece of writing. If a book's title is boring, readers may not pick up that book. They may miss out on a good story because they do not think it will be interesting. Write "My Vacation" on the board. Have children talk about things they would like to do on a vacation. Then have them use details from their discussion to brainstorm more interesting titles.

Summarize/Apply Have children take another look at their revised drafts to see if they can make their titles more interesting.

Writer's Craft

Reader Interest—Writing an Attention-Grabbing Beginning

Introduce Talk about choosing a book at the library. Ask children how they decide whether a book will be fun to read. If needed, offer these suggestions: *Look for an author you like. Look for an interesting title. Look at the pictures. Read the first page.*

Model Point out that the beginning of a story should grab the reader's attention right away. If it does not, the reader may not finish the story. The beginning should make the reader want to know more. Read aloud an interesting story beginning. Ask children what the beginning makes them want to know.

Summarize/Apply Have pairs of children talk about how they could make the beginning of current story drafts more interesting.

Rhyme

Introduce Say: *Now it's time to make a rhyme.* Right *time* and *rhyme* on the board and explain that they are rhyming words because their endings sound the same, even though the spelling is different.

Model Invite children to help you make up some poems with pairs of rhyming words. Have children suggest rhyming word pairs. List the words they say and then choose one pair to use in a short poem. With children's help, write a short, easy rhyme such as *In the spring, the robins sing.* Explain that rhymes are often used by poets and other writers who want to make their writing more interesting.

Summarize/Apply Remind children that words that end with the same sound rhyme. Have partners check to see if current drafts of poems could be improved by adding rhyming words.

Rhythm

Introduce Beat out a short rhythm pattern on your desk and have children echo it by clapping. Tell children they clapped out a rhythm pattern. Explain that songs and poems have rhythm.

Model Have children sing "The Farmer in the Dell." Repeat the first two lines as children clap along. Clap the rhythm without the song and point out that some claps are louder. Those claps stand for accented syllables. Write on the board *The FARmer in the DELL.* Point out that the syllables written with capital letters are accented syllables or words. Explain that writers of songs, poems, and other works often choose their words very carefully to create a special rhythm. Using rhythm keeps readers interested and makes writing more interesting and fun to read.

Summarize/Apply Remind children that many songs and poems have a rhythm. You may want to have children review their descriptive writing to see if rhythm would make the writing more interesting.

Sentence Variety— Beginnings

Introduce Ask children why they like to play different games. Elicit that playing the same game all the time would become boring. Tell children that writers use variety to keep their writing from becoming boring. One thing they can change is the way they begin their sentences, such as not beginning every sentence with the word *I* in a personal narrative.

Model Tell children they can make their writing more interesting if they change the order of the words in some of the sentences. Write *I play soccer every Saturday* on a sentence strip. Cut the strip apart between *soccer* and *every*. Model how to arrange the sentence parts to form two different sentences: *I play soccer every Saturday* and *Every Saturday I play soccer.* Write the sentences on the board, capitalizing and punctuating them correctly.

Summarize/Apply Have children check their writing to see if changing the beginning of some of their sentences might give their writing more variety and interest.

Writer's Craft

Sentences—Combining Short, Choppy Sentences

Introduce Write on the board *We packed the picnic basket. We walked to the park. It rained. We went home*. Ask a volunteer to read the paragraph. Elicit from children that it is choppy because the sentences are all short.

Model Tell children that writing is smoother and has a better rhythm when it has both short and long sentences. Model how to combine the first two sentences that have the same subject by writing a sentence with two predicates: *We packed the picnic basket and walked to the park*. Model how to combine the last two sentences by joining them with a comma and *so*: *It rained, so we went home*.

Summarize/Apply Have children look through their writing portfolios to find writing that could be made better by combining short, choppy sentences.

Sentences—Expanding by Adding Details and Description

Introduce Hold up an animal picture or a stuffed toy and say a short sentence such as *This is a teddy bear*. Ask children to name words that describe the animal picture or toy. List their adjectives in a word web.

Model On the board, write *The teddy bear is cute*. Point out that the sentence does not tell much about the teddy bear. Ask for suggestions about how children can use the describing words in the web to expand the sentence and paint a word picture of the teddy bear. Write the new sentence under the first sentence. Your sentence may be similar to this one: *The small, brown, fuzzy teddy bear is cute*.

Summarize/Apply Invite children to look through their current drafts to see if there are sentences that could be expanded with descriptive details.

Simile

Introduce Hold up an orange and ask children to name things that have the same shape, such as a basketball, the sun, a full moon, and a bubble. Tell children they can compare the orange to the objects they mentioned.

Model Explain that writers use comparisons to help readers picture an object they are writing about. When the comparison includes the word *like* or *as*, the comparison is called a simile. Write these similes on the board:

> *The sun is like an orange, bright and round.*

> *That orange is as round as a basketball.*

Ask volunteers to underline *like* and *as*. Call on other children to draw arrows between the two objects that are being compared *(sun > orange, orange > basketball)*.

Summarize/Apply Invite children to review current drafts to see if their writing could be improved by adding similes.

Grammar and Usage

Adjectives—Common

Introduce Hold up a book and ask questions about it, such as *What color is the book? Is it thick or thin? Is it simple or hard to read? Is it funny or serious?* List children's answers on chart paper, leaving space at the top for a title.

Model Explain that the list shows describing words, or adjectives. Write *Adjectives* at the top of the chart. Tell children that adjectives are words that describe people, places, things, or ideas and come before the nouns they describe. Write the sentence patterns below. Complete the first sentence with a word from the chart. Ask volunteers to complete the others.

> The _____ flower is pretty.

> That was a _____ test.

> The _____ joke made me laugh.

Summarize/Apply Have children review their drafts to see if they could add adjectives to make the writing more interesting.

Grammar and Usage

Adverbs—Where, When, How

Introduce Give children directions, such as *stand up now, stay there, wave wildly,* and *clap loudly.* Explain that they knew where, when, and how to do the actions because of the adverbs *there, now, wildly,* and *loudly.*

Model Tell children that adverbs are words that describe verbs—they tell how, where, or when a subject does an action. Writers often use adverbs to describe how, when, or where a character is doing something. Write these on the board:

> *A turtle moves slowly.*
>
> *The game starts early.*
>
> *My grandmother lives here.*

Ask volunteers to circle the adverbs. *(slowly, early, here)* Have other children write *where, when,* or *how* beside the sentence to show what the adverb tells. *(how, when, where)*

Summarize/Apply Have partners look through their drafts to find examples of each kind of adverb and perhaps add a few more.

Complete Sentences

Introduce Ask two volunteers to pantomime playing baseball. Have another child narrate the action. Write a complete sentence the narrator uses on the board.

Model Tell children that the words on the board form a sentence because they tell a complete thought. They tell what is done and who or what does it. Write the following on the board: *Andy and Jim. Jen pitched the ball. Ran around the bases.* Point out that the only complete sentence is *Jen pitched the ball* because it tells a whole thought. It tells who did something (Jen) and what Jen did (pitched the ball).

Summarize/Apply Have children check their current drafts to make sure all their sentences are complete.

Declarative Sentences

Introduce Choose a science topic children are studying and call on volunteers to tell a fact about the topic. Tell children that the sentences they used are telling sentences, or declarative sentences, because they make a statement.

Model Explain that telling sentences give information. Other kinds of sentences ask a question, give a command, or share a strong feeling. Telling sentences begin with a capital letter and end with a period. Write one of the children's facts on the board as an example. Then read aloud from an easy reader, pausing after each sentence to let children tell whether or not the sentence they heard is a declarative sentence.

Summarize/Apply You may wish to have children find telling sentences in their own writing. Remind them that their telling sentences should begin with capital letters and end with periods.

Exclamatory Sentences

Introduce Tell children that if someone dropped a book in a quiet room, you might say *That noise scared me!* Tell children that the sentence you just said was an exclamatory sentence—a sentence that shows strong feeling.

Model Explain that writers use exclamatory sentences to show strong feelings like surprise and anger. Write these on the board:

> *That really makes me angry!*
>
> *What a great catch!*
>
> *I love that song!*
>
> *Help, the tiger is escaping!*

Have volunteers circle the exclamation points. Explain that exclamatory sentences end with exclamation points. An exclamation point tells a reader to read the sentence with expression. Read each sentence above and have children repeat it, matching your intonation.

Summarize/Apply Have children revisit their current writing to see if they used or could add exclamatory sentences to show strong feeling.

Grammar and Usage

Interrogative Sentences

Introduce Walk around the room and ask a volunteer *What is your name?* Continue asking other volunteers questions, such as *How old are you? What is your favorite color? Which school subject do you like best? Why do you like that subject?*

Model Explain that the questions you asked are interrogative sentences, or asking sentences. Write one of the sentences on the board. Point out that interrogative sentences begin with a capital letter and end with a question mark. Add that questions often begin with special words, such as *what, who, when, where, why*, and *how*. Writers often use questions in dialogue or in making a point for the reader to consider.

Summarize/Apply Have children review their drafts to see if they have used interrogative sentences to ask questions, and if so, to check that the sentences end with a question mark.

Nouns—Common

Introduce Say: *A boy and a girl went up the hill to get a pail of water.* Ask: *Which words in the sentence name people?* (boy, girl) *Which word names a place?* (hill) *Which words name things?* (pail, water) Tell children that these words are called nouns, or common nouns.

Model Write *Nouns* at the top of a sheet of chart paper. Then make three columns headed *Person, Place, Thing*. Have volunteers write the nouns they named *(boy, girl, hill, pail, water)* in the correct column. Ask children to name other common nouns that can fit in each column. If needed, explain that common nouns do not name specific people, places, or things.

Summarize/Apply Have children revisit their drafts to find all the common nouns and tell whether they name people, places, or things.

Nouns—Plural

Introduce Write *s* on a note card. Then write these words in a column on the board or chart paper: *dog, cat, boy, girl.* Call on volunteers to read a word, hold the *s* card at the end, and read the new word. Ask another volunteer to use the two words in sentences.

Model Point out that adding the letter *s* gave each word a whole new meaning. The letter changed a word that names one thing to a word that names more than one. Write *Singular* above the column of words you wrote. Write *Plural* beside it. Add *s* to *dog*, explaining as you write that you are adding *s* to change *dog* into a plural noun. Have volunteers write the plural forms of the other words. Encourage them to follow your model of explaining what they are doing as they write.

Summarize/Apply Remind children that they can add *s* to many nouns to make them plural. You may wish to have children find examples in their own writing.

Nouns—Plural Irregular

Introduce Remind children that *plural* means "more than one" and that most singular nouns can be made plural by adding -*s*. Say: *There are (number of students) childs in this class.* Have children tell you what is wrong with the sentence.

Model Explain that some nouns do not follow the usual rules when they are made plural—they change their spelling and do not add *s*. Write *child, man, woman, goose,* and *mouse* in a column on the board. Have children tell you the plural form of each word. Write *children, men, women, geese,* and *mice* beside the singular forms. Tell children that they will usually recognize a word that doesn't follow the rules when they read it in a sentence, because it will not sound right if they add an *s*. Suggest that children add difficult plural nouns to a word wall, personal dictionary, or learning log to refer to when they write.

Summarize/Apply Have children reread their current drafts to see if they have formed irregular plural nouns correctly.

Grammar and Usage

Nouns—Possessive

Introduce Choose a child whose name does not end with *s* and hold up that child's book. Say, for example, *This is the book of Jim.* Ask children to tell you a shorter and simpler way to say that the book belongs to Jim. *(This is Jim's book.)*

Model Explain that making a noun show that it owns something is called making it possessive. Write *Jim's book* on the board and circle the apostrophe. Have children repeat the word *apostrophe* while drawing one in the air with a finger. Then write *the tail of the dog* and *the game of the boys*. Write *dog's tail* and say that you added an apostrophe and *s* to show one dog's tail. Write *boys' game*. Point out that *boys* is a plural noun. Tell children that to show that the game belongs to more than one boy, you wrote an apostrophe after the *s*.

Summarize/Apply Remind children that to make nouns possessive, they should add an apostrophe and an *s* after singular nouns, an apostrophe after plural nouns that end in *s*, and an *s* plus an apostrophe after nouns that are spelled differently when they are made plural.

Nouns—Proper

Introduce Ask children to name their city or town. On the board, write *city* and the city's name beside it. Add other common nouns, such as *school, teacher, state*, and *street*. Have children name specific nouns for each category.

Model Ask what children notice about the words in the column on the right. *(They all begin with capital letters.)* Explain that the nouns on the left are common nouns because they could name any number of people, places, or things. The nouns on the right name specific people, places, and things, so they are called proper nouns. Important words in proper nouns are always capitalized.

Summarize/Apply Remind children to use capital letters when they write proper nouns.

Nouns—Singular

Introduce Play "I Spy" with children. Choose an object in plain sight in the classroom and give clues about the object until children guess what it is. Write the name of the object and play the game a few more times until you have a short list of singular nouns.

Model Read the list, and write the adjective *one* before each word. Explain that the nouns on the list are called singular nouns because they name one person, place, or thing. Read aloud from an easy reader. Have children raise a hand when they hear a singular noun. Pause after each sentence and have children name the singular noun or nouns.

Summarize/Apply Invite children to find the singular nouns in a current writing draft. Have partners check each other's work.

Predicates

Introduce Write predicates such as *walk on a tightrope, dance across the rug, skip rope, laugh out loud*, and *talk to a friend* on note cards. Invite volunteers to choose a card and act it out for the other children to guess. Write each phrase on the board as children guess the action.

Model Tell children that the phrases on the board start with "doing words." Explain that doing words belong in the part of a sentence that tells what the subject does. The doing part, or action part, of a sentence is called the predicate. Write a complete sentence using a predicate from the list: *Molly skipped rope.* Underline *skipped rope* and explain that this is the complete predicate because it tells what Molly did. Circle *skipped* and tell children that *skipped* is the action word, or verb, in the predicate.

Summarize/Apply Have children use a colored pencil to underline each predicate in a current writing draft. If they find "sentences" that do not have predicates, ask them what they would need to write to add predicates.

Grammar and Usage

Pronouns—Personal

Introduce Write this story on chart paper: *Austin is learning to swim. Austin learned to float, and then Austin learned to kick. Now Austin is learning the dog paddle. Soon Austin will be a real swimmer.* Elicit that the story is repetitive because the name *Austin* is used over and over.

Model Tell children that using pronouns to replace nouns makes writing flow more smoothly. List the personal pronouns *I, me, he, she, you, it, they,* and *we* on the board. Ask which pronoun they would use to replace a boy's name. *(he)* Then write *he* on three sticky notes, and have volunteers replace Austin's name any time but the first time. Reread the story to see how the pronouns improved it.

Summarize/Apply Have children review their writing drafts to see if there are nouns that could be replaced with pronouns.

Pronouns—Possessive

Introduce Pick up a pencil that belongs to you and say: *Is this your pencil? Is it his? Is it hers? It must be mine.*

Model Tell children that the words *your, his, hers,* and *mine* are all pronouns, or words that stand for nouns. Explain that these pronouns are special pronouns that stand for possessive nouns. They are called possessive pronouns because they show who owns something. Write two groups of possessive pronouns on the board: *my, your, his, her, its, our, their* and *mine, yours, his, hers, its, ours, theirs.* Explain that the first group of pronouns come before a noun, as in *Is this your sweater?* The second group stand alone, as in *The sweater is yours.*

Summarize/Apply Have partners review each other's drafts to find any possessive pronouns used. You may wish to have them underline the pronouns with a different-colored pencil.

Subjects

Introduce Ask a volunteer to say a sentence about something that is happening outside or has just happened in the classroom. Write the sentence on the board and circle the complete subject. For example, you might write *The first graders are playing kickball* and circle *The first graders.*

Model Tell children that the words in a sentence that tell who or what is doing the action are called the subject. Write on the board: *The cat chased the mouse. My dad likes dogs. I love butterflies.* Have children find the subject in each sentence. *(The cat, My dad, I)*

Summarize/Apply You may wish to have children revisit a piece of writing and circle all the subjects in a different-colored pencil. If children find just subjects, or incomplete sentences, encourage them to figure out what is missing and write it in.

Verbs—Action

Introduce Play "Simon Says," giving one-word commands, such as *stand, sit, march, hop,* and *wink.* When the game ends, tell children that the words that named the actions they performed are called verbs.

Model Write the sentence patterns below on the board. Model how to fill in the sentences with action verbs. Then have children fill in the sentences with as many different verbs as they can. Examples are provided.

Ben _____ quickly. (runs, walks, races, talks)

Tran _____ loudly. (yells, shouts, claps, sings)

Summarize/Apply Suggest children use action verbs particularly when they write instructions and descriptions. Children can brainstorm action words in a web or list, and then use them in their writing.

Grammar and Usage

Verbs—Irregular

Introduce Look out the window and say: *I see a bird outside. Yesterday I saw one, too. I have seen those birds before.* Write *see, saw,* and *seen* on the board and tell children that all three words are forms of the same verb. *See* is a verb that tells what is happening now; *saw* and *have seen* tell what happened in the past.

Model Explain that *-ed* is added to many verbs when talking about something that happened in the past or when using a helping verb. However, some verbs, called irregular verbs, use different forms. On chart paper, make a three-column chart with the headings *Present, Past,* and *Past with Helping Verbs*. Say: *Today I see* as you write *see* in the first column. Say: *Yesterday I saw* as you write *saw* in the second column. Say: *I have seen* as you write *seen* in the last column. Continue the chart, adding the high-frequency verbs *come, go, give, run,* and *take*.

Summarize/Apply Have partners check each other's drafts for correctly formed irregular verbs. If desired, have children add difficult irregular verbs to a word wall, personal dictionary, or learning log.

Verbs—Past Tense

Introduce Talk with children about an experience the class shared in the past. Tell children that the action verbs they used were past-tense verbs because they described actions that already happened.

Model Explain that past-tense verbs tell about things that happened in the past. Most past-tense verbs are formed by adding *-ed*. Write these sentences on the board: *We walked into the zoo. We looked at the animals.* Have volunteers underline the past-tense verbs.

Summarize/Apply Have partners read one another's drafts of personal narratives or other writing that tells about something that happened in the past. Ask them to check that all the verbs are in past tense.

Verbs—Present Tense

Introduce Invite two volunteers to pretend to make a book. Ask another child to narrate what the actors are doing, using sentences such as *Susan gets a piece of construction paper. Eliot folds it in half. They put the story pages inside.*

Model Write some of the present-tense verbs the narrator used, including verbs that end with *-s* and those that do not. Explain that the verbs used are in the present tense. They tell about something that is happening right now. To decide whether or not to add *-s* to a verb, children must know who is doing the action. If the subject is only one person or thing, the present-tense verb ends with *-s*, as in *Eliot folds it in half.* If the subject is two or more people or things, the verb does not end in *-s*, as in *They put the story pages inside.*

Summarize/Apply Have children check that their present-tense verbs are all formed correctly in their writing.

Mechanics

Apostrophes—to Show Possession

Introduce Show a picture of a dog and ask what things might belong to the dog (collar, bowl, toys). Write *the dog's toys* on the board. Then show a picture of two or more dogs and write *the dogs' toys*.

Model Tell children that nouns that show ownership, or possession, need an apostrophe. If the noun is singular, or names only one thing, writers add an apostrophe and *s*. If the noun is a plural noun that ends with *s*, writers just add an apostrophe. Write on the board: *the girls' shoes* and *the cat's food*. The plural possessive noun *girls'* names more than one girl. The singular possessive noun *cat's* names only one cat. Writers place the apostrophe or apostrophe and *s* based on whether the noun is singular or plural.

Summarize/Apply Remind children to use apostrophes when they write possessive nouns.

Mechanics

Capitalization—Pronoun *I*

Introduce Invite a child to say a sentence that tells what he or she likes to do at school. Write the sentence on the board, but make the word *I* lowercase. Ask what is wrong. Help children understand that the word *I* should always be capitalized since it stands for a person's name.

Model Read this sentence aloud: *Roy and I like to play soccer.* Read it again and ask children to raise their hands when they hear a person's name or a word that stands for a person's name. Write the sentence on the board and ask a volunteer to circle the word *I*. Remind children that the pronoun *I* is capitalized because it stands for a person's name.

Summarize/Apply Ask children to exchange current drafts and check for the correct capitalization of the pronoun *I*.

Capitalization—Calendar Items

Introduce Direct children's attention to your class calendar and invite a volunteer to name a holiday and the month and day it takes place. Write a sentence using all the information. Help children understand that the first letter in the days of the week, the names of months, and important holidays are capitalized.

Model On the board, write: *thanksgiving is on thursday, november 27 this year*. Invite volunteers to read the sentence, then capitalize letters that are the first letter in the name of a holiday, day, or month.

Summarize/Apply Ask children to check current drafts of friendly letters, invitations, and other writing forms that contain calendar items to make sure they have correctly capitalized days, months, and holidays.

Capitalization—States, Streets, Cities

Introduce Write the address of the school, then read it aloud. Invite volunteers to come up and circle each letter that is capitalized and identify the words that name the street, city, and state.

Model Write on the board: *huron avenue, fairfax, virginia*. Guide children to understand that the first letter in the names of streets, cities, and states should be capitalized. Invite volunteers to make the changes. Then write the names of streets, cities, and states on slips of paper. Use lowercase letters instead of capital letters. Call on volunteers to choose words and write them on the board with the correct capitalization.

Summarize/Apply Ask children to exchange drafts with partners to check that the names of streets, cities, and states are capitalized correctly.

Capitalization—Titles of People

Introduce Invite children to introduce themselves with the following titles: Judge, President, King, Queen, Mayor. Write the titles and names on the board. Ask children to read aloud their titles and names and circle each capital letter. Explain that capital letters show that the titles are special and that they are proper nouns—specific names of people.

Model Write these words on the board.

the president	*the queen*
President Lincoln	*Queen Elizabeth*

Discuss the difference between the two uses of a title. Guide children in understanding that a capital letter is not needed when a title is not used with a name.

Summarize/Apply Remind children to write titles of specific people using capital letters at the beginning of the title and the name.

Mechanics

Comma—In Addresses

Introduce Display a sentence with an imaginary address, such as *I live at 43 Storybook Lane, Fun Town, Ohio.* Ask a volunteer to circle the commas. Point out that the commas between the street and the city and between the city and the state make the address easier to read. Explain that in addresses written on envelopes, the street is written on one line and the city and state on a second line, so a comma is not needed at the end of the street name.

Model Write the following on the board, omitting the commas: *Write me at 412 West Branch Road Elk Iowa*. Write a comma on two sticky notes. Invite volunteers to place the commas correctly in the address. Help children understand that a comma is inserted after the name of the street and after the name of the city.

Summarize/Apply Have partners check drafts of friendly letters, invitations, and other writing forms to make sure commas are placed correctly in addresses.

Comma—In Dates

Introduce Write today's date on the board, such as *Monday, March 15, 2002.* Invite volunteers to circle the commas and label the parts (day, month, date, year). Help children understand that the commas make the parts of the date easier to read.

Model Write on the board *I was born on Monday April 17 1993*. Invite volunteers to add the commas using colored chalk. Then invite children to look at a class calendar and tell about recent school events, including the date. Record their sentences on the board, omitting the commas in the date. Have volunteers add the commas and explain their use.

Summarize/Apply Have partners exchange drafts of invitations and other writing forms to make sure commas in dates are placed correctly.

Exclamation Point—At End of Exclamatory Sentence

Introduce Write on the board *We won the game. We won the game!* Read the sentences aloud, the first one with a monotone and the second one using an excited tone. Ask children which version showed excitement (*the second one*). Point out the exclamation point and explain that when a sentence shows strong feeling, it should have an exclamation point rather than a period at the end.

Model Write this sentence on the board:

> *What a great game it was*

Write an exclamation point on a sticky note. Have a child place the exclamation point at the end of the sentence and read it with expression. Remind children that an exclamation point signals strong feelings, such as excitement, joy, fear, pain, or surprise.

Summarize/Apply Remind children to use exclamation points in their writing when they want to show strong feelings.

Period—at the End of a Sentence

Introduce Write two short sentences on the board. Invite volunteers to read aloud each word in both sentences, one at a time. When the end of a sentence is reached, the child saying the last word should put out his or her hand to indicate *stop*. Explain that writers often use a period to signal a stop at the end of a sentence.

Model Write on the board:

> *It will rain all day Wear your raincoat*

Invite volunteers to come to the board, read aloud each sentence, and add a period at the end. Guide children to understand that writers use periods at the ends of sentences to make them easier to read.

Summarize/Apply Invite children to revisit current drafts to make sure they've included periods at the ends of their sentences.

Mechanics

Period—With Initials

Introduce Write the following name on the board, omitting the periods: *L F Hunt*. Explain that the *L* and *F* are the initial letters in the person's first and middle names. Ask volunteers what the initials might stand for, such as *Lawrence Francis*. Add the missing periods after the *L* and *F* and point out that each period takes the place of the missing letters in a name.

Model Write children's first and last names on slips of paper, using initials for their first names. Omit the period in the initial. Ask children to take turns choosing a name, writing it on the board, and adding the period. Invite them to tell what the whole name is and what letters are missing.

Summarize/Apply Invite children to review their writing to make sure that names written as initials end in periods.

Question Mark

Introduce Ask: *How big is an elephant?* Write the sentence on the board, and call on a volunteer to circle the question mark. Help children understand that a question mark is used at the end of a sentence that asks a question.

Model Write on the board:

> *What is your name*
>
> *How old are you*

Invite volunteers to read each question aloud and write a question mark at the end. Have them answer the questions, and then erase the question marks so another child can take a turn. Remind children that a question ends with a question mark.

Summarize/Apply Have children make sure that questions in their drafts end in question marks. Encourage them to check their work with partners.

Quotation Marks—In Conversation

Introduce Ask children questions such as *What is your favorite game? Why?* Record their answers as dialogue, then invite children to underline the exact words the speakers said. Point out the quotation marks and explain that they are used to show the speaker's exact words.

Model Write on the board:

> *The picnic is this Saturday, Ms. Ramirez said.*
>
> *Ken asked, What should we bring?*

Have volunteers read each sentence, underline the speaker's exact words, and add quotation marks. Remind children that quotation marks make dialogue easier to read.

Summarize/Apply Ask children to check their own writing to make sure they have used quotation marks correctly in dialogue.

Spelling

Antonyms

Introduce Pantomime being sleepy, and invite children to describe what they see. Write *sleepy* on the board. Then act out being awake. Write *awake* on the board. Tell children that *sleepy* and *awake* are antonyms—words that have the opposite or almost opposite meaning. Antonyms are often used when contrasting two things. Explain that writers use antonyms to make their writing more interesting.

Model Write these words on the board.

happy	*sit*
stand	*cold*
hot	*sad*

Invite a volunteer to choose a word from the left column and act it out. Have another child draw a line from that word to a word in the right column that is opposite in meaning.

Summarize/Apply Encourage children to think of antonyms when they describe things. They can brainstorm opposites in a list to refer to.

Spelling

Compound Words

Introduce Write the following word equation on the board: *sun + shine = sunshine*. Ask a volunteer to read the equation aloud and then use the word *sunshine* in a sentence. Help children understand that a compound word is one word made up of two or more smaller words.

Model Say the word *earthworm*. Invite children to name the smaller words in it. *(earth* and *worm)* Explain that figuring out the smaller words in a compound word can make it easier to spell. Work with children to spell the compound words *bluebird* and *homework* by creating word equations.

Summarize/Apply Have partners check current drafts for compound words. Encourage them to use a dictionary or word wall to verify spellings.

Consonant Digraphs

Introduce Say: *I'm thinking of a piece of furniture that you sit on.* When children guess *chair*, write *chair* on the board. Read the word aloud, emphasizing the *ch* consonant digraph. Call on a volunteer to circle the two letters that form /ch/. Help children understand that consonants like *c* and *h* together can stand for one sound. Explain that some words contain two or three letters whose sounds come together to make one sound. Examples at the beginning or end of words include *ch, sh, th,* and *wh*.

Model Write on the board: *teeth, shell, dish, peach, chimp, that, white, while.* Invite volunteers to read the words aloud and circle the two letters that stand for /th/, /sh/, /wh/, or /ch/. Have children brainstorm other words that fit in these categories.

Summarize/Apply Have partners read one another's papers and circle words with consonant digraphs. Encourage them to check that the words are spelled correctly.

Consonant Blends

Introduce Clap your hands and ask children what you just did. Write *clap* on the board. Read the word aloud, emphasizing the *cl* consonant blend. Explain that some words have *consonant blends*—two or three letters whose sounds are blended together. Have a volunteer circle the two-letter consonant blend in *clap*. Help children understand that if they have trouble spelling a word like *clap*, they can say the word and think about what sounds they hear as they write the word.

Model Write these words on index cards: *green, trap, blue, play, smoke, stop, string, belt, kilt.* Hand out the cards and have children categorize the words into these categories: consonant + *r* blend, consonant + *l* blend, *s* + consonant blend, and *lt* blend. Brainstorm other words that fit in these categories.

Summarize/Apply Have children read current writing drafts, checking for words with consonant blends. Have them circle the words, then check them for correct spelling with partners.

Endings *-s, -es, -ed, -ing*

Introduce Invite children to act out this phrase: *brush your teeth*. Write *brush* on the board. Then write *brushes, brushed,* and *brushing* under *brush*. Invite children to say each word and circle the ending. Point out that the endings *-s, -es, -ed,* and *-ing* help a verb match a singular or plural noun, or tell if an action happens now, happened in the past, or will happen in the future.

Model Give a child a book and ask the child to hand it to a classmate. Say: *(Name 1) hands the book to (Name 2).* Repeat the demonstration, this time saying *(Name 1) passes the book to (Name 2).* Write *hands* and *passes* on the board. Ask what is different about the endings. (*hands* ends in *-s* and *passes* ends in *-es*.) Explain that if a word ends in a consonant, the spelling of the word does not change before adding *s, ed,* or *ing*. If a word ends in *ss, sh, ch, x,* or *zz*, add *es*. Do not change the spelling to add *ed* or *ing*.

Summarize/Apply Invite partners to look through their writing to find verbs that end with *s, es, ed,* or *ing*. Encourage them to check that the words are spelled correctly.

Spelling

Endings -s, -ed, -ing (Double Final Consonant)

Introduce Invite children to hop on one foot. Write *hopping* on the board. Help a volunteer circle the verb *hop* in *hopping* and tell what letter was doubled before adding the ending *-ing* (p). On the board, write the word equation *hop + p + ing = hopping*.

Model Write on the board *Yesterday, the crow _____ its wings. (flap)* Ask a volunteer to change the verb *flap* to make it tell about the past *(flapped)*. Ask which letter was doubled before adding the ending *-ed* (p). Explain that for most one-syllable words that end in a vowel and a consonant, the final consonant is doubled when adding *-ed* or *-ing*. The final consonant is not doubled when adding *-s*.

Summarize/Apply Have children write about this spelling rule in their learning logs, then refer to it when checking their spelling.

Endings -es, -ed, -ing (Drop the Final e)

Introduce Ask children if they like riding a bike. Write *I like riding a bike* on the board. Help children figure out what was changed in the word *ride* before the ending *-ing* was added. (The final e was dropped.) On the board, write the word equation *ride – e + ing = riding*.

Model Write on the board: *Last night, Jason _____ at the puppy. (smile)* Ask a volunteer to change the verb *smile* to make it tell about the past. *(smiled)* Ask which letter was dropped before adding *-ed* (the final letter e). Help children understand that if a word ends in silent e, they should drop the e before adding *-es, -ed,* or *-ing*.

Summarize/Apply Ask children to work with partners to check their writing for this spelling rule. Encourage them to write about the rule in their learning logs.

High-Frequency Words

Introduce Ask children: *Do you have a brother or a sister?* Write the question and children's responses on the board, such as *Peter has a sister*. Then draw children's attention to the words *have* and *has*. Explain that words like *have* and *has* are words that people use quite often when talking and writing, and they are important to know how to spell. Cover the words and invite volunteers to spell them.

Model Write on slips of paper and put in a paper bag high-frequency words like *are, blue, come, here, said*. Invite children to choose a word, read it aloud, and use it in a sentence. Then write the words on the board and ask children to copy them in their personal dictionaries. Encourage children to memorize words like *here* and *come*, since writers often use these common words.

Summarize/Apply Have partners think of other high-frequency words that they could add to their personal dictionaries or a word wall.

Homonyms and Problem Words

Introduce Write on the board *I have ____ pens. (two, to)* Ask children which word completes the sentence, *two* or *to*. Explain that the words sound the same but have different meanings and spellings. Writers have to be careful to use the correct spelling of a word or the meaning of the sentence can change entirely, or even become nonsense.

Model Write on the board *You're having a party at your house.* Ask a volunteer to underline the two words that sound the same. *(you're, your)* Explain that *you're* is a contraction standing for *you are*, and *your* is a possessive pronoun showing whose house it is. Help children understand that how the word is used in the sentence will help them decide if they have the correct word.

Summarize/Apply Encourage children to add problem words like *two/to/too, you're/your, hear/here,* and *they're/there/their* to word walls or personal dictionaries. Invite them to refer to these resources when checking their writing for spelling.

Spelling

Long Vowel Sounds

Introduce Ask two children to perform a simple task. Give these directions: *Go, Stop.* Then write the words on the board. Invite a child to circle the word with a long *o* sound. *(go)* Explain that in *go,* the letter *o* stands for the long *o* sound. Review the long vowel sounds. Explain that when writing, children should think about the long vowel sounds they hear in words to help them spell the words correctly.

Model Write on the board: *be, he, hi, so, go, no, me, we, I, a, flu.* Read the words aloud with children, emphasizing the long vowel sound in each. Ask children to take turns copying the words onto a class chart that has these categories: *long* e, *long* a, *long* i, *long* o, and *long* u.

Summarize/Apply Invite partners to exchange drafts and look for words in which one vowel stands for a long vowel sound.

Long Vowel Sounds in Letter Combinations

Introduce Ask children what can fall from the sky. Jot down these words on the board: *snow, rain, hail, sleet.* Read the words aloud. Draw attention to the letters *ow* in *snow,* the *ai* in *rain* and *hail,* and the *ee* in *sleet.* Explain that two letters can be combined to form long vowel sounds. Talk about the "silent *e* rule" with words such as *snake, rope, bike, these,* and *rude.*

Model Write the following words on the board: *hope, train, say, key, teeth, dream, pie, road, low.* Read the words aloud with children. Help children identify the letters that stand for the long vowel sounds. *(o-e, ai, ay, ey, ee, ea, ie, oa, ow)* Tell children that when writing, it is important to think about the long vowel sounds they hear in words so the words can be spelled correctly.

Summarize/Apply Invite children to brainstorm words with long vowel sounds made with letter combinations and add them to the word wall. Have them refer to the list when writing or editing.

Phonograms and Word Families

Introduce Prepare word cards for final *-an, -et, -ig, -ot, -ut,* and for initial *c-, f-, g-, h-, b-,* and *s-.* Place the word cards on the chalkboard ledge or in a pocket chart. Invite children to form new words by placing the single consonants in front of the phonograms. Explain that many words can be formed by adding letters to units of sound, so writers must be careful to listen to each sound in a word as they spell.

Model Write these words on the board: *bat, cat, rat, sat.* Call on volunteers to read the words aloud and circle the two letters that stand for /at/. Work with children to brainstorm and spell other words that rhyme with /at/.

Summarize/Apply Invite children to make mobiles based on word families. Children will need word cards, string, a hole puncher, and hangers. Suggest they use these phonograms: *-at, -op, -in, -et, -un.*

Prefixes *un-, dis-, re-*

Introduce Ask a child to untie his or her shoes. Write *untied* on the board. Explain that the prefix *un-* means "not" and is added to *tied* to make a new word that means "not tied." Invite children to complete this word equation: _____ + *tied* = *untied.* Review the meanings of the prefixes *re-* ("to do again") and *dis-* ("the opposite of"). Explain that knowing the meanings of prefixes and how to spell them can help children become better readers, writers, and spellers. (Have child tie his/her shoes.)

Model Write these equations on the board:

> *re + open =* _____
> *un + happy =* _____
> *dis + appear =* _____

Ask children to copy the equations and form new words. Discuss each new word's meaning.

Summarize/Apply Remind children of the importance of knowing the meaning of prefixes and how to spell them. Children can write about them in their learning logs or personal dictionaries or add them to the class word wall for reference.

Spelling

Rhyming Words

Introduce Write on the board *Buddy has a red bed. Yesterday, he ate bread in bed.* Ask volunteers to read the sentences aloud and circle the rhyming words in each. *(red/bed, bread/bed)* Point out that many rhyming words have the same end sound. Some are spelled almost the same, but others are spelled quite differently.

Model In a left column on the board, write *road, lake,* and *bead.* In a right column, write *take, toad,* and *need.* Ask volunteers to draw lines between the rhyming pairs. Ask which pair has different spellings for the same long vowel sound *(bead/need).* Write *The frog jumps off the log and takes a leap into the deep water.* Ask volunteers to circle the rhyming words that have the same vowel spelling and underline the rhyming words that have different vowel spellings.

Summarize/Apply Remind children that the vowel sounds in rhyming words are sometimes spelled with different letter combinations. Encourage them to add rhyming words to their logs, personal dictionaries, or word walls.

Short Vowel Sounds

Introduce Review the short vowel sounds for *a, e, i, o,* and *u.* Write *hot* on the board. Ask children to circle the letter that stands for the short *o* sound. Explain that many one-syllable words with a short vowel sound are spelled with a consonant-vowel-consonant, or CVC, pattern.

Model Write these words on the board: *got, hat, bet, sit, cut.* Invite volunteers to write them in a class chart in these categories: *short* a, *short* e, *short* i, *short* o, *short* u. Brainstorm other words with short vowel sounds that follow the CVC spelling pattern to add to the chart.

Summarize/Apply Have pairs of children go on a word hunt using current writing drafts to find words with short vowel sounds. As partners read, have them record words they find and then share their lists.

Short Vowel Sounds in Letter Combinations

Introduce Write *heavy* on the board. Invite children to read the word and name the two letters that stand for the short *e* sound *(ea).* Explain that sometimes two vowels can stand for a short vowel sound, rather than the more common long vowel sound.

Model Write on the board and read aloud the following words in random order: *said, head, breath, build, flood, rough.* Tell children that each word has a short *e, i,* or *u* sound, which is made by a combination of two vowels. Ask volunteers to read the words and circle the letters in each one that stand for a short vowel sound.

Summarize/Apply Invite pairs of children to look through current drafts to see if they can find words that have short vowel sounds that are spelled with the letter combinations of *ai, ea, ui, oo,* and *ou.* Children can copy the words into their personal spelling dictionaries or onto word wall charts.

Suffixes

Introduce Ask children what someone who writes is called. Write the word *writer* on the board and explain that it means "a person who writes." Circle the suffix -*er* and explain that it often means "one who." Point out that suffixes like -*er* are added to words to make new words. Help children understand that recognizing suffixes can help them spell many words.

Model Talk about the meanings of the suffixes -*ful* ("full of") and -*less* ("without"), then write these equations on the board:

   paint + *er* = _____

   care + *ful* = _____

   hope + *less* = _____

Ask children to complete the word equations and use each word in an oral sentence.

Summarize/Apply Have children work with partners to find words with suffixes in their writing. Encourage pairs to explain what each word means and check for correct spelling.

Spelling

Reference Resources

Syllables in CVC and CVCe Words

Introduce Say: *I'm thinking of a two-syllable word that names something you use to keep your clothes neat when you eat. What is it?* Write *napkin* on the board and read it. Ask children what short vowel sounds they hear. (short *a* and short *i*) Point out the CVC pattern in each syllable. Explain that they can use what they know about the spellings of vowel sounds to help them spell two-syllable words. Repeat the activity with the word *pancake*, stressing the combination of CVC and CVCe syllables.

Model Write the following word parts on index cards: *sun, pot, sit, pipe, rise, up, hole, line.* Ask volunteers to match syllables to form words. *(sunrise, pothole, situp, pipeline)* Help children identify the CVC and CVCe patterns in the syllables.

Summarize/Apply Invite children to add two-syllable words that use the CVC and CVCe patterns to the word wall. They can then refer to the word wall when they check spelling.

Synonyms

Introduce Ask children: *Which is another word for* happy: glad *or* sad? Write *happy* and *glad* on the board. Explain that *happy* and *glad* are synonyms, or words with the same or almost the same meaning.

Model Write the following on the board: *The tiny dog ran after the bone. (huge, little)* Ask children which word in parentheses can take the place of *tiny* without changing the meaning of the sentence *(little)*. Explain that writers use synonyms to make their writing more interesting, more descriptive, and clearer.

Summarize/Apply Invite partners to find two or three words in their writing that could be replaced with synonyms. Encourage them to brainstorm possible synonyms for the words or use a children's thesaurus to find the synonyms.

Dictionary

Introduce Ask children: *If I'm not sure how to spell or say a word or what it means exactly, where can I look to find the answer?* When children mention a dictionary, hold one up and explain that writers use dictionaries to tell them what words mean, how they are spelled, and how they are pronounced.

Model Write the guide words *hat/hope* and *hot/hurry* on the board. Explain that a dictionary has guide words such as these at the tops of the pages to help writers find words quickly. Write *head* on the board. Ask: *Between which two pairs of guide words might you find the word* head? (between *hat* and *hope*) Then point to words in the dictionary, and help children use the pronunciation key to pronounce them correctly.

Summarize/Apply Remind children that they can use the dictionary when they are unsure of a word's meaning or how to spell or pronounce it.

Encyclopedia

Introduce Ask: *I want to find information about penguins. What set of books in our classroom or library might have what I want?* When children mention an encyclopedia, hold up the *P* volume and explain that they can look up *penguins* in the *P* volume since the word *penguin* begins with *p*. Point out that there are also computer encyclopedias.

Model Write the guide words *diamond/Dutch* on the board, and next to them the words *diving, dentist,* and *dog.* Ask which two topics might be found on a page with these guide words. (*diving* and *dog*) Display an encyclopedia article on dogs, and point out the headings, illustrations, and captions. Explain that children can use articles like this when they need information to write a report, a description, or a comparison. Encyclopedias can provide background information for story ideas as well.

Summarize/Apply Encourage children to look in an encyclopedia when they need facts and information for their writing.

Reference Resources

Index

Introduce Hold up a social studies textbook and say: *I want to find out if holidays are discussed in this book. Where can I quickly check?* When children mention the index, help a volunteer find the index at the back of the book, and then use *ABC* order to look up *holidays*. Explain that an index goes more in-depth than a table of contents—it provides names of smaller, specific topics and the page numbers on which you can find the information.

Model Have children open a textbook to the index. Guide them to look up key terms from a recent topic of study. Invite them to share what they find, including the page numbers. Have them turn to those pages to see where the key terms are mentioned.

Summarize/Apply Remind children to look in a book's index when they want to know where in the book they can find a specific word or topic.

Maps

Introduce Say: *I want to know where the nearest river is. What can I use to find that out?* When children say a map, direct their attention to a state map. If possible, identify your community and the nearest river. Ask children how they can tell what a river is on a map. *(It usually is a blue line.)* Help children understand that a map is a drawing or chart that shows where things are and is used to help people get to places.

Model On your state map, put a pushpin in the state capital and one in another city. Help children use the compass rose to figure out which direction to follow to go from the capital to the other city. You may also wish to help them use the scale to measure the distance between the two cities.

Summarize/Apply Remind children that maps can help people find things. You may wish to encourage children to draw maps when writing things such as instructions and reports.

Outline

Introduce On the board draw a simple tree. Add the labels *Branches, Trunk,* and *Roots*. Tell children that this is a picture outline of a tree. Explain that they can also write outlines with words that tell about a topic.

Model On the board, write the following.

Manatees

  I. *Where they live*
     A. *Warm shallow water*
     B. *The ocean*

 II. *What they eat*
     A. *Water hyacinth*
     B. *Sea grass*

Explain that this is the beginning of an outline. The Roman numerals I and II state main ideas. The first word following each Roman numeral begins with a capital letter. The letters A and B list details or facts about each main idea. Have children identify the details, then point out that the first word in each detail begins with a capital letter.

Summarize/Apply Explain that outlines can help writers organize information. You may wish to have children make outlines to use when they draft their reports or other informative writing.

Table of Contents

Introduce Hold up a textbook and ask: *How would I find out where Chapter 2 starts?* When children mention the table of contents, help a volunteer find the table of contents in the front of the book. Ask the child to find the chapter title and the page on which the chapter starts, and then turn to that page.

Model Have children open a textbook to the table of contents and look up the names and starting pages of Chapters 3 and 4. Then have them turn to those pages. Explain that readers use a table of contents to find out the chapters or topics in a book. Tell children that writers often make a table of contents for their portfolio so that they and others will know what's in it.

Summarize/Apply You may wish to have children each create a table of contents for their portfolio or for a long piece of writing.

Index

Teacher Notes

Teacher Notes

Teacher Notes

Teacher Notes

Teacher Notes

Teacher Notes

Teacher Notes

Teacher Notes

Teacher Notes

Teacher Notes

Art & Photo Credits

Illustrations: Front cover, title page, v, xxix: Bernard Adnet.

Photo: All photographs ©Modern Curriculum Press unless otherwise noted.
v: *l.* Courtesy of Dr. Sharon Elizabeth Sicinski-Skeans. *r.* Courtesy of Dr. Lindamichelle Baron. xxxii: Steven Ferry for Modern Curriculum Press. xxxviii: Nancy Ferguson for Modern Curriculum Press.

Big Book of Writing Models Acknowledgments

"Breakfast Sundae" reprinted with permission from *Kids Cook!* by Sarah Williamson and Zachary Williamson. © 1992, Williamson Publishing Company.

"Kaboom!" by Laura C. Girardi from *Time for Kids* magazine, March 10, 2000, issue. Reprinted by permission of *Time for Kids* magazine.

Excerpts from "Seals and Sea Lions" reprinted from the June 2000 issue of *Ranger Rick* magazine, with the permission of the publisher, the National Wildlife Federation. Copyright 2000 by the National Wildlife Federation. Roseate Spoonbill Portrait Copyright © Deborah Lipsky/DRK PHOTO. Seal photo © C. Allan Morgan/Peter Arnold, Inc. Sea lion photo © Breck P. Kent/Animals Animals.

Why the Sun and the Moon Live in the Sky by Blair Lent and Elphinstone Dayrell. Illustrations copyright © 1968 by Blair Lent, Jr. Reprinted by permission of Houghton Mifflin Company. All rights reserved.

ZB Font Copyright © 1996 Zaner-Bloser.

NOTE: Every effort has been made to locate the copyright owner of material reprinted in this book. Omissions brought to our attention will be corrected in subsequent editions.

Big Book of Writing Models Art and Photo Credits

Illustrations: Front cover, 1 *t.*, pencil person: Bernard Adnet. 35: Rebecca Thornburgh. 46: *b.r.* Loretta Trezzo-Braren/Williamson Publishing Co.

Photo credits: All photographs ©Modern Curriculum Press unless otherwise noted.
8: *t.r.* AP Photo/Bullit Marquez. *b.l.* Courtesy of *Time for Kids*. *b.r.* Mayon Volcano Photo © Val Rodriguez/Reuters. 25, 31, 38, 42, 48: Steven Ferry for Modern Curriculum Press. 32: David Lorenz Winston for Modern Curriculum Press. 35: Courtesy of Lindamichelle Baron/Harlin Jacque Publications. 43: Earl Fansler for Modern Curriculum Press. 44: *t.* C. Allan Morgan/Peter Arnold, Inc. *b.* Roseate Spoonbill Portrait © Deborah Lipsky/DRK PHOTO. 45: Breck P. Kent/Animals Animals. 46: Courtesy of Williamson Publishing Co. 47, 50: Richard Nowitz for Modern Curriculum Press. 52, 60: Bob Boyer for Modern Curriculum Press.